TRANSPORTATION ISSUES, POLICIES AND R&D

CRUISE INDUSTRY SAFETY AND SECURITY

DEVELOPMENTS AND CONSIDERATIONS

TRANSPORTATION ISSUES, POLICIES AND R&D

Additional books in this series can be found on Nova's website
under the Series tab.

Additional e-books in this series can be found on Nova's website
under the e-book tab.

CRUISE INDUSTRY SAFETY AND SECURITY

DEVELOPMENTS AND CONSIDERATIONS

BRENNAN T. PRESTON

EDITOR

New York

For permission to use material from this book please contact us:
Telephone 631-231-7269; Fax 631-231-8175
Web Site: http://www.novapublishers.com

Library of Congress Cataloging-in-Publication Data

ISBN: 978-1-63117-882-5

Published by Nova Science Publishers, Inc. † New York

CONTENTS

PREFACE

This book reviews the extent to which the cruise vessel industry and federal agencies have implemented the CVSSA, and any actions taken following the Costa Concordia accident to enhance the safety of cruise vessels visiting U.S. ports.

Chapter 1 - In 2011, almost 11 million passengers took a cruise from a U.S. port. Media reports about passenger personal safety while aboard cruise vessels— including those related to the January 2012 grounding of the cruise vessel *Costa Concordia* off the coast of Italy, which resulted in 32 deaths— combined with the increasing number of passengers taking cruises has raised questions about passenger safety and security. With the enactment of the CVSSA in 2010, cruise vessels that visit U.S. ports were required to meet certain security and safety requirements, such as having rail heights of at least 42 inches and reporting allegations of certain crimes to the FBI. GAO was asked to review cruise vessel safety as well as security issues—related to keeping passengers safe from crime.

GAO reviewed (1) the extent to which the cruise vessel industry and federal agencies have implemented the CVSSA, and (2) any actions taken following the *Costa Concordia* accident to enhance the safety of cruise vessels visiting U.S. ports.

GAO reviewed the CVSSA and related agency and industry documents, and interviewed officials from the Coast Guard, FBI, CLIA, five cruise lines which accounted for over 80 percent of North American cruise vessel passengers in 2012, and two crime victim advocacy groups. The cruise lines were selected based on several factors including their volume of North American passengers. Crime victim advocacy groups were selected based on their knowledge about cruise ship crime issues. GAO is not making any recommendations in this report.

Chapter 2 - Testimony of Rear Admiral Joseph Servidio, Assistant Commandant for Prevention Policy, U.S. Coast Guard.

Chapter 3 - Testimony of Ross A. Klein, Professor, Memorial University of Newfoundland, Canada.

Chapter 4 - Testimony of Mark Rosenker, Panel of Experts Member, Cruise Line International Association.

Chapter 5 - Testimony of Gerald Cahill, President and CEO, Carnival Cruise Lines.

Chapter 6 - Statement of Adam M. Goldstein, President and CEO, Royal Caribbean International.

In: Cruise Industry Safety and Security
Editor: Brennan T. Preston

ISBN: 978-1-63117-882-5
© 2014 Nova Science Publishers, Inc.

Chapter 1

CRUISE VESSELS: MOST REQUIRED SECURITY AND SAFETY MEASURES HAVE BEEN IMPLEMENTED, BUT CONCERNS REMAIN ABOUT CRIME REPORTING[*]

United States Government Accountability Office

WHY GAO DID THIS STUDY

In 2011, almost 11 million passengers took a cruise from a U.S. port. Media reports about passenger personal safety while aboard cruise vessels— including those related to the January 2012 grounding of the cruise vessel *Costa Concordia* off the coast of Italy, which resulted in 32 deaths— combined with the increasing number of passengers taking cruises has raised questions about passenger safety and security. With the enactment of the CVSSA in 2010, cruise vessels that visit U.S. ports were required to meet certain security and safety requirements, such as having rail heights of at least 42 inches and reporting allegations of certain crimes to the FBI. GAO was asked to review cruise vessel safety as well as security issues—related to keeping passengers safe from crime.

GAO reviewed (1) the extent to which the cruise vessel industry and federal agencies have implemented the CVSSA, and (2) any actions taken following the *Costa Concordia* accident to enhance the safety of cruise vessels visiting U.S. ports.

GAO reviewed the CVSSA and related agency and industry documents, and interviewed officials from the Coast Guard, FBI, CLIA, five cruise lines which accounted for over 80 percent of North American cruise vessel passengers in 2012, and two crime victim advocacy groups. The cruise lines were selected based on several factors including their volume of North American passengers. Crime victim advocacy groups were selected based on their knowledge about cruise ship crime issues. GAO is not making any recommendations in this report.

---

[*] This is an edited, reformatted and augmented version of the United States Government Accountability Office publication, GAO-14-43, dated December 2013.

WHAT GAO FOUND

The cruise industry and federal agencies have implemented 11 of 15 Cruise Vessel Security and Safety Act (CVSSA) provisions, but implementation of 4 provisions requires the development of regulations and policy, and is underway. Officials from all five cruise lines GAO met with said most required measures were in place when the CVSSA was enacted. According to U.S. Coast Guard officials, a notice of proposed rulemaking is in development to address 3 of the 4 remaining provisions. The 3 provisions relate to technologies to (1) detect a person going overboard, (2) maintain a video surveillance system to assist in documenting crimes on the vessel, and (3) transmit communications and warnings from the ship to anyone in surrounding waters. A policy linked to the fourth provision on the certification of trainers who provide the CVSSA course on crime scene preservation to cruise line personnel, is, as of December 2013, undergoing review at the Department of Transportation. With respect to CVSSA crime-reporting requirements, the Federal Bureau of Investigation (FBI) and the Coast Guard have implemented these provisions as required. Accordingly, the agencies publish on a website information on reported crimes that are no longer under investigation. However, GAO identified some limitations in the usefulness of the publicly reported data. Specifically, (1) allegations for which investigations are not opened are never published; (2) the data are not timely—due to the length of the criminal justice process—and thus, crime data may be posted months or years after the alleged crime occurred and (3) the data reported are not put into context, such as a city's crime rate, to provide the public with the information needed to compare rates and make decisions. However, some cruise lines are making efforts to improve reported crime data. In August 2013, several cruise lines began voluntarily disclosing alleged crime data on their websites. Also, in July 2013, legislation was introduced to amend the CVSSA that would revise and expand crime-reporting requirements, among other items. As of November 2013, however, these actions were either new or pending. Thus, GAO could not assess whether, or to what extent, the voluntary reporting or potential legislation might provide more useful data than current requirements.

Following the *Costa Concordia* accident, the cruise industry, an international maritime organization, and the Coast Guard took actions to improve passenger safety. The Cruise Lines International Association (CLIA)—which represents over 98 percent of cruise lines in the United States—identified 10 safety-related policies in 2012 that were adopted by all member cruise lines by July 2013. These policies include improvements to vessel passage planning and life jacket stowage, among other things. The International Maritime Organization (IMO)—a United Nations agency responsible for maritime matters—has also adopted a regulation, effective January 2015, requiring passengers to participate in a safety and evacuation exercise (muster drill) prior to or immediately upon departure— rather than within 24 hours of departure. CLIA member cruise lines adopted a similar muster policy weeks after the *Costa Concordia* accident. The Coast Guard is monitoring IMO's consideration of additional regulations. The agency has also started witnessing predeparture muster drills and has reported no major concerns. In addition, the Coast Guard has worked with the cruise industry for several years to plan and hold disaster exercises, including one in April 2013 to practice a mass rescue from a cruise vessel.

ABBREVIATIONS

AAJ	American Association for Justice
BRM	Bridge Resource Management
CBP	Customs and Border Protection
CCTV	closed circuit television
CEO	chief executive officer
CLIA	Cruise Lines International Association
CVSSA	Cruise Vessel Security and Safety Act
FBI	Federal Bureau of Investigation
ICV	International Cruise Victim's Association
IMO	International Maritime Organization
ISM Code	International Safety Management Code
MARAD	Maritime Administration
MSC	Maritime Safety Committee
NPRM	Notice of Proposed Rulemaking
NTSB	National Transportation Safety Board
OMB	Office of Management and Budget
RFI	Request for Information
SMS	safety management system
SOLAS	International Convention for the Safety of Life at Sea
STD	sexually transmitted disease
UCR	Uniform Crime Reports

December 20, 2013

The Honorable John D. Rockefeller IV
Chairman
The Honorable John Thune
Ranking Member
Committee on Science, Commerce and Transportation
United States Senate

The Honorable Bennie Thompson
Ranking Member
Committee on Homeland Security
House of Representatives

The Honorable Doris O. Matsui
House of Representatives

The popularity of cruise vessels as a vacation option continues to grow. Since 1980, the cruise industry has had an average annual passenger growth rate of 7.6 percent, and in 2011, over 16 million passengers traveled aboard cruise vessels worldwide.[1] About 10.9 million of these passengers traveled from U.S. ports.[2] Media reports about passenger personal safety while aboard cruise vessels, combined with the increasing number of cruise vessel passengers and the January 2012 *Costa Concordia* cruise vessel grounding off the coast of Italy, which claimed 32 lives, raised questions about personal security and passenger safety when aboard cruise vessels. According to the Federal Bureau of Investigation (FBI), from 2005 through 2010, sexual assaults and physical assaults on cruise vessels were the leading cruise vessel crimes investigated and reported by the FBI. However, the public was often not aware of these crimes because the federal government did not require information about them to be published. Moreover, cruise vessels carrying U.S. passengers often travel to foreign ports before returning to the United States, a fact that can introduce the possible involvement of law enforcement from a variety of foreign countries—in addition to the federal and local law enforcement agencies that may be involved if a crime occurs during a voyage. The involvement or potential involvement of foreign governments can add to the confusion of crime victims as they attempt to navigate various justice systems.

The Cruise Vessel Security and Safety Act (CVSSA), enacted in July 2010, requires cruise lines operating ships that visit U.S. ports and the federal government to take certain actions related to these issues.[3] For example, the CVSSA requires the cruise lines to report allegations of certain crimes to the FBI and the United States Coast Guard as well as to ensure that passengers have key information available to them—such as U.S. embassy contact information for all of the countries on the cruise vessel itinerary—and to implement specific personal security measures onboard such as ensuring that all stateroom doors have peepholes, among other things.[4] The CVSSA also requires that the Coast Guard maintain a website that provides a numerical accounting of certain crimes that have been reported by cruise lines, but are no longer under FBI investigation.[5] The CVSSA places much of the responsibility for implementing the law with the Coast Guard and FBI. The Coast Guard is the federal agency responsible for a wide array of maritime safety and security activities, including those involving cruise vessels and their landside facilities, while the FBI is responsible for investigating certain cruise vessel crimes, among other responsibilities.

In addition to the issue of personal security of passengers, the January 2012 grounding of the cruise vessel *Costa Concordia* off the coast of Italy raised questions about vessel management and the procedures for safeguarding passengers in emergency situations. For example, although international maritime law requires all passengers to be evacuated within 30 minutes of an order to abandon a vessel, the Italian government reported that the evacuation of the *Costa Concordia* took over 6 hours. The accident resulted in the death of 32 passengers. The Italian government investigated the accident and reported in May 2013 on numerous lapses in emergency procedures and management, including problems with vessel evacuation, voyage planning, and emergency communication.

You requested that we review the implementation of the CVSSA as well as any safety actions taken by federal government agencies and the cruise industry following the *Costa Concordia* accident. This report examines the following questions:

- To what extent have the cruise industry and federal agencies taken actions to implement the requirements of the CVSSA?
- What actions, if any, have federal agencies and the cruise industry taken to enhance the safety of cruise vessels visiting U.S. ports as a result of the *Costa Concordia* accident?

To address both objectives, we conducted visits to four cruise vessel ports, which we selected in large part because of their high cruise traffic and passenger embarkation volume, among other things—Los Angeles, California; Miami, Florida; Fort Lauderdale, Florida; and Seattle, Washington. To understand how the Coast Guard checks for CVSSA compliance and other safety issues on cruise vessels, we accompanied Coast Guard officials on cruise vessel exams in the Port of Los Angeles and Port Everglades, the port for Fort Lauderdale. During these visits, we interviewed security and safety officials from five cruise lines to understand how they implemented the provisions of the CVSSA and what safety changes they have implemented as a result of the *Costa Concordia* accident.[6] Additionally, we interviewed Coast Guard officials in the field and in headquarters on their role in implementing the CVSSA, any challenges encountered during implementation, and any actions taken following the *Costa Concordia* accident. We also interviewed officials from the Cruise Lines International Association (CLIA)—which currently represents over 98 percent of the cruise industry operating in the United States—for their perspective on the impact of the CVSSA and to discuss the safety changes they have implemented among their members as a result of the *Costa Concordia* accident. Finally, during our visits to cruise vessel ports, we also interviewed FBI and local law enforcement agency officials to discuss their role in handling crime aboard cruise vessels. The information we obtained from personnel at the ports and the cruise lines cannot be generalized across all U.S. ports and the cruise industry—although CLIA does represent a substantial portion of the industry—but the information provided us with a perspective on the implementation of the CVSSA as well as any changes resulting from the *Costa Concordia* accident.

To address the first objective, we reviewed relevant documents, guidance, and policy from federal agencies, such as the Coast Guard's policy letter on CVSSA implementation procedures. Additionally, we reviewed the provisions in the CVSSA and assessed the extent to which federal agencies and cruise lines were implementing those provisions. We also analyzed alleged and published cruise vessel crime data obtained from the FBI. Specifically, we analyzed all CVSSA crimes reported to the FBI from January 2008 through September 2013 (pre- and post-CVSSA implementation) as well as analyzed for the same time period the number of closed cases that appeared on the Coast Guard's public website. To determine the reliability of these data, we interviewed FBI and cruise line officials familiar with the data regarding their procedures for obtaining, analyzing, and reporting cruise vessel crime data. We determined that the data were sufficiently reliable for our purposes.[7] While the publication of the CVSSA crime data is consistent with the law, these data have some limitations. These limitations were identified through our independent analysis, as well as through comments from officials at the FBI, CLIA, the cruise lines we met with, and a crime victim advocacy groups. We discuss these limitations later in this report.

We interviewed Coast Guard officials as well as representatives of two victim advocacy groups and two academic researchers who have written extensively on cruise vessel crime for their perspectives on the implementation of the CVSSA. The interest groups and researchers were selected based on their knowledge about cruise vessel crime—either advocating for victims or researching cruise crime trends.[8] We also interviewed officials from the the Department of Transportation's Maritime Administration (MARAD)—which works to improve and strengthen the U.S. marine transportation system—to determine its role in implementing the CVSSA and discuss any challenges MARAD had encountered.

To address the second objective, we reviewed relevant documents and policies from CLIA and the selected cruise lines, including the safety measures that CLIA introduced after the *Costa Concordia* accident. We also reviewed documents from the International Maritime Organization (IMO)—a United Nations agency that specializes in maritime issues—as well as the *Costa Concordia* marine casualty investigation report issued by the Italian government in 2013. We interviewed Department of State and National Transportation Safety Board (NTSB) officials to understand their agencies' roles in relation to cruise vessel safety and the *Costa Concordia* accident. During our port visits, we also interviewed officials from two classification societies to better understand their roles in ensuring cruise vessel safety.[9] We also witnessed a cruise vessel mass rescue exercise, conducted by the Coast Guard, which involved numerous cruise line personnel, federal agency personnel, and local authorities in the Bahamas. The exercise was part of a series of mass rescue operation–based exercises designed to educate and prepare participants for a potential catastrophic event—similar to the *Costa Concordia* accident—involving a mass rescue operation at sea.

We conducted this performance audit from January 2013 to December 2013 in accordance with generally accepted government auditing standards. Those standards require that we plan and perform the audit to obtain sufficient, appropriate evidence to provide a reasonable basis for our findings and conclusions based on our audit objectives. We believe that the evidence obtained provides a reasonable basis for our findings and conclusions based on our audit objectives.

BACKGROUND

Many Stakeholders Involved in Cruise Vessel Safety and Security Regulation

International, national, state, and local requirements regulate maritime safety and security. At the international level, IMO is responsible for developing an international maritime regulatory framework. IMO member states (nations) have adopted the International Convention for the Safety of Life at Sea (SOLAS), which is designed to help ensure maritime security and safety worldwide. Among other things, SOLAS provides that companies and vessels should comply with the requirements of the International Safety Management Code (ISM Code), which was adopted by IMO in 1993. Federal laws, regulations, and guidance direct federal agencies and vessel operators within U.S. ports and waters, and state and local requirements may also further direct activities of vessel operators within their jurisdictions.

The enforcement of safety and security requirements for all maritime vessels is governed by two different systems: flag state control and port state control. A flag state that signed on to the SOLAS Convention has responsibility for verifying that vessels flying its flag meet international safety and security standards and that the flag state's standards are at least as stringent as those included in the convention's ISM Code. A port state is the country where a port is located. Port state control is the process by which a nation exercises its authority over foreign-flagged vessels operating in waters subject to the port state's jurisdiction. Port state control is generally intended to ensure that these visiting vessels comply with the various international and domestic requirements established to help ensure the safety of the visited port, its environment, and its personnel. Figure 1 shows the regulatory oversight regime affecting cruise vessels; however, there are many additional international and domestic stakeholders with roles contributing to the security and safety of cruise vessels. For a list of key stakeholders and their activities, see appendix I.

The Coast Guard administers the U.S. port state control program for foreign-flagged cruise vessels that enter U.S. waters or a U.S. port, to enforce maritime safety and security in the United States.[10] The Coast Guard exercises this enforcement through port state control activities, which include initial, annual, and periodic examinations of foreign flag cruise vessels. These exams allow the Coast Guard to examine vessels at various times:

- **Initial exams:** Conducted on vessels with potential U.S. itineraries, these exams include concept reviews during the very earliest stages of design, preconstruction plan reviews by Coast Guard naval architects and fire protection engineers, and mid-construction inspections at the shipbuilder's yard by Coast Guard marine inspectors.
- **Annual inspection:** The Coast Guard inspects each cruise vessel visiting the United States at least twice a year. The first inspection, an annual inspection, focuses on the vessel's fire protection, lifesaving, and emergency systems as well as any modifications to the vessel that would affect its structural fire protection and means of escape.
- **Periodic inspection:** The second Coast Guard inspection, a periodic inspection, focuses on the performance of the officers and crew, with specific attention paid to their training and knowledge of the vessel's emergency procedures, fire fighting, lifesaving systems, and performance during drills.

From January 2008 through March 2013, the Coast Guard performed 1,208 cruise vessel examinations (71 initial, 673 annual, and 464 periodic) and identified 1,802 deficiencies. Nearly half of these deficiencies were related to fire-fighting systems. For example, according to the Coast Guard's Cruise Ship National Center of Expertise, the most common deficiency identified in 2012 was the improper operation of fire screen doors. In 2011, the most commonly identified deficiency was the improper stowage of combustibles. According to Coast Guard officials, most deficiencies are corrected on the spot or within the time frames allowed by the Coast Guard. Moreover, officials reported that the Coast Guard rarely detains cruise vessels based on substandard compliance— for example, from January 2008 through March 2013, they have detained seven cruise vessels as a result of their 1,208 cruise vessel examinations. Four of the seven cruise vessels made corrections and were released from detention the same day, while the others took 2, 3, and 8 days to make corrections.[11]

As part of its regulatory role, the Coast Guard also maintains data on marine casualties (accidents) that occur upon the navigable waters of the United States and its territories or possessions, or whenever an accident involves a U.S. vessel. Coast Guard regulations require that certain types of accidents be reported to the Coast Guard—including accidents that result in the loss of main propulsion or primary steering, or that materially and adversely affect the vessel's seaworthiness, among other things.[12] Our analysis of Coast Guard data shows that from January 2008 through March 2013, there were 256 marine casualties that involved cruise vessels: 128 of these were classified as failures of equipment or material; 64 were classified as accidents that caused damage to the environment (mostly discharge of oil); and 64 were classified in a variety of other categories—such as fire, loss of electrical power, or collision.[13]

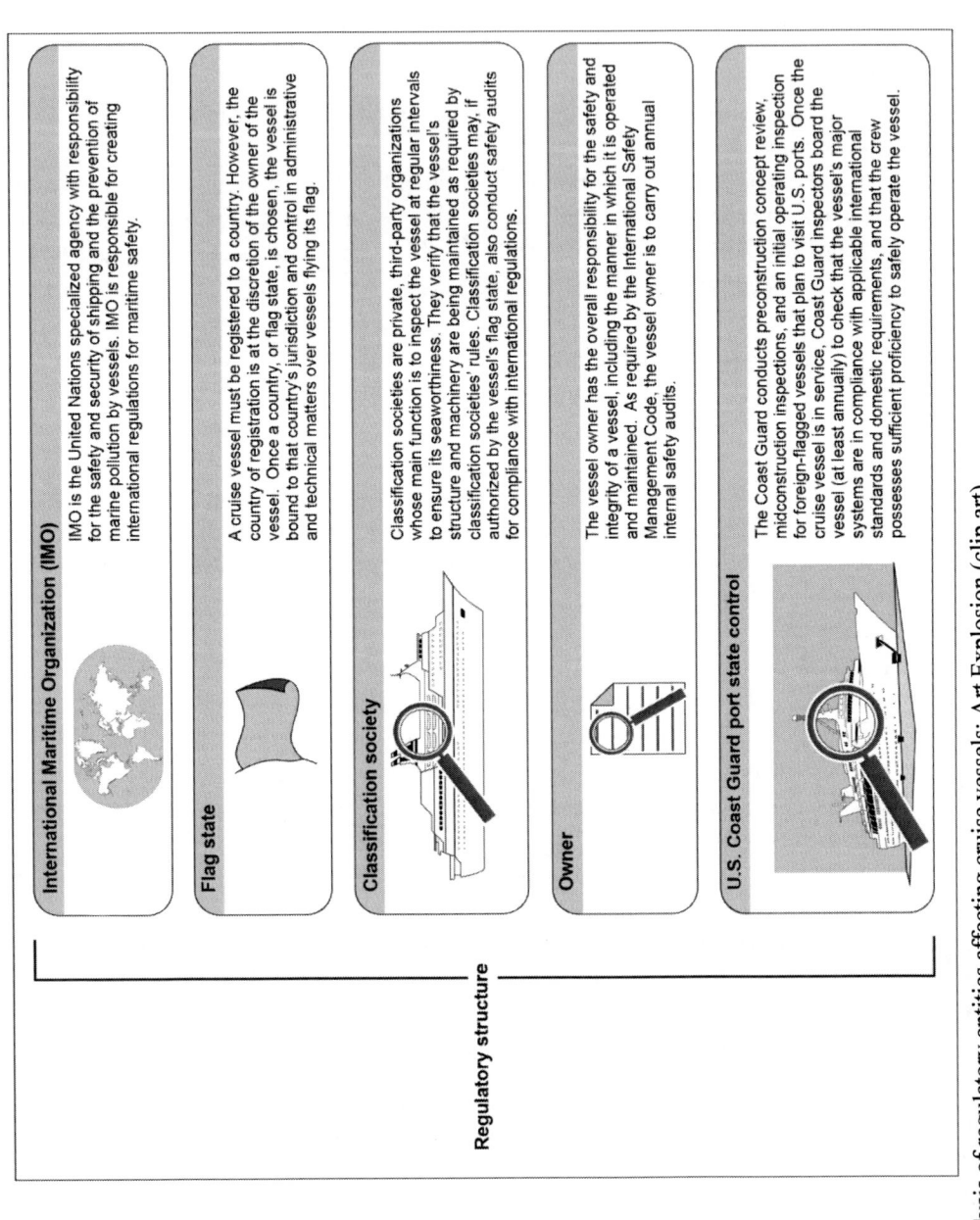

International Maritime Organization (IMO)

IMO is the United Nations specialized agency with responsibility for the safety and security of shipping and the prevention of marine pollution by vessels. IMO is responsible for creating international regulations for maritime safety.

Flag state

A cruise vessel must be registered to a country. However, the country of registration is at the discretion of the owner of the vessel. Once a country, or flag state, is chosen, the vessel is bound to that country's jurisdiction and control in administrative and technical matters over vessels flying its flag.

Classification society

Classification societies are private, third-party organizations whose main function is to inspect the vessel at regular intervals to ensure its seaworthiness. They verify that the vessel's structure and machinery are being maintained as required by classification societies' rules. Classification societies may, if authorized by the vessel's flag state, also conduct safety audits for compliance with international regulations.

Owner

The vessel owner has the overall responsibility for the safety and integrity of a vessel, including the manner in which it is operated and maintained. As required by the International Safety Management Code, the vessel owner is to carry out annual internal safety audits.

U.S. Coast Guard port state control

The Coast Guard conducts preconstruction concept review, midconstruction inspections, and an initial operating inspection for foreign-flagged vessels that plan to visit U.S. ports. Once the cruise vessel is in service, Coast Guard inspectors board the vessel (at least annually) to check that the vessel's major systems are in compliance with applicable international standards and domestic requirements, and that the crew possesses sufficient proficiency to safely operate the vessel.

Regulatory structure

Source: GAO analysis of regulatory entities affecting cruise vessels; Art Explosion (clip art).

Figure 1. Regulatory Oversight Regime Affecting Cruise Vessels.

Cruise Vessel Security and Safety Act Added to Regulatory Framework

Enacted in July 2010, the CVSSA, as discussed above, required cruise lines and federal agencies to take certain actions designed to further bolster the security and safety of U.S. passengers aboard cruise vessels. The CVSSA applies to all passenger vessels that are authorized to carry at least 250 passengers, have onboard sleeping facilities for each passenger, are on voyages that embark or disembark passengers from the United States, and are not engaged on coastwise voyages.[14] The CVSSA includes 15 provisions aimed at, among other things, increasing information available to passengers—such as requiring cruise lines to provide contact information in passenger staterooms for local embassies and providing crime victims with free and immediate access to sexual assault hotlines—as well as provisions requiring training to increase the capability of a cruise vessel's crew to document crimes and preserve crime scenes. Many CVSSA requirements are aimed at the cruise lines and were effective with CVSSA enactment or by January 27, 2012—18 months after CVSSA's enactment. The topics addressed by these 15 provisions are listed below (for a more detailed summary of these provisions please see app. II):

- Rail heights
- Peepholes
- Security latches and time-sensitive keys
- Capture of images/detection of passengers who have fallen overboard
- Acoustical hailing and warning devices
- Video recording requirements
- Availability of passenger safety information
- Medical treatment for victims of sexual assault
- Access to information and communications for victims of sexual assault
- Confidentiality of sexual assault examination and support information
- Logbook details and requirement to report alleged crimes
- Crew access to passenger staterooms
- Crime data on Coast Guard website and link on cruise line websites
- MARAD certification of crew training on crime scene preservation
- Crew training on crime scene preservation

Costa Concordia Accident Identified Numerous Potential Safety Shortcomings

On January 13, 2012, an Italian-flagged cruise vessel, the *Costa Concordia,* ran aground with over 4,000 passengers and crew onboard off the coast of Giglio Island, Italy. The vessel was so badly damaged that five contiguous watertight compartments—which housed machinery and equipment vital for the propulsion and steering of the vessel—rapidly flooded. The vessel then lost propulsion and suffered intermittent power outages, as the emergency backup systems could not handle an emergency on such a scale. The accident resulted in 32 deaths, including 2 U.S. citizens.

The *Costa Concordia* accident triggered an investigation led by the Italian government to ascertain the reasons that the vessel went aground. In May 2013, the Italian government issued its findings and recommendations. The investigation found that the root cause of the accident rested with the vessel's master for transiting too close to the coastline. According to the investigation, the accident was compounded because of poor emergency management by the master, some staff deck officers, and the vessel's hotel director. However, the report also offered additional recommendations, including improvements in bridge resource management, emergency power generation, and search and rescue operations, among other things.[15]

CRUISE INDUSTRY AND FEDERAL AGENCIES HAVE IMPLEMENTED MOST CVSSA PROVISIONS, AND ADDITIONAL CRIME- REPORTING EFFORTS ARE UNDER WAY

In 2011, the Coast Guard issued guidance on most of the provisions in the CVSSA, and the cruise lines had already implemented most of the safety measures required by the law. However, as of December 2013, the Coast Guard and MARAD were in the process of developing and publicizing new regulations before moving forward with the implementation of the remaining provisions related to items such as new technology and training certifications required or authorized by the CVSSA. Provisions regarding the publication of information on crimes on cruise vessels have been fully implemented by the FBI and Coast Guard in accordance with the law. Even so, efforts are under way that could address remaining concerns related to the thoroughness, timeliness, and context of reported crime data.

The Coast Guard Issued CVSSA Guidance, and Cruise Lines Have Implemented Most CVSSA Requirements

The Coast Guard issued guidance for 11 of the 15 CVSSA provisions in June 2011.[16] The Coast Guard guidance was issued in the form of internal Coast Guard policy letters with the main purpose of providing instructions to Coast Guard port state control officers regarding CVSSA requirements.[17] Guidance was provided in the following 11 areas: (1) rail heights; (2) peepholes in passenger stateroom doors, (3) security latches and time-sensitive keys for stateroom doors, (4) safety information provided to passengers, (5) medical licensing and proper equipment to perform sexual assault exams, (6) patient access to information and communications in the event of sexual assault, (7) confidentiality of sexual assault examination and support information, (8) crew access to passenger staterooms, (9) logbook and reporting requirements for CVSSA crimes, (10) availability of crime data on the Coast Guard's website and the link on cruise lines' webpages to the Coast Guard's website,[18] and (11) training standards and curricula—which resulted in the development of the required course on crime scene preservation.[19] Coast Guard officials stated that the guidance was necessary to help clarify some aspects of the CVSSA, especially in those areas that are outside the Coast Guard's normal area of expertise. For example, the guidance provides specific questions for inspectors to ask medical personnel to verify that adequate training, equipment, and medicine are in place in the event of a sexual assault.

Officials from all five of the cruise lines we spoke with, as well as CLIA, told us that there were minor issues with implementing these 11 CVSSA requirements and that most of the safety and security measures required by the law were already in place when the CVSSA was enacted, in July 2010. For example, each of the cruise line officials we met with told us that their vessels already were in compliance with most CVSSA provisions including having peepholes in stateroom doors, using certified medical personnel for sexual assault exams, and carrying rape kits onboard. As a result, according to all of the cruise lines we spoke with, meeting the CVSSA deadline for most of the requirements was not difficult. In the case where a modification was needed to meet a CVSSA requirement, the cruise lines we spoke with described the modification as minor. For example, officials from CLIA stated that, for the most part, the rail heights on their members' vessels already met the 42-inch height specified in the CVSSA. In one case, officials from a cruise line identified isolated locations where the rail height was below the requirement—such as around entrance gangways and by lifeboat stations—and thus they took steps to modify the railing height to meet the new standard. CLIA officials also reported that developing security information guides for passenger staterooms required a moderate amount of effort for the cruise lines because of the variations in their vessels' itineraries, which required cruise lines to collect and update information for all of their vessels' ports of call. Additionally, officials from one cruise line we spoke with discussed going beyond what the CVSSA requires. For example, this cruise line told us it was involved in discussions with officials from a victim advocacy group to evaluate and enhance the cruise line's procedures for preventing sexual assault and responding to sexual assault allegations. Additionally, this cruise line also told us it uses strict criteria to credential its professional staff to meet at least the minimum guidelines of the American College of Emergency Physicians and uses outside vendor software to help ensure credentials are kept up to date. Furthermore, these officials stated that an electronic medical record system is being introduced to improve the documentation and accessibility of health care information for guests and crew.

The Coast Guard and MARAD Are in the Process of Developing Regulations and Policy for Four CVSSA Provisions

There are four CVSSA provisions that require the development of regulations and policy for enforcement, and these are in development by the Coast Guard and MARAD. These provisions are (1) man overboard technology, which detects and alerts the crew to a person falling overboard; (2) video recording requirements, which are to assist in documenting crimes on the vessel and in providing evidence for the prosecution of such crimes; (3) acoustical hailing and warning devices, which provide communication capability around a vessel operating in high-risk waters; and (4) certification of training providers that teach the CVSSA training course on crime prevention, detection, evidence preservation, and reporting.[20] The Coast Guard is responsible for developing regulations for the first three provisions, while MARAD is responsible for developing policy for the training certification provision.

Coast Guard CVSSA Provisions

The Coast Guard issued a Request for Information (RFI) in May 2011 to obtain the public's input on the CVSSA requirements on man overboard technology and video recording because they involved complex technology and the CVSSA language was not specific enough, according to Coast Guard officials, for them to use it to verify compliance on cruise vessels. In response to its RFI, the Coast Guard received comments from nine entities: CLIA, two cruise victim advocacy groups, five companies stating that they had effective technology in these areas, and one private citizen. In addition to the RFI responses, officials that we interviewed from CLIA, cruise lines, and cruise victim advocacy groups also provided insights on some of the challenges associated with two of the technology provisions of the CVSSA. Comments from the RFI as well as additional information provided to us from interested stakeholders are discussed in tables 1 and 2:

Table 1. Differing Viewpoints on the Cruise Vessel Security and Safety Act's (CVSSA) Man Overboard Technology Provision

Man overboard technology	
CVSSA language: The vessel shall integrate technology that can be used for capturing images of passengers or detecting passengers who have fallen overboard, to the extent that such technology is available.[a]	
Cruise Lines International Association's (CLIA) request for information (RFI) comments	CLIA noted that there are two different parts to the man overboard technology: image capturing and detection. CLIA stated that the technology exists to reliably capture images of people falling overboard through closed circuit television (CCTV), thermal imaging, and so forth. However, the technology to reliably detect persons as they are in the process of going overboard does not presently exist. CLIA believes the technology is not yet reliable in a maritime environment because of the movement of a vessel, weather and sun glare, and lens encrustation caused by saltwater, among other things.
Cruise victim advocacy group's RFI comments	An official from the International Cruise Victim's Association (ICV) stated that all CCTV systems of public areas should be monitored at all times and recorded by qualified shipboard security personnel in a dedicated watch center. Such a system would provide a safety blanket that envelops the vessel, making it impossible for someone to go overboard without being seen on a video camera.
Five cruise lines interviewed comments	All five of the cruise lines we met with agreed with CLIA's perspective that the technology to detect persons as they are in the process of going overboard is not yet reliable. However, officials from four of the five cruise lines we met with have or are currently testing different technologies onboard their cruise vessels. Officials from four of the five cruise lines also said one problem with the technology relates to the potential impact of false readings, both positive and negative. Specifically, one cruise line official commented that if cruise lines are going to be required to invest significant amounts of money in man overboard technology they want to be sure it does not produce inaccurate results that could result in increased operational costs such as conducting unnecessary searches or disrupting an itinerary, among other costs. Similarly, if the technology failed to detect a passenger who had gone overboard, and as a result the vessel failed to conduct a search for that person, this type of error could expose the cruise line to costly litigation.

Source: RFI comments provided to Coast Guard and GAO interviews.
[a] 46 U.S.C. § 3507(a)(1)(D).

Table 2. Differing Viewpoints on the Cruise Vessel Security and Safety Act's (CVSSA) Video Recording Requirements Provision

Video recording requirements
CVSSA language: *Requirement to maintain surveillance.—The owner of a vessel to which this section applies shall maintain a video surveillance system to assist in documenting crimes on the vessel and in providing evidence for the prosecution of such crimes, as determined by the Secretary.*[a]

Cruise Lines International Association's (CLIA) request for information (RFI) comments	CLIA said that two main factors must be considered in developing regulations for a video surveillance system: locations on the vessel that should be under video surveillance and the length of time that images should be retained. CLIA commented that each vessel is different in size, layout, and design as well as the number and demographics of its passengers, and the type and location of prior crime allegations. As a result, CLIA commented that there should be a risk-based approach, rather than arbitrary standards, that guide video recording requirements. CLIA also recommended a video retention period of 7 days, as the average cruise length of its member lines is 7.2 days.
Cruise victim advocacy groups' RFI comments	Cruise victim advocacy groups state they would like to see more video cameras onboard, and the cameras monitored continuously. Two advocacy groups that provided RFI comments on the video recording requirements differed about how long video recordings should be kept. One group stated that the video recordings should be retained for 30 days; another stated the recordings should be retained for 90 days.
Five cruise lines interviewed comments	Officials from two cruise lines we spoke with said that most crimes are reported within 1 to 2 weeks after they occur, so video retention requirements longer than that would be unnecessary. Specifically, officials from one cruise line we spoke with commented that its current retention storage is 14 days, but if it was to double the retention period to 28 days, it would be at a one-time cost of $21.7 million. This cruise line also noted that it is standard practice to keep video footage indefinitely if it is tied to an ongoing investigation. This cruise line also reported that ensuring that video footage of a crime is maintained is generally not an issue, as 95 percent of crimes are reported to it within 24 hours. Officials from two cruise lines also said that because of the large number of cameras onboard it is not feasible to have continuous monitoring.

Source: RFI comments provided to Coast Guard and GAO interviews.
[a] 46 U.S.C. § 3507(b).

The Coast Guard's RFI did not solicit feedback on the final provision, on acoustical hailing; however, Coast Guard officials told us that this provision would still be part of the final regulation as the technology already exists for acoustical hailing and warning devices. The term "high- risk waters" used in the provision was problematic to some cruise victim advocacy groups, according to Coast Guard officials, as they perceived the definition to be different from the Coast Guard's definition. For example, Coast Guard officials said that some cruise victim advocacy groups believe that those places that may be high-risk terrorism targets near land should be considered high-risk waters (e.g., New York Harbor and waterways). However, Coast Guard officials told us they have a long- standing definition of high-risk waters, and that they are typically waters where terrorism, piracy, and armed robbery occur (i.e., the waters off the Horn of Africa, etc.). Therefore, Coast Guard officials said that they felt it was necessary to include this provision in the proposed rule to allow for public comments because it was not clear from the law how the provision should be implemented.

In July 2013, Coast Guard officials told us that they had drafted a Notice of Proposed Rulemaking (NPRM) that will encompass these three provisions of the CVSSA. They added that the regulation will likely be performance based—focusing on what must be achieved—rather than prescriptive. Coast Guard officials noted that the NPRM is currently going through final agency review. According to the website of the Office of Management and Budget (OMB), which is the final reviewer in the rulemaking process, the NPRM will be issued in June 2014. There is no timetable for when the final regulation will be issued.

All cruise line officials we spoke with reported that one of their key frustrations with the implementation of the CVSSA was not having timely information related to these three technology areas of the CVSSA. They expressed concern with how long it has taken to develop the regulations as well as concern about the lack of interim communication from the Coast Guard on the status of the rulemaking process. Cruise line officials stated that this affects their business, and that they want to be in full compliance with the law. Coast Guard officials commented that the time they have taken to develop the proposed rule was to ensure that they were adequately addressing CVSSA requirements and incorporating all viewpoints, while MARAD officials said that the time they took was to determine the best approach for implementation. Furthermore, Coast Guard officials told us that once a rulemaking process is under way, federal agencies generally do not discuss it with outside parties to avoid concerns regarding ex parte communications. According to Coast Guard officials, engaging with outside parties to update them on the process, as cruise line officials wished had been done, could hinder transparency, unless the agency gave all parties and the public the same opportunity to comment and provide information.

While the Coast Guard is drafting its NPRM to address these three outstanding CVSSA provisions, in July 2013, legislation was introduced that would amend the video recording requirements of the CVSSA, among other items.[21] The proposed bills detail requirements for placement of video surveillance equipment on cruise vessels, access to video records, and video retention standards, among other items. As of December 2013, the two bills have been referred to the Senate Committee on Commerce, Science and Transportation and the House Committee on Transportation and Infrastructure's Subcommittee on Coast Guard and Maritime Transportation, respectively, and have not been voted on. It is unclear what effect these bills may have on the impending regulation from the Coast Guard if they become law.

MARAD CVSSA Provision

For the fourth CVSSA provision, MARAD issued a notice of proposed new policy in the *Federal Register* in May 2013 for certifying providers of the CVSSA training course on crime prevention, detection, evidence preservation, and reporting.[22] While the CVSSA did not mandate that MARAD develop a training provider certification—the language of the CVSSA states that MARAD "may" develop a certification—MARAD officials stated that they were intent on pursuing certification because there were requests from both the Coast Guard and CLIA to provide clarity on the certification portion of the CVSSA. MARAD proposed a voluntary certification program for training providers to assure the general public that passenger cruise vessel security and safety personnel have received training that is in strict compliance with the CVSSA-mandated model training course. According to MARAD, certification would serve to assist the cruise industry in identifying and obtaining qualified training services. Training providers seeking to be certified by MARAD would be required to submit training plans and supporting information for review. If the training provider's plans meet the CVSSA model course criteria, the agency would offer its certification subject to the training provider entering into an agreement that, in addition to other terms, would subject the organization to program audits. Four comments were received on the proposed policy from CLIA, ICV, the American Association for Justice, and a practicing maritime attorney. Their comments on the proposed policy are summarized in table 3. MARAD is reviewing the comments, and officials said that it will promulgate a final policy as soon as practicable.

The FBI and the Coast Guard Have Fully Implemented CVSSA Crime Data Reporting Requirements

The FBI and the Coast Guard have fully implemented the CVSSA provisions regarding crime data reporting. Specifically, the FBI is responsible for implementing two main areas of the CVSSA: reviewing safety guides that the cruise lines prepare[23] and reporting CVSSA crime data (regarding crimes that occur onboard cruise ships) to the Coast Guard which publishes it on a public website.[24] FBI officials reported that they provide data for cases no longer under investigation, as stated in the CVSSA. The CVSSA identifies eight crimes that, if within the FBI's jurisdiction, cruise lines must report to the FBI.[25] These crimes are homicide, suspicious death, missing U.S. national, kidnapping, assault with serious bodily injury, firing or tampering with the vessel, theft of money or property in excess of $10,000, and certain sexual assault offenses.[26] The CVSSA then requires the Coast Guard to publish on its website a statistical compilation of all allegations of CVSSA crimes reported to the FBI that are no longer under FBI investigation.[27] The data are to be updated at least quarterly, aggregated by cruise line, and each type of crime is to be identified including whether it was committed by a passenger or a crew member. Figure 2 explains the FBI's general process for receiving a CVSSA-related crime report and, if appropriate, opening and closing its investigation of a CVSSA-related crime.

FBI Involvement—"Pre- opening" Period
When an alleged crime occurs aboard a cruise vessel, according to cruise line officials, the security officer onboard the vessel typically receives notification of the alleged crime. If the alleged crime is believed to be a CVSSA-related crime, the security officer is usually required to notify the vessel owner, since under the CVSSA it is the owner's responsibility to report any CVSSA crime to the FBI and the Coast Guard as soon as possible.[28] FBI officials stated that initial reports of crimes can come in varying forms, but generally for CVSSA crimes, they are notified within 24 hours by telephone. FBI officials also stated that, in most instances, they are relying on cruise vessel personnel to preserve the crime scene aboard the vessel since the FBI cannot typically get to a cruise vessel until it arrives in a United States port.[29] To help address these circumstances, the FBI has provided the cruise lines with a standard form for detailing initial information about the alleged crime that includes a description of the incident; the names of victims, witnesses, and suspects; any statements made by those involved; and any evidence preserved (rape kits, video recordings, photos, etc.). The cruise lines are to send this form to the FBI and Coast Guard as soon as possible after the crime is reported. The FBI considers the information as it determines what further actions need to be taken.

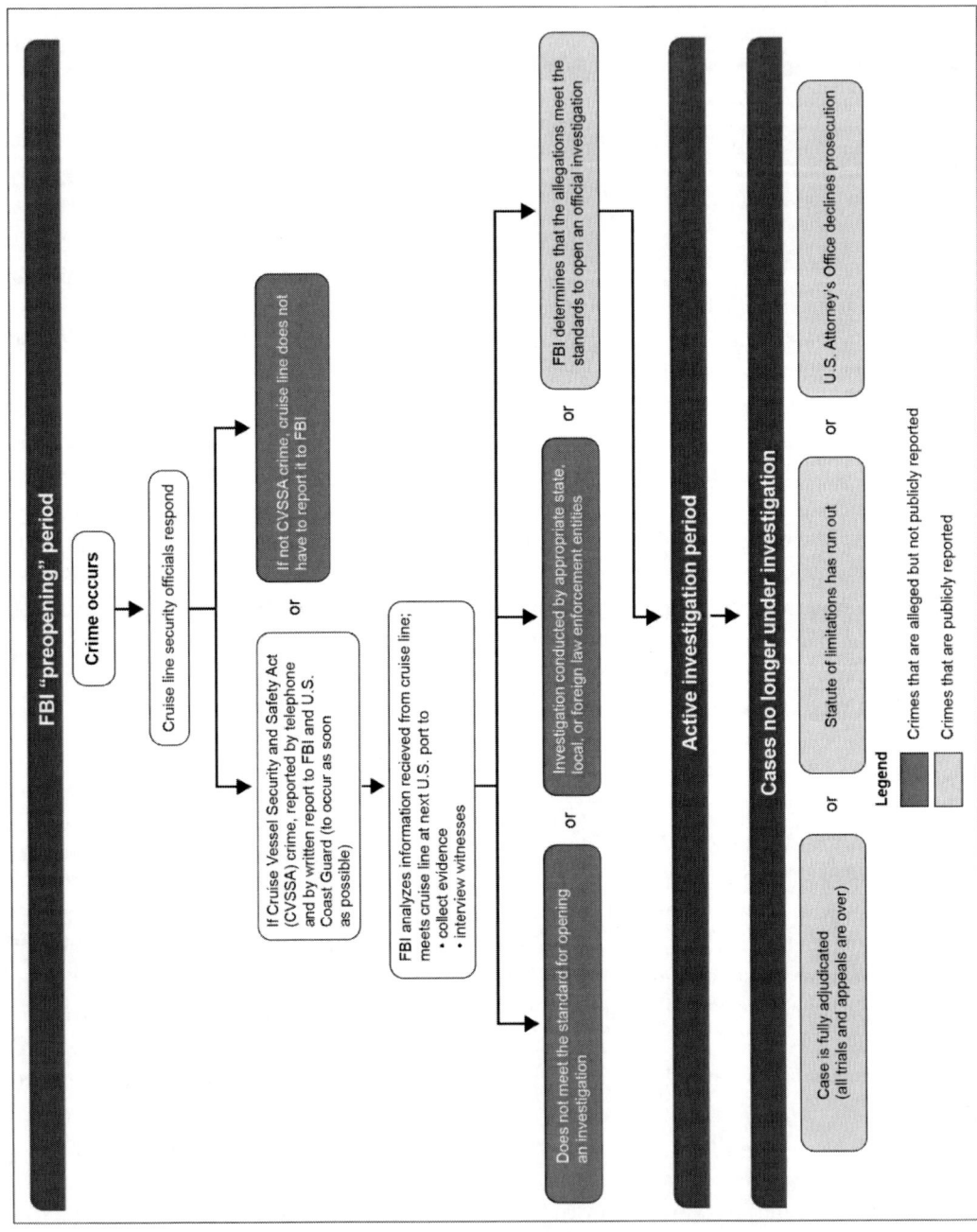

Source: GAO analysis of FBI interviews.

Note: Figure 2 describes the general process law enforcement might use to investigate a cruise vessel crime. However, each case is different and the facts and circumstances will drive how the case is approached. Additionally, the FBI continues to gather information and evidence during the "active investigation period." However, we did not include specific methods the FBI uses because the purpose of this graphic is to show which alleged crimes are eventually reported publicly, and not to detail the FBI's investigative methods.

Figure 2. Law Enforcement Process for Investigation of Cruise Crime within FBI's Jurisdiction.

Table 3. Differing Viewpoints on the Cruise Vessel Security and Safety Act (CVSSA) Training Certification Provision

Maritime Administration (MARAD) training certification	
CVSSA language: The Administrator of the Maritime Administration may certify organizations in the United States and abroad that offer the curriculum for training and certification [for crime prevention, detection, evidence preservation and reporting].[a]	
Cruise Lines International Association (CLIA)	CLIA had both questions and suggested changes for MARAD to consider when developing its final policy. Specifically, CLIA addressed the process MARAD plans to use to certify training providers that may have already been independently certified, and requested that MARAD provide additional details on the qualifications it will be looking for in a training provider in order to obtain certification, among other items. CLIA also made numerous suggestions including a request for a quicker turnaround for certification approval and for MARAD not to publicize the course materials of certified training providers for proprietary reasons, among other items.
Cruise victim advocacy group's perspective	International Cruise Victims' (ICV) comments included a request to make the certification mandatory, as well as for MARAD to have responsibility for issuing uniform course completion certificates to training providers. ICV also asked about the criteria MARAD plans to use to evaluate training providers. Additionally, ICV sought more clarity from MARAD on the frequency of the compliance audits that MARAD plans to perform for training providers, among other items.
Other interested parties' perspectives:	Two others commented on MARAD's proposed policy. These included the American Association for Justice (AAJ) as well as a maritime attorney. First, AAJ commented that the certification program does not provide immunity to cruise lines for failure to preserve evidence; instead it is simply a certification of a training standard and nothing more. Second, AAJ urged caution in relying on the certification program to successfully and skillfully preserve evidence, as those that are certified remain cruise line personnel and are not agents of the government. The maritime lawyer had one main concern about the transparency of the training provider, and would like to see MARAD require cruise lines to post on their websites their training providers and the names of the crew who are certified.

Source: Notice of proposed new policy comments provided to MARAD.
[a] 46 U.S.C. § 3508(a).

According to a cruise victim advocate group's official, this "pre-opening" phase has been a stated source of concern for the group because of the following issues:

- **Law enforcement response:** At sea, unlike on land, generally, a crime victim cannot call 911 to reach an independent local law enforcement authority. Instead, it is the responsibility of the cruise line's security personnel to respond. This can be disconcerting to the victim of a crime, particularly if the alleged perpetrator is a cruise line employee. An ICV official stated that the group realizes that it is the cruise line's responsibility to respond initially, but the ICV believes that victims should be given immediate access to a private phone and contact information to call the FBI directly, and other support organizations.[30]
- **Jurisdiction:** Cruise vessels generally sail through multiple local and foreign jurisdictions during a cruise. A cruise victim advocate group official stated that this can result in a victim feeling confused in dealing with the different legal systems.[31]

Depending on where the reported crime occurs, there can be several foreign ports that the cruise line may visit before arriving back in the United States. Each of these foreign jurisdictions may investigate the crime if it so chooses.

- **Evidence integrity:** Cruise vessel personnel preserve crime scene evidence until law enforcement personnel board the vessel to begin reviewing the allegations, generally upon the vessel arriving at a U.S. port. For cruise victim advocates, this raises questions about evidence preservation, conflict of interest, the feasibility of conducting an investigation days after a crime may have occurred, and the potential contamination of a crime scene if other jurisdictions investigate prior to the vessel arriving back in the United States.

In response to these concerns, FBI officials stated that they believe it is important to have cruise line security officials begin some evidence preservation work. They added that this is important given that there is no law enforcement agency onboard and that the FBI interviews and evidence collection are generally conducted when the cruise vessel has arrived in a U.S. port. To help support this effort, the FBI has provided CLIA with information on how to preserve crime scenes.[32] FBI officials in all field offices we visited told us they have never been concerned about the information they received or the integrity of an investigation as a result of the security officer being a cruise line employee. Most cruise line officials mentioned that the circumstances of an international cruise— where no independent law enforcement agency is available in international waters—may make it necessary for their security personnel to begin preserving evidence and collecting information while the vessel is still at sea to assist law enforcement personnel. FBI officials in one port city noted that they had seen an improvement in evidence preservation since the CVSSA came into law.

FBI Investigation—Active Investigation Period
Upon boarding the vessel, the FBI can more readily gather evidence, interview witnesses, and survey the crime scene. If the alleged crime meets the standard for opening an investigation, the FBI will open an investigation and certain statistics about the case are to be published on the Coast Guard's website when the case is closed. Whether the FBI opens an investigation depends on a number of factors related to the facts and circumstances of each case. However, for a crime allegation to eventually appear on the Coast Guard's public website, under the law, an investigation would have to have been officially opened by the FBI.

FBI Investigation—Cases No Longer under Investigation, or "Closed" Cases
According to FBI officials, an open case may no longer be under investigation if (1) the case has reached a final disposition in court (e.g., a verdict was rendered and appeals have concluded); (2) the statute of limitations has run out; and (3) at some point following the opening of an official investigation, the U.S. Attorney declines prosecution. Once a case is closed, FBI provides statistics on these closed cases to the Coast Guard for posting on the website.

Table 4. Alleged CVSSA Crimes Reported to the FBI by Cruise Lines from January 2010 through September 2013

Crime	2010	2011	2012	2013 (January-September)	Total
Homicide	0	0	0	0	**0**
Death-suspicious	1	3	0	2	**6**
Missing U.S. national	3	5	7	7	**22**
Kidnapping	0	0	0	0	**0**
Assault with serious bodily injury	12	3	10	12	**37**
Firing or tampering with vessel	1	0	1	1	**3**
Theft greater than $10,000	19	16	15	13	**63**
Sexual assault	50	43	30	33	**156**
Total allegations	**86**	**70**	**63**	**68**	**287**

Source: GAO analysis of FBI data.

Note: According to FBI officials, the FBI receives reports of alleged serious violations of U.S. law directly from the cruise lines in accordance with the CVSSA. The FBI then assesses the reports and classifies the allegations into one of the eight serious violations outlined in the CVSSA.

Table 5. Alleged CVSSA Crimes No Longer under Investigation by the FBI (Published on Coast Guard Website) from January 2010 through September 2013

Crime	2010	2011	2012	2013 (January-September)	Total
Homicide	0	0	0	0	**0**
Death-suspicious	4	0	1	0	**5**
Missing U.S. national	0	0	0	1	**1**
Kidnapping	0	0	0	0	**0**
Assault with serious bodily injury	3	3	0	2	**8**
Firing or tampering with vessel	0	0	1	0	**1**
Theft greater than $10,000	0	0	2	0	**2**
Sexual assault	28	13	11	12	**64**
Total crimes no longer under investigation	**35**	**16**	**15**	**15**	**81**

Source: GAO analysis of Coast Guard data.

However, there is a difference between the number of reported cases and the number of closed cases. Table 4 identifies alleged CVSSA crimes reported to the FBI by year, and table 5 identifies closed CVSSA cases published on the Coast Guard's public website by year. As tables 4 and 5 demonstrate, there were 287 alleged CVSSA crimes reported to the FBI during this nearly 4-year time period and 81 CVSSA crimes that were published on the website as closed.

Efforts Are Under Way to Provide Additional Data in Crime Reporting

While the FBI reporting of CVSSA crime data is consistent with the law, these data have some limitations. For example, the crime data currently reported are limited in that (1) allegations for which investigations are not opened are not reported, (2) the data reported are not timely, and (3) the data reported are not put into context that would provide the public with the magnitude of crime on vessels, as discussed below.

- **Allegations for which investigations are not opened are never published:** As shown in tables 4 and 5, there are more than three times the number of alleged crimes reported to the FBI by the cruise lines than the CVSSA requires the FBI to post publicly. The data in table 4 on alleged crimes are not available publicly. According to a cruise victim advocate we interviewed, and to some members of Congress, there are questions about whether the public is adequately informed about the numbers of alleged CVSSA crimes on cruise lines. An official from a cruise victim advocacy group we interviewed stated that without complete data on the crimes that have occurred on cruise vessels, the public may not have the necessary information to make informed decisions about cruise travel. However, information on allegations of crime also may not accurately reflect crime on cruise vessels, as some allegations may be unfounded.

- **Data reported are not timely:** There can be a lag between the time an alleged crime is reported to the FBI and the time a case is closed. According to an FBI official, the crime data that are posted on Coast Guard's website represent incidents that may have occurred months or years in the past. Depending on the progression of a case, this may be due to the length of the investigation, criminal trial, or any appeals. As a result, crimes published on the public website often do not align with the quarter, and sometimes the year, in which the crime occurred. An official from a cruise victim advocacy group we interviewed commented that the significant time lapse from when a crime allegedly occurs to when it is ultimately reported on the public website results in the public getting less valuable information about crimes that may have occurred onboard cruise vessels.

- **Data reported without any context for comparison:** According to a CLIA official, appropriate context is needed when presenting the CVSSA crime data figures so that the public can determine how cruise vessel crime rates compare with land-based crime rates. The FBI's Uniform Crime Reports (UCR) collects crime statistics from over 18,000 city, university and college, county, state and tribal, and federal law enforcement agencies.[33] In an effort to provide more detail on the comparative prevalence of cruise crimes, one cruise line and CLIA have included data that compare cruise line crime rates for homicide, rape, and assault with serious bodily injury with similar land- based crime rate statistics from the UCR for homicide, forcible rape, and aggravated assault.[34] As we discuss below, while the UCR comparison has some limitations, CLIA officials commented that providing this comparison would provide potential cruise passengers with more transparent and comprehensive crime statistics. In addition to using rates to compare the prevalence of cruise vessel crime with the prevalence of land-based crime, presenting cruise crime data in a rate-based format may also be useful in comparing crime statistics among cruise lines.

In July 2013, CLIA officials stated that certain cruise lines would begin reporting additional crime data on their websites. According to CLIA, in August 2013, six cruise lines—which account for over 90 percent of the North American cruise passengers—began to voluntarily report on their respective websites the number of alleged CVSSA crimes that had been reported onboard their cruise vessels.[35] Officials from one of these cruise lines stated that they were volunteering to report this information to be more transparent about alleged crimes reported on their vessels. The data presented on their respective websites provide more information than they are required to report to the FBI—as the cruise line website information includes all alleged CVSSA crimes that have been reported regardless of FBI jurisdiction, even if the allegation of a crime is later determined to be unfounded.

However, methodological factors may limit the usefulness of these data for consumers. For example, there are some limitations associated with the UCR data comparisons that one cruise line and CLIA are making, in that, only certain CVSSA crimes—violent crimes—can be reasonably compared with the UCR crimes because of definitional differences and the lack of comparison crimes identified in the UCR. In addition, some factors that explain the relatively low rate of alleged cruise vessel crimes compared with UCR land-based crime rates include the fact that passengers are in a confined cruise vessel environment where all persons and items brought onboard are screened, camera surveillance is ubiquitous, security personnel are present, and the demographic profile of the passengers on cruise vessels does not necessarily compare well with the profile of a major U.S. city (average income, for example). As a result, the differences presented by these two environments make the comparison between a cruise vessel environment and a land-based community challenging. A CLIA official commented that despite these limitations, the UCR is still viewed as the only national data set of reported crimes that can be used to make crime comparisons. According to a criminal justice researcher familiar with the cruise industry data, the UCR is being used as a comparison baseline in part because of the lack of an alternative baseline for comparing crime data, and while there may be some limitations, the comparative analysis is appropriate.[36] While the presentation of the data on the cruise lines' and CLIA's websites may have limitations, the methodology for comparison generally appears sound and this voluntary crime data reporting is more comprehensive than what CVSSA currently requires.

In July 2013, legislation was introduced in the Senate and House that would amend the CVSSA, including the FBI's crime-reporting requirements, among other provisions.[37] These bills propose amending the CVSSA so that a statistical compilation of all alleged crimes, including non-CVSSA crimes, reported by cruise lines to the FBI, irrespective of their investigative status, would be publicly posted, quarterly, on a new website maintained by the Department of Transportation. Under the proposed legislation, the allegation data would identify whether each crime was committed (or allegedly committed) by a passenger or crew member and whether it was against a minor. The bills also propose that cruise lines report CVSSA-type crimes within the FBI's jurisdiction to the FBI and the nearest U.S. consulate within 4 hours of the crime occurring, among other items.[38] In July 2013, these bills were referred to the Senate Committee on Commerce, Science and Transportation and the House Committee on Transportation and Infrastructure's Subcommittee on Coast Guard and Maritime Transportation, respectively.

The efforts of both the cruise lines and Congress could improve the completeness, timeliness, and context for crime data on cruise vessels. However, as previously stated, the cruise lines are publishing their information voluntarily, and it is unknown if they will continue to do so. Also, there are some consistency issues in how the data are reported, with one cruise company reporting its data in aggregate—combining the crime data of all of its North American subsidiary cruise lines into a single data set for reporting—while other cruise companies report crime data by individual company or by subsidiary cruise line. In addition, the cruise lines currently do not report crime in a rate-based format, which would allow for easier comparison among cruise lines. If enacted into the law, the proposed amendments to the CVSSA, introduced in July 2013, could also improve the timeliness, relevance, and transparency of cruise vessel crime data available to the public. As of November 2013, however, the cruise lines' voluntary reporting had just begun and the CVSSA bills remained in committee, and thus we cannot assess whether, or to what extent, these efforts may address the data limitations.

THE CRUISE INDUSTRY MADE CHANGES AFTER THE COSTA CONCORDIA ACCIDENT AND POTENTIAL INTERNATIONAL REGULATIONS REMAIN UNDER CONSIDERATION

The cruise industry responded to the *Costa Concordia* accident by reviewing safety practices and implementing changes across the industry and potential international regulatory actions are under consideration at the IMO. The Coast Guard began witnessing passenger musters in February 2012, soon after the *Costa Concordia* accident, and has participated in a mass rescue exercise involving a cruise vessel.[39]

The Cruise Industry Adopted Safety-Related Policies Identified following the *Costa Concordia* Accident

In response to the *Costa Concordia* accident, CLIA initiated an operational safety review and member cruise lines adopted 10 safety- related policies.[40] According to CLIA's Operational Safety Review Executive Summary, the review was guided by cruise industry members with the advice and input of an independent panel of safety experts.[41] Suggested policies were discussed and developed within CLIA's Operational Safety Review's Task Force, made up of senior industry executives from CLIA's member lines with responsibility for maritime safety, and approved by the chief executive officers (CEO) of member lines. The resulting 10 policies relate to various safety enhancements, such as improvements to passenger musters, vessel passage planning, and life jacket stowage. CLIA announced these policies throughout 2012, as shown in figure 3.

As a condition of CLIA membership, CEOs of all member cruise lines had to attest in writing that their companies had adopted the 10 policies and had included them in their companies' safety management systems (SMS), according to CLIA officials.[42] These officials said they expected cruise lines to implement most of the policies upon the dates of their announcement.[43] Officials noted that they received written attestations from member cruise line CEOs at different times following the announcements; however, all had provided them as of July 2013. As a matter of international regulation, once a policy has been included in a company's SMS, the policy is subject to routine external audits. These audits are conducted by vessels' flag states (or classification societies acting on their behalf), which are responsible for ensuring that a vessel's SMS is in compliance with the ISM Code and that the company operates the vessel in accordance with the SMS, among other things.[44] Almost all cruise vessels visiting U.S. ports are registered (flagged) in other countries, and are therefore subject to SMS compliance audits by their flag states. When foreign-flagged cruise vessels visit U.S. ports, their SMSs are also subject to verification by the Coast Guard in its role as a port state control authority.[45] Coast Guard officials said their port state control boarding officers review the validity of the certificates issued by a vessel's flag state and also perform spot checks of a vessel's compliance with its SMS, and noted that their review of a vessel's SMS is less in-depth than a flag state's review. Officials also explained that the Coast Guard may check items in a vessel's SMS that go beyond domestic or international regulations—such as the 10 CLIA policies shown in figure 3—but said that any deficiencies found would merely be subject to correction rather than vessel detention because such items are self imposed rather than part of any regulation. However, Coast Guard officials noted that a series of such deficiencies might indicate a lack of implementation of the SMS which could result in more serious actions by Coast Guard.

To facilitate CLIA's operational safety review following the *Costa Concordia* accident, each member cruise line was to conduct a review of its own safety practices and procedures and collaborate to share best practices. The reviews conducted by the five cruise lines we interviewed varied in scope and outcomes. For example, according to a document provided by one company, it conducted a safety review that examined nine areas of its cruise operations—such as emergency management and damage control—and officials said this review resulted in over 500 recommendations. Another cruise line provided documentation showing that its review, conducted by an outside entity, focused on six objectives that in many cases relate to the human aspect of safety and emergency response—such as leadership involvement, teamwork and training, and safety culture—and the review resulted in 26 observations for further consideration. Representatives of the five cruise lines we spoke with identified some examples of changes they have made, or are making, after reviewing their safety procedures following the *Costa Concordia* accident. They include the following:

- One cruise line, as part of its quality assurance processes, reported that it has its most qualified captains visit vessels and observe staff to determine whether they are fostering an open atmosphere on the bridge. These captains are to ensure that senior bridge officers are making their thoughts and intentions known, and that junior bridge officers challenge senior officers if they are unclear about orders or have concerns. This emphasis on bridge team management aligns with the new CLIA "Passage Planning" policy where, among other things, bridge team members are encouraged to raise operational concerns without fear of retribution.
- Another cruise line reported that it changed the duty of managing the vessel mustering process from the captain of the vessel to the hotel director, to alleviate extra burden on the captain during an emergency. It also changed its mustering policy, so if a passenger refuses to muster prior to departure, then that passenger is not allowed to travel.
- Another cruise line reported that it sent its officers to receive testing to assess how they will react during the stress of an emergency; the suitability of their leadership style; and human factors such as approachability, reliability, and acceptance of change. CLIA officials also said testing of crew to assess how they will react during the stress of an emergency was a topic of in-depth discussion during its operational safety review following the *Costa Concordia* accident.

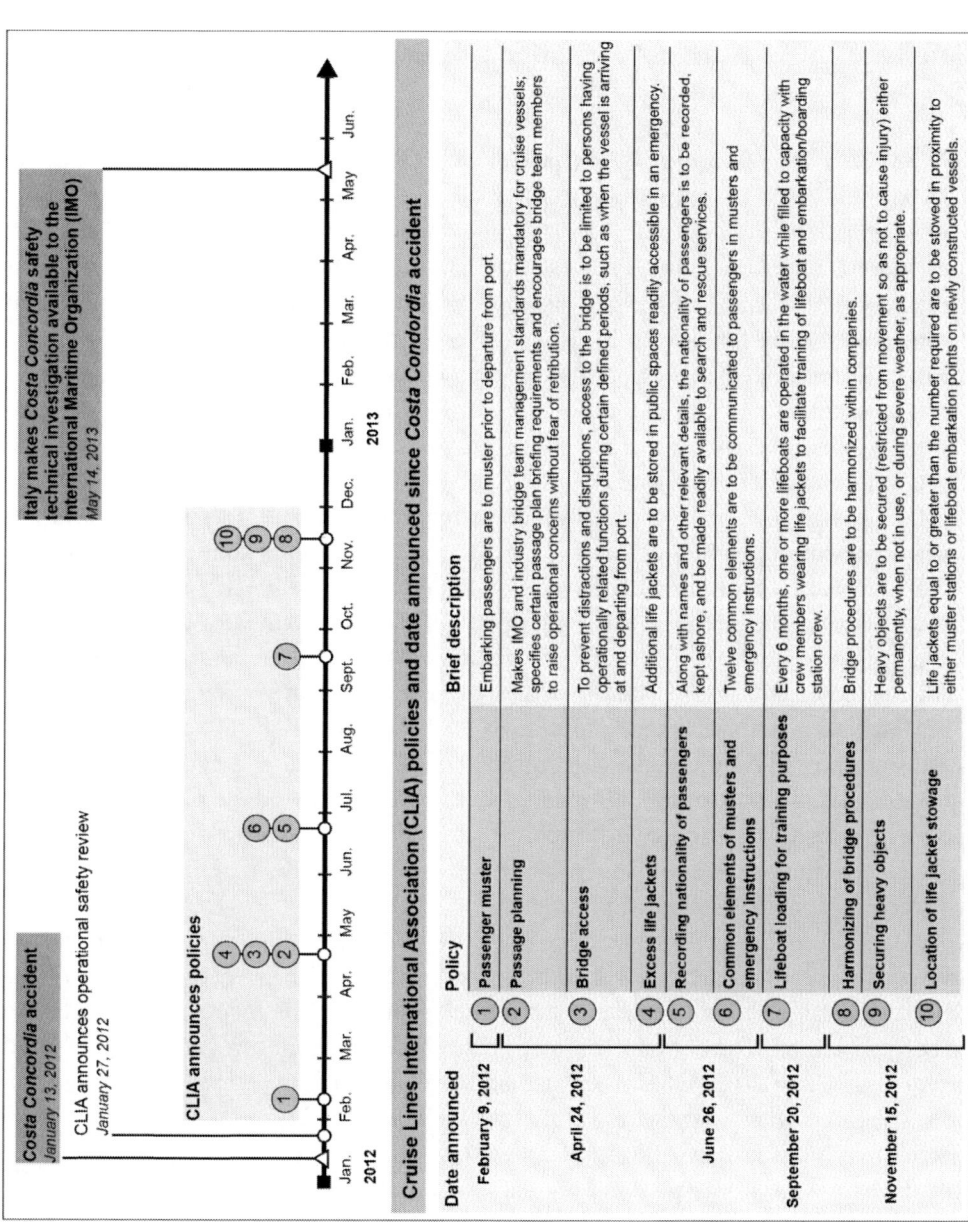

Source: GAO analysis of CLIA policies.

Figure 3. Timeline of CLIA Actions Relative to the Costa Concordia Accident.

Representatives from all five cruise lines we spoke with said they have included, or plan to include, the safety-related changes they have made as a result of their internal reviews into their SMSs.

International Safety Measures Are Under Consideration and the Coast Guard Has Taken Some Initial Actions

IMO Adopted Muster Regulation and Is Considering Other Potential Measures

IMO's Maritime Safety Committee (MSC)—a key IMO committee charged with addressing all matters related to the safety of shipping—has adopted one regulation, issued 18 interim safety recommendations, and is considering additional safety-related measures that it may take following the *Costa Concordia* accident. Specifically, MSC adopted a regulation in June 2013 to be effective on January 1, 2015, which requires that newly embarked passengers muster prior to or immediately upon departure, instead of within 24 hours, as stated in current regulations.[46] According to a Coast Guard official, in the case of the *Costa Concordia* accident, the passengers that had embarked at the previous port had not yet participated in a muster drill before the accident occurred.[47]

IMO's MSC has also issued 18 interim safety recommendations for passenger vessel companies to implement on a voluntary basis.[48] Many of these recommendations closely align with the 10 CLIA policies discussed above. For example, as with CLIA's policy, IMO recommends that companies record the nationality of persons onboard for purposes of coordination during emergencies.[49] However, in some cases the IMO recommendations offer additional guidance. For example, in addition to recommending that passenger vessels carry additional life jackets in public spaces (similar to CLIA's policy), IMO recommends that companies consider providing life jackets that are similarly designed and can be donned in a similar manner to avoid confusion. Following the release of the *Costa Concordia* safety technical accident investigation report in May 2013, the MSC working group responsible for developing these 18 interim recommendations expressed the view that, in the future, a decision will need to be made on their final status.

Following the *Costa Concordia* accident, the MSC created a long-term action plan to facilitate the consideration of measures resulting from the accident. According to a MSC report, MSC uses the action plan to document proposals from IMO member governments and international organizations. The action plan is not publicly available; however, a Coast Guard official present at the June 2013 MSC meeting said the plan contains about 20 items and can be viewed as a list of issues—similar to the list of 18 interim safety recommendations—on which the MSC may take further action.[50] This action could include a variety of outcomes, including the development of international regulations. Figure 4 summarizes the main actions of IMO following the *Costa Concordia* accident.

Although IMO is considering additional measures that may become regulations, it could be years before they take effect, and the Coast Guard can then enforce them through its port state control inspections.[51] In the interim, the one new regulation, adopted in June 2013, requires newly embarked passengers to muster prior to or immediately upon departure.

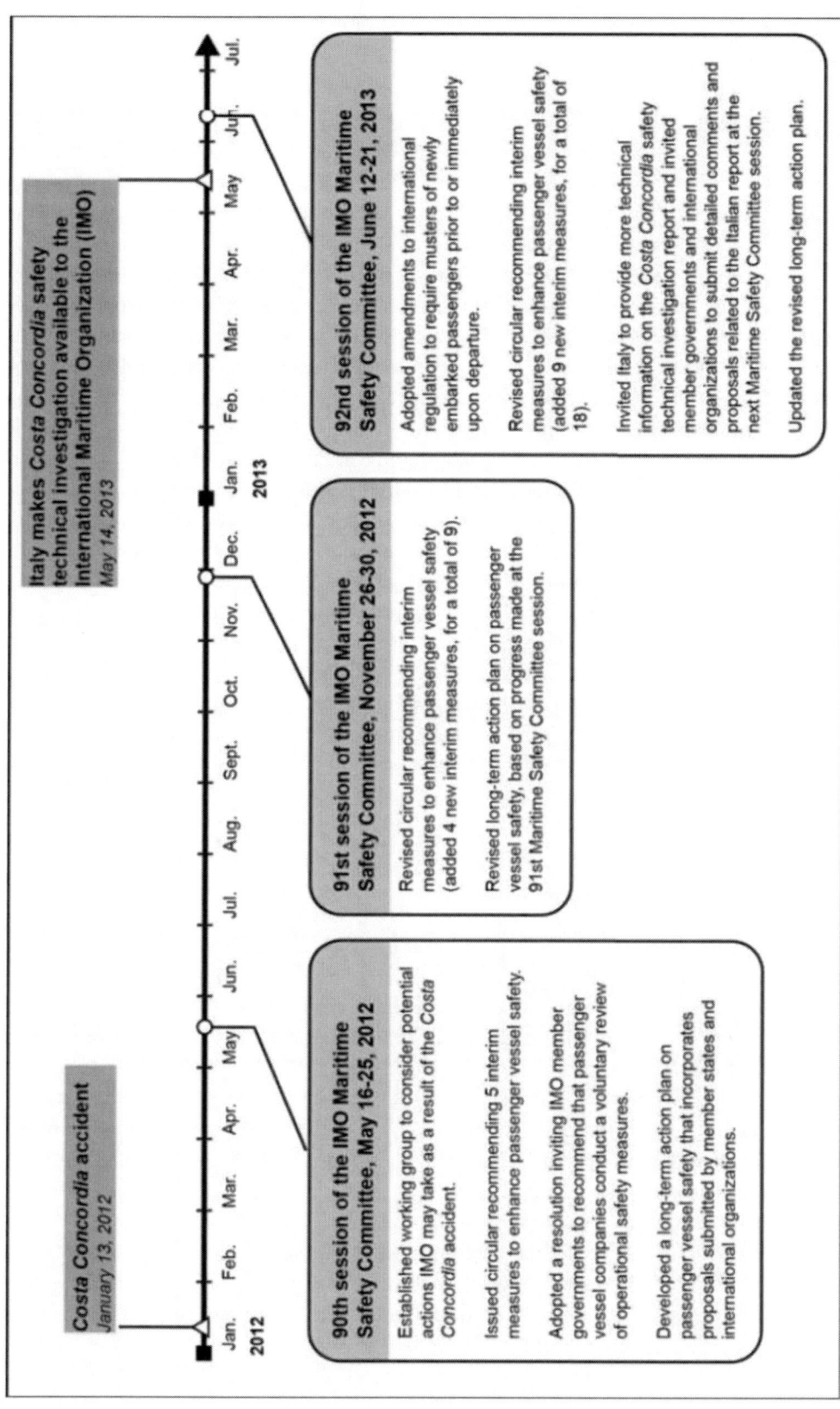

Source: GAO analysis of IMO actions.

Figure 4. Timeline of IMO MSC Actions following the Costa Concordia Accident.

Coast Guard Witnesses Passenger Musters and Coordinated Mass Rescue Exercise

Although the new muster requirement does not go into effect until January 2015, the Coast Guard initiated the practice of witnessing passenger musters as part of its mandatory vessel examination program in February 2012, just weeks after the *Costa Concordia* accident. Coast Guard officials acknowledged that they are, in effect, regulating by policy; however, they said the industry is supportive of this effort and has developed a similar policy to perform passenger musters prior to departure. Coast Guard officials said that when witnessing passenger musters, the Coast Guard actively ensures they contain the elements required by current regulation. For example, they check to ensure that crew members are appropriately directing passengers to their muster stations and that passengers are instructed in how to wear a life jacket, among other things. The Coast Guard reported it has witnessed about 280 musters since its policy went into effect, and agency officials said they have not had any major concerns with the musters they have witnessed.[52]

The Coast Guard reported that it is also continuing to monitor developments resulting from the *Costa Concordia* accident and may make additional policy changes in the future. For example, the Coast Guard and the NTSB represented the United States as a "substantially interested state" in the Italian-led *Costa Concordia* accident investigation, consistent with international law.[53] Coast Guard and NTSB officials said they contributed to the investigation by interviewing U.S. passengers and providing comments on a draft of the report. A senior Coast Guard official noted some of the general lessons that all parties with an interest in the investigation have learned. For example, the official said that muster drills should be held prior to departure, vessel route changes should not be made as unilateral decisions by the captain, better control of a vessel's environment can help alleviate human error, proper training of crew to handle emergency situations is essential, and extra life jackets should be available at locations convenient to evacuating passengers. Coast Guard officials said they are also monitoring actions being taken by CLIA and IMO, and may make policy changes in the future as they continue to review the final *Costa Concordia* report and wait for the results of the vessel salvage.[54]

Additionally, the Coast Guard has also been active in exercising scenarios related to cruise vessel evacuation and rescue. In April 2013, the Coast Guard coordinated an offshore cruise vessel rescue exercise in an effort to prepare for large-scale disasters similar to the *Costa Concordia* accident.[55] Although the Coast Guard has participated in mass rescue exercises involving cruise vessels before, the Coast Guard reported that this exercise was the largest in terms of scale and complexity in the history of the international maritime community and the Coast Guard.[56] The exercise was conducted in Freeport, Bahamas, and included Coast Guard collaboration with CLIA, three cruise lines, and the National Emergency Management Agency of the Bahamas, among others. One cruise line provided a cruise vessel that was used for the abandon vessel portion of the exercise, where we observed individuals posing as passengers boarding lifeboats that were lowered to the water and driven to shore. The second cruise line led the landing site and transportation element of the exercise, and the third cruise line led the sheltering operations element of the exercise where we observed passenger services— such as providing access to embassy consular affairs services, counseling, and minor medical services— being exercised.

In addition to witnessing the above actions as part of the mass rescue exercise, we observed efforts by the Department of State and Customs and Border Protection (CBP) as they exercised their respective responsibilities for managing passengers under the cruise vessel mass rescue scenario. For example, Department of State officials established a meeting room at the Freeport Airport, where they interacted with U.S. passenger evacuees to process their required passport documentation. Additionally, because Freeport is a CBP preclearance location—where departing U.S. passengers are processed through U.S. customs and immigration prior to departure to the United States—we witnessed CBP's approach for processing the surge of evacuees at the airport.[57] The Coast Guard characterized the 2013 exercise as a success, and noted that the exercise had effectively and interactively put into effect the full spectrum of vessel-to-shore mass rescue operations and identified strengths and weaknesses in existing procedures.

AGENCY COMMENTS

We provided a draft of this report to the Department of Homeland Security, the Department of Justice, the Department of Transportation, the National Transportation Safety Board, and the Department of State for review and comment. The Department of Homeland Security, Department of Justice, and Department of State provided technical comments, which we incorporated as appropriate.

Stephen L. Caldwell, Director
Homeland Security and Justice Issues

APPENDIX I: KEY STAKEHOLDERS WITH MARITIME SAFETY AND SECURITY ACTIVITIES

This appendix provides information on the international and domestic organizations that play a role in the safety and security of cruise vessels. The non-U.S. stakeholders are diverse; have wide-ranging roles and responsibilities; and include international organizations, governments of nations where cruise vessels make stops or are registered, and private organizations that help ensure the safe operation of vessels. See table 6 for a list of some of the relevant international and domestic stakeholders involved in implementation of the Cruise Vessel Security and Safety Act of 2010 (CVSSA) and cruise vessel safety and security issues.

Table 6. Stakeholders with Maritime Safety and Security Activities

Organization or agency	Maritime security or safety activities
International organizations	
International Maritime Organization (IMO) IMO is a specialized agency of the United Nations with 170 member states that is responsible for developing an international regulatory framework addressing, among other things, maritime safety and security.	• Responsible for developing and maintaining a comprehensive regulatory framework for cruise vessels. • Responsible for developing international standards for vessel security and safety.
Flag state The flag state is the country in which the vessel is registered, and a flag state's control or authority	• Responsible for ensuring that vessels flying its flag meet all international safety standards.

Table 6. (Continued)

Organization or agency	Maritime security or safety activities
over a vessel flying its flag can generally extend anywhere in the world that the vessel operates.	
Port state The port state is the country where the port is located. Port state control is the process by which a nation exercises its authority over foreign-flagged vessels operating in waters subject to the port state's jurisdiction.	• Inspects foreign vessels in national ports to verify that the condition of the vessel and its equipment complies with the requirements of international regulations and that the vessel is manned and operated in compliance with these rules.
Classification societies Classification societies are independent organizations that verify the structural strength and integrity of essential parts of the vessel's hull and its appendages, and the reliability and function of the propulsion and steering systems, power generation, and those other features and auxiliary systems that have been built into the vessel in order to maintain essential services onboard. Additionally, they verify the functionality of safety equipment and systems during inspections and verify operational procedures through audit programs.	• Develop and apply their own rules and verify compliance with international and national statutes on behalf of flag states. • Perform periodic surveys, carried out onboard the vessel, to verify that the vessel continues to meet relevant requirements.
Cruise Lines International Association (CLIA) CLIA is a trade association composed of 26 major cruise lines and represents 98 percent of the cruise line businesses operating in the United States.	• Responsible for acting as the coordinating body and conduit of information for its members in meetings with U.S. agencies at the national level. • Serves as a nongovernmental consultative organization to IMO.
Federal agencies[a]	
U.S. Coast Guard	• Ensures vessels in U.S. ports comply with domestic and international maritime security and safety standards. • Conducts initial, annual, and periodic exams of foreign-flagged cruise vessels calling in U.S. ports. This regime allows the Coast Guard to determine that the vessel is in substantial compliance with all applicable international and domestic standards. • Investigates marine casualties that occur on foreign cruise vessels in the navigable waters of the United States and its territories or possessions. The Coast Guard may also represent the United States as a "substantially interested state" in certain marine casualty investigations outside of U.S. jurisdiction. Furthermore, the Coast Guard and the National Transportation Safety Board have agreed to coordinate investigative responses for certain marine casualties. • Primary U.S. representative to IMO for all maritime policy development.
Maritime Administration (MARAD)	• MARAD is the agency within the U.S. Department of Transportation dealing with waterborne transportation. Among other things,

Organization or agency	Maritime security or safety activities
	it promotes the viability of U.S.-registered (flagged) vessels moving in domestic and international commerce. Almost all cruise vessels servicing the United States, however, are foreign flagged. • Responsible for developing a training curriculum for mariner use of force against piracy, and may certify organizations that offer a curriculum for training in the prevention, detection, evidence preservation, and reporting of criminal activities in the international maritime environment.
Federal Bureau of Investigation (FBI)	• Responsible for investigating alleged serious crimes listed in the CVSSA that occur aboard cruise vessels and meet the jurisdictional requirements of the CVSSA. • Employs maritime liaison agents who are responsible for coordinating with other organizations that share responsibility for security at the nation's ports, and facilitate the sharing of information on threats and security measures. • Employs victim specialists who provide information and crisis intervention/ emergency assistance to victims of violations that fall under FBI's investigative authority, whether charges are filed or not, to include referrals to counseling and other services available in the victim's home community.
National Transportation Safety Board (NTSB)	• NTSB's Office of Marine Safety investigates major marine accidents on or under the navigable waters, internal waters, or the territorial sea of the United States as well as accidents involving U.S.-flagged vessels worldwide to determine the probable cause and identify safety recommendations that will prevent similar events in the future.
Department of State	• Administers the Consular Information Program to inform U.S. citizens about potential threats to their health or safety abroad. • Provides assistance to U.S. citizens on cruise vacations in the event of a crime, medical issue, death, or loss of passport, among other things. • Works with foreign embassies and cruise companies in the event of a disaster to ensure U.S. citizens are accounted for and provided assistance—such as accommodations, clothing, and transportation home.
State and local governments	
Law enforcement agencies	• Conduct investigations into cruise vessel crime occurring within their maritime jurisdictions. • Except in those instances where the FBI has lead jurisdiction, coordinate with the FBI regarding alleged crimes and investigations, as appropriate.

Source: GAO analysis of organization and agency documents.

ª There are numerous federal agencies that play a role with respect to cruise safety and security, including: (1) Customs and Border Protection, which is responsible for screening vessels, passengers, and cargo as well as extraditing suspects to law enforcement officials and making admissibility decisions for non-U.S. citizens involved in crimes, among other things; (2) Centers for Disease Control and Prevention, which conducts the vessel sanitation program to assist the cruise vessel industry in preventing and controlling the introduction, transmission, and spread of gastrointestinal illnesses on cruise vessels; and (3) United States Department of Agricultural Animal and Plant Health Inspection Service, which regulates garbage arriving from outside the United States. However, for the purposes of this report, we focus on the agencies listed in table 4 because they have significant responsibilities for implementing the CVSSA, addressing crime, and ensuring the structural safety of cruise vessels.

APPENDIX II: PROVISIONS IN THE CRUISE VESSEL SECURITY AND SAFETY ACT

This appendix provides summary information on the provisions of the Cruise Vessel Security and Safety Act, including time frames for implementation.

Table 7. Summary of Provisions in the Cruise Vessel Security and Safety Act (CVSSA)

Category	Provision	Implementation time frame
Rail heights	The vessel shall be equipped with rails that are located not less than 42 inches above the cabin deck.	Eighteen months after enactment of the CVSSA.
Peepholes/other means of identification	Each passenger stateroom and crew cabin shall be equipped with entry doors that include peepholes or other means of visual identification.	Eighteen months after enactment of the CVSSA.
Security latches and time- sensitive keys	Each passenger stateroom and crew cabin shall be equipped with security latches and time-sensitive key technology.	Required for any vessel constructed after July 2010.
Capturing images of passengers/ detecting persons fallen overboard	The vessel shall integrate technology that can be used for capturing images of passengers or detecting passengers who have fallen overboard, to the extent that such technology is available.	Eighteen months after enactment of the CVSSA. Per Coast Guard Policy Letter 11-09, the Coast Guard is using a phased implementation plan to accommodate analysis and research and development. This provision is to be addressed by regulation or updated policy guidance.ª
Acoustical hailing and warning devices	Vessels shall be equipped with a sufficient number of operable acoustic hailing or other such warning devices to provide communication capability around	Eighteen months after enactment of the CVSSA. Per Coast Guard Policy Letter 11-09, the Coast Guard is using a phased implementation plan to

Category	Provision	Implementation time frame
	the entire vessel when operating in high-risk waters.	accommodate analysis and research and development. This provision is to be addressed by regulation or updated policy guidance.
Video recording requirements	(1) The owner of the vessel shall maintain a video surveillance system to assist in documenting crimes on the vessel and in providing evidence for the prosecution of such crimes, as determined by the Secretary of Homeland Security. (2) The owner of the vessel shall provide to any law enforcement official performing official duties in the course and scope of an investigation, upon request, a copy of all records of video surveillance that the official believes may provide evidence of a crime reported to law enforcement officials.	Per Coast Guard Policy Letter 11-09, the Coast Guard is using a phased implementation plan to accommodate analysis, research, and development. This provision is to be addressed by regulation or updated policy guidance.
Safety information	The owner of the vessel shall have available for each passenger a guide that provides a description of medical and security personnel onboard with 24-hour contact instructions and describes the jurisdictional authority applicable to, and the law enforcement processes available for, CVSSA crimes that arise in the territorial waters of the United States, on the high seas, or in any country to be visited on the voyage. The owner of the vessel shall also provide passengers with U.S. embassy and consulate information for each country the vessel will visit during the course of the voyage.	Effective immediately upon enactment of the CVSSA.
Sexual assault	The owner of the vessel shall (1) maintain adequate antiretroviral medications to prevent sexually transmitted diseases (STD) after a sexual assault; (2) maintain on-vessel equipment and materials to perform a sexual assault medical evaluation; (3) make available at all times	Effective immediately upon enactment of the CVSSA.

Table 7. (Continued)

Category	Provision	Implementation time frame
	medical staff who have proper credentialing; and (4) prepare, provide to the patient, and maintain documentation of the exam findings.	
Sexual assault, patient access to information and communications	The owner of the vessel shall provide patients free access to contact information for local law enforcement, FBI, Coast Guard, nearest U.S. embassy/consulate, and sexual assault hotline, as well as private phone line and Internet.	Effective immediately upon enactment of the CVSSA.
Confidentiality of sexual assault examination and support information	The master or other individual in charge of a vessel shall treat all information concerning an exam and post-assault counseling confidential.	Effective immediately upon enactment of the CVSSA.
Crew access to passenger staterooms	The owner of the vessel shall establish and implement procedures and restrictions concerning which crew members have access to passenger staterooms and periods during which they have access.	Effective immediately upon enactment of the CVSSA.
Logbook and reporting requirements	The owner of the vessel shall record in a logbook all complaints of CVSSA crimes, all complaints of theft of property in excess of $1,000, and all complaints of other crimes committed on any voyage that embarks or disembarks passengers in the United States. The owner of the vessel shall make the logbook available upon request to the FBI, any members of the Coast Guard, and any law enforcement officer performing official duties in the course and scope of an investigation. Logbook details shall include vessel operator, name of cruise line, flag state, age/gender of victim and assailant, description of alleged crime, vessel's position, time/date/method of initial report and law enforcement authority to which it was made, time/date of incident, total number of passengers and crew members,	Effective immediately upon enactment of the CVSSA.

Category	Provision	Implementation time frame
	and case number. Additionally, the owner of the vessel shall contact the FBI by phone to report alleged CVSSA crimes, and shall furnish a written report to the Coast Guard Internet portal.	
Availability and access of incident data via Coast Guard website	(1) The Secretary of Homeland Security shall maintain statistical compilation on the Internet of CVSSA crimes that are no longer under investigation by the FBI. Information shall be updated quarterly and aggregated by cruise line, and each crime shall be identified as to whether it was committed by a passenger or a crew member. (2) Each cruise line taking or discharging passengers in the United States shall include a link on its website to the website maintained by the Coast Guard described above.	Effective immediately upon enactment of the CVSSA.
Maritime Administration (MARAD) certification of crew training on crime scene preservation	MARAD may certify organizations in the United States and abroad that offer a curriculum for training and certification.	No implementation requirement for MARAD. Final policy under development as of December 2013.
Crew training on crime scene preservation	The Secretary of Homeland Security, in consultation with the FBI and MARAD, shall develop minimum training standards and curricula to allow for the certification of passenger vessel security personnel, crew members, and law enforcement officials on the appropriate methods for prevention, detection, evidence preservation, and reporting of criminal activities in the international maritime environment. Beginning 2 years after standards are established, no vessel may enter a U.S. port unless there is at least one crew member onboard who is certified as having completed training.	Within 1 year of the enactment of the CVSSA.

Source: GAO summary of Cruise Vessel Security and Safety Act.

^a The Coast Guard used Policy Letter 11-09 to set dates for compliance with CVSSA provisions in cases where the act did not provide specific time frames.

End Notes

1 Cruise Lines International Association (CLIA), *2011 CLIA Cruise Market Overview* (Fort Lauderdale, Florida: 2011). Passenger numbers for various years can be found on CLIA's website at http://www.cruising.org/regulatory/industry-welcome.

2 U.S. Department of Transportation Maritime Administration, *North American Cruise Statistical Snapshot, 2011*(Washington, D.C: March 2012). Data on the number of cruise passengers for 2012 were not available because the Department of Transportation's Maritime Administration no longer collects this information.

3 Pub. L. No. 111-207, 124 Stat. 2243. The CVSSA applies to cruise vessels that are authorized to carry at least 250 passengers, have onboard sleeping facilities for each passenger, are on a voyage that embarks or disembarks passengers in the United States, and are not engaged on a coastwise voyage. 46 U.S.C. § 3507(k)(1). Security, as it relates to the CVSSA and this report, is concerned with personal security from crime rather than threats of terrorism. We have previously reported on the issue of cruise vessel security as it relates to threats of terrorism. See GAO, *Maritime Security: Varied Actions Taken to Enhance Cruise Ship Security, but Some Concerns Remain*, GAO-10-400 (Washington, D.C.: Apr. 9, 2010).

4 46 U.S.C. §§ 3507(g)(3)(A), 3507(c)(2), 3507(a)(1)(B).

5 Id. at § 3507(g)(4).

6 Throughout the report we refer to these companies as cruise lines. However, they include two cruise corporations that are parent companies to several cruise lines or brands. Additionally, we conducted an interview with a subsidiary company of one corporation related to CVSSA implementation and security, but for purposes of this report, we have categorized this interview under the corporation. The five cruise lines we interviewed represent over 80 percent of North American cruise vessel passengers in 2012.

7 The data posted on the Coast Guard website were provided to the Coast Guard from the FBI and were a subset ("cases no longer under investigation") of the information provided to us for analysis. The Coast Guard reported that it had no role in verifying the accuracy of the information.

8 While the information we obtained from these groups and individuals cannot be generalized across the entire cruise industry, it provided us with varying perspectives on issues associated with cruise vessel crime and CVSSA implementation.

9 A classification society verifies the structural strength and integrity of essential parts of a vessel's hull and appendages, and the reliability and function of the propulsion and steering systems, power generation, and those other features and auxiliary systems that have been built into the vessel in order to maintain essential services onboard. Classification societies do this through the development and application of their own rules and by verifying compliance with international and national statutory regulations. We interviewed two classification societies that were headquartered in the Miami area—the location of one of our visits. While the information we obtained from the classification societies cannot be generalized across the entire cruise industry, it did provide us with a perspective on issues associated with cruise vessel safety.

10 Almost all cruise vessels operating in and out of U.S. ports are foreign flagged.

11 According to Coast Guard officials, analysis shows that foreign cruise vessels have roughly 70 percent fewer deficiencies than other types of foreign-flagged vessels, and are less likely to be detained. Additionally, given the quick turnaround that can occur with cruise vessels at ports and the amount of time needed to conduct an inspection, Coast Guard inspections are scheduled in advance.

12 46 C.F.R. pt. 4.

13 This analysis excludes 786 marine casualties that were classified as "personnel casualties," where one or more individuals were injured or died as the result of existing medical conditions or contact with the vessel as a result of a fall, among other things. Although in some instances personnel casualty data may be related to CVSSA crimes— such as when injury or death is the result of a CVSSA crime—we did not include a comparison of marine casualty data to CVSSA crime data for two reasons. First, there is overlap but not a direct correlation between some of the data associated with personnel casualties and the required crime-reporting categories in the CVSSA. Second, there are differences in reporting requirements for marine casualties versus CVSSA crime, based on the ownership and registry of the vessel, the nationality of the person(s) involved, and the location of the vessel at the time of the incident.

14 46 U.S.C. § 3507(k)(1). A coastwise voyage is defined as a voyage in which a vessel in the usual course of her employment proceeds from one port or place in the United States to another port or place in the United States or from a port or place in a possession to another port or place in the same possession, and passes outside the line dividing inland waters from the high seas (a voyage exclusively on the Great Lakes excepted), as well as a voyage in which a vessel proceeds from a port or place in the United States or its possessions and passes

outside the line dividing inland waters from the high seas and navigates on the high seas, and then returns to the same port or place.

[15] A vessel's bridge is the part of the vessel from which it is steered and navigated. Bridge Resource Management (BRM) is the effective management and utilization of all resources, human and technical, available to the bridge team (those employed on the bridge) to ensure the safe completion of the vessel's voyage. BRM focuses on bridge officers' skills such as teamwork, team building, communication, leadership, decision making, and resource management and incorporates these into the larger picture of organizational and regulatory management.

[16] CVSSA required Coast Guard to issue guidelines, training curricula, and inspection and certification procedures necessary to carry out the requirements of the law. 46 U.S.C. § 3507(i). Pursuant to the guidance, two of the provisions (rail heights and peepholes or other means of identification on stateroom doors) were not to be enforced by Coast Guard inspectors during their exams until January 2012; the remaining provisions were to be enforced from the date of enactment of the CVSSA, in July 2010 (although implementation guidelines from the Coast Guard did not come out until June 2011). The requirement for security latches/time-sensitive keys on stateroom doors applies only to those vessels where the keel was laid on or after July 27, 2010.

[17] The Coast Guard posted the policy guidance on its external website, so it was publicly available to cruise lines and others as well.

[18] Policy guidance was not issued in this area; however, Coast Guard officials told us they maintain a website with the FBI's cruise vessel crime data and that they did an initial check of all cruise lines' webpages to ensure they had a link to this Coast Guard crime data website.

[19] Three federal agencies were involved in creating the required course on crime scene preservation: the Coast Guard, the FBI, and MARAD. The Coast Guard coordinated the development of the course, the FBI provided much of the content for the course, and MARAD contributed its expertise in writing and structuring training courses, according to Coast Guard officials.

[20] High-risk waters are defined by the Coast Guard as waters with a high risk of terrorism, piracy, or armed robbery against vessels.

[21] S.1340, 113th Cong. (2013); H.R. 2800, 113th Cong. (2013).

[22] 78 Fed. Reg. 30,956 (May 23, 2013).

[23] 46 U.S.C. § 3507(c)(1). FBI officials told us that after the CVSSA was enacted, the cruise lines sent them their safety guides for the FBI to review, and the FBI provided comments back to the cruise lines, as required.

[24] Id. at § 3507(g)(4). While both the Coast Guard and the FBI have implementation responsibilities for the crime-reporting requirements in the CVSSA, the vast majority of the work in implementing the crime reporting provision of the CVSSA falls to the FBI. The Coast Guard's role is ensuring that the crime statistics that the FBI provides to it are posted on the Coast Guard's website in a timely manner, and it has done so. The website where the crime statistics are posted is http://www.uscg.mil/hq/cg2/cgis/CruiseLine.asp.

[25] 46 U.S.C. § 3507(g)(3)(A). The FBI has jurisdiction to investigate an alleged crime if (1) the vessel, regardless of registry, is owned, in whole or in part, by a United States person, regardless of the nationality of the victim or perpetrator, and the incident occurs when the vessel is within the admiralty and maritime jurisdiction of the United States and outside the jurisdiction of any state; (2) the incident concerns an offense by or against a United States national committed outside the jurisdiction of any nation; (3) the incident occurs in the Territorial Sea of the United States, regardless of the nationality of the vessel, the victim, or the perpetrator; or (4) the incident concerns a victim or perpetrator who is a United States national on a vessel during a voyage that departed from or will arrive at a U.S. port. 46 U.S.C. § 3507(g)(3)(B).

[26] The sexual assault offenses are aggravated sexual abuse, sexual abuse, sexual abuse of a minor, and abusive sexual contact. Prior to the CVSSA, in March 2007, the FBI, the Coast Guard, and CLIA reached an agreement on voluntary, standardized protocols for CLIA member lines to report allegations of serious violations of U.S. law committed aboard cruise vessels. The agreement listed eight categories of incidents that are to be reported by CLIA members to the nearest FBI field office or legal attaché office. These incidents are identical to those listed in the CVSSA.

[27] 46 U.S.C. § 3507(g)(4).

[28] 46 U.S.C. § 3507(g)(3)(A). The CVSSA also gives the cruise lines discretion to report any serious incident that does not meet the reporting requirements of the law if they wish. Officials from one cruise line we spoke with said it generally reports all crimes that occur onboard, including minor offenses, to the FBI.

[29] If the next port is a U.S. port, the FBI is to meet the vessel upon arrival. If the next port is a foreign port, the FBI works with the local foreign authorities to decide who has jurisdiction over the case. If it is determined that a foreign country has jurisdiction, it would be less likely the FBI would also open its own investigation, according to the FBI.

[30] The CVSSA does require cruise lines to provide victims of alleged sexual assault with free and immediate access to contact information for law enforcement, hotline services, and others and a private telephone line and Internet connection by which the individual may confidentially access law enforcement, an attorney, and information and support services. 46 U.S.C. § 3507(d)(5).

[31] If a crime occurs outside the United States' jurisdiction, State Department officials said that if they are notified of a cruise vessel crime involving a U.S. citizen, the local embassy or consulate will provide assistance to that U.S. citizen, if needed, and coordinate with the FBI.

[32] However, in the information provided to CLIA, the FBI cautions that cruise line personnel should not be "collecting evidence" nor does their effort to preserve a crime scene create an agency relationship such that cruise vessel or other maritime vessel personnel are deemed to be acting as agents of the government, or vice versa.

[33] The UCR was conceived in 1929 by the International Association of Chiefs of Police to meet the need for reliable uniform crime statistics for the nation. In 1930, the FBI was tasked with collecting, publishing, and archiving those statistics. The FBI produces three annual publications: *Crime in the United States, Law Enforcement Officers Killed and Assaulted,* and *Hate Crime Statistics.* The crime data are submitted either through a state UCR program or directly to the FBI's UCR Program.

[34] Although the crime data on CLIA's website are presented through the end of 2012, the UCR's definition of forcible rape was updated in January 2013 to be more broad and include rape of a male or a female. CLIA indicated that it would require its members to update their definitions as the UCR definitions change.

[35] CLIA reports a subset of these data on its website as well. One of the six cruise lines is a corporation that reported the crime data in aggregate for its four North American–based cruise line subsidiaries.

[36] There is precedent for the collection of alleged crime information across institutions for comparison purposes. For example, the Jeanne Clery Disclosure of Campus Security Policy and Campus Crime Statistics Act requires colleges and universities participating in federal financial aid programs to maintain and disclose statistics on certain alleged crimes. 20 U.S.C. § 1092(f). According to the Department of Education, the goal of this regulation is to provide students, and their families, as higher education consumers, with accurate, complete, and timely information about safety so they can make informed decisions.

[37] S.1340, 113th Cong. (2013); H.R. 2800,113th Cong. (2013).

[38] Currently, CVSSA requires an alleged crime to be reported to the FBI "as soon as possible," and it does not require the nearest U.S. consulate to be notified. 46 U.S.C. 3507(g)(3)(A).

[39] Musters are mandatory exercises conducted on cruise vessels to ensure passengers are informed of safety protocols while onboard the vessel, including emergency evacuation procedures.

[40] CLIA announced its Operational Safety Review on January 27, 2012, about 2 weeks after the *Costa Concordia* accident. CLIA officials said they completed their review in December 2012.

[41] CLIA, *Operational Safety Review Executive Summary,* accessed June 14, 2013, http://www.cruising.org/ regulatory/cruise-industry-policies/cruise-industry-operational-safety-review. The panel of experts included a former chairman of the U.S. NTSB; a former rear admiral in the Royal Navy and head of the United Kingdom's Marine Accident Investigation Branch; a former director, Office of Marine Safety, U.S. NTSB; and a former head and executive director of the European Maritime Safety Agency.

[42] An SMS is a structured and documented system enabling company personnel to implement effectively the company safety and environmental protection policy.

[43] One policy—the location of life jacket stowage policy—went into effect on July 1, 2013, for newly constructed cruise vessels. CLIA officials said that they did not expect cruise lines to implement the harmonization of bridge procedures policy and the securing heavy objects policy upon the dates of their announcement (November 15, 2012).

[44] As part of enforcing the ISM Code, flag states (or organizations recognized by the flag administrations, such as classification societies) audit company and vessel compliance with its SMS, and issue documents of compliance and safety management certificates that are valid for 5 years, subject to periodic verification. The ISM Code also requires that companies perform annual internal safety audits to ensure compliance with their SMSs.

[45] As previously discussed, through its Port State Control Program, the Coast Guard routinely boards foreign-flagged vessels operating in U.S. waters to verify that they are in compliance with applicable international conventions and U.S. laws and regulations. When the Coast Guard identifies vessels that are not in substantial compliance with applicable laws or regulations, it is responsible for imposing controls to ensure the vessels are brought into compliance.

[46] In June 2013, the IMO Marine Safety Committee adopted amendments to the SOLAS convention, regulations III/19.2.2 and III/19.2.3.

[47] According to the Italian government report on the safety technical investigation for the *Costa Concordia* accident, 1,270 of the 3,206 passengers had participated in a muster drill, while the remaining passengers received safety instructions by video.

[48] In June 2012, IMO's MSC issued a circular with 5 interim recommendations, and has subsequently updated the circular twice, for a total of 18 interim recommendations. These 18 recommendations address life jackets onboard passenger vessels, emergency instructions for passengers, common elements of musters and emergency instructions, passenger muster policy, access of personnel to the navigating bridge and avoiding distractions, harmonization of bridge navigational procedures, voyage planning, recording the nationality of persons on board, lifeboat loading for training purposes, securing heavy objects, and inclinometer (rolling

motion) data for the voyage data recorder. More complete information can be accessed by creating a public account on http://webaccounts.imo.org, and searching for the circular that lists the 18 interim recommendations (MSC.1/Circ.1446/Rev.2).

[49] Department of State officials said they had a difficult time determining who the U.S. citizens were that were onboard the *Costa Concordia* at the time of the accident. Officials said the vessel's manifest contained only last names and first initials of passengers and did not have citizenship information, making it difficult for them to determine who the U.S citizens were so they could render assistance.

[50] This same Coast Guard official noted that the long-term action plan was not intended to include only issues that can be linked directly to the *Costa Concordia* accident. He said the plan also includes issues that were already under consideration by MSC when the accident occurred. At the most recent MSC meeting (June 2013), MSC instructed the IMO Secretariat to revise the long-term action plan with a view to clearly identify whether proposed actions are related to existing issues or are new issues arising from the loss of the *Costa Concordia*. The Coast Guard informed us that this revision has been completed, but noted that the action plan has not been finalized and therefore continues to not be publicly available.

[51] The Coast Guard generally focuses its enforcement activities on U.S. and international regulations. However, as of September 2013, we identified one international regulation and no U.S. regulations that have been adopted as a result of the *Costa Concordia* accident.

[52] Coast Guard officials said they do not separately track the number of musters they have witnessed. However, the Coast Guard conducted 301 cruise vessel examinations from the beginning of the muster policy (February 2, 2012) through July 1, 2013. Officials estimated that they witnessed musters at about 280 of these examinations, and did not witness musters at the roughly 20 examinations where passengers had embarked on the vessel elsewhere.

[53] See IMO Resolution MSC.255(84). The investigating state should allow substantially interested states to interview witnesses, view and examine evidence and make copies of documents, make submissions in respect of the evidence, comment on and have their views properly reflected in the final report, and be provided with the draft and final reports.

[54] As a result of the accident, the *Costa Concordia* turned on its side and rested on the ocean floor, with a significant portion of the vessel still above water. Vessel salvage refers to the process of removing the vessel wreck. The owner of the vessel plans to have the vessel removed in one piece by refloating it and having it towed away from the coast of the Island of Giglio, Italy, where the accident occurred.

[55] This operation was the first in a 5-year mass rescue exercise series known as Black Swan. Future mass rescue operations are scheduled in Hawaii in 2015, and Norfolk, Virginia, in 2017.

[56] The Coast Guard noted that all offshore mass rescue events require significant search and rescue efforts including international communications; coordination of rescue resources; local emergency management stakeholders; international health care systems to support medical surge capacities to care for large numbers of injured personnel; coordinated landing site management; sustained care for the rescued with clothing, food, and counseling services; and transportation travel documentation and logistics planning to return the rescued to their homes.

[57] Preclearance operations are part of CBP's Office of Field Operations, which has the responsibility of managing 329 ports of entry nationwide. These operations are established via a formal agreement between the United States and host country, which allows CBP to staff officers at host airports and facilitate the customs and immigration process for passengers prior to arrival in the United States. As of September 2013, preclearance is in effect in Aruba, Bermuda, Bahamas (two locations), Ireland (two locations) and Canada (nine locations).

In: Cruise Industry Safety and Security   ISBN: 978-1-63117-882-5
Editor: Brennan T. Preston   © 2014 Nova Science Publishers, Inc.

Chapter 2

TESTIMONY OF REAR ADMIRAL JOSEPH SERVIDIO, ASSISTANT COMMANDANT FOR PREVENTION POLICY, U.S. COAST GUARD. HEARING ON "CRUISE INDUSTRY OVERSIGHT: RECENT INCIDENTS SHOW NEED FOR STRONGER FOCUS ON CONSUMER PROTECTION"*

INTRODUCTION

Good morning Mr. Chairman, Ranking Member Thune, and distinguished members of the committee. Thank you for the opportunity to appear before you to discuss issues related to cruise ship safety. I would like to provide background into the Coast Guard's oversight of the cruise industry, highlight what we've learned and implemented from recent casualties, and discuss the effectiveness of our Port State Control system in holding cruise industry companies and their vessels accountable for safe passenger operations.

In my role as the Coast Guard's Assistant Commandant for Prevention Policy, I am responsible for setting standards for safety, security, and environmental stewardship for commercial vessels, facilities, and mariners, ensuring compliance with those standards, and conducting investigations of violations and accidents.

Over the past three years we've seen a number of high profile ship casualties within the cruise industry, fires aboard the *Carnival Splendor*, *Carnival Triumph* and *Grandeur of the Seas* highlight serious questions about the design, maintenance and operation of fire safety equipment on board these vessels, as well as their companies' safety management cultures. As the United States' lead as a Port State for holding foreign companies accountable for the safe and secure design and operation of these vessels, I am very concerned about these failures. I am working to ensure that the Coast Guard thoroughly reviews each incident to determine causes and identify corrective actions and hold the cruise lines accountable for improving safety aboard vessels through increased examination and oversight. Additionally

---

* This is an edited, reformatted and augmented version of testimony presented July 24, 2013 before the Senate Committee on Commerce, Science, and Transportation.

we will work through the International Maritime Organization (IMO) to update the design and operational standards for cruise ships based on these incidents.

We recently completed our investigation into the *Carnival Splendor* engine explosion and debilitating fire. We are treating the recommendations for Coast Guard action in that report as requirements, and based on that report, the Coast Guard is changing its examination program for foreign cruise ships to examine CO_2 system installations and arrangements more closely. Additionally, we have increased our expectations for successful fire drills. We have also made recommendations to Carnival Corporation to improve their training programs. I will cover these recent developments in more detail a bit later in my testimony.

In late June, I led the U.S. delegation to the 92nd session of the IMO Maritime Safety Committee. At this session, we adopted new rules governing cruise ship passenger safety briefings which will become mandatory in July 2015. These new rules ensure that whenever U.S. passengers board a Safety of Life at Sea (SOLAS) regulated passenger ship for more than 24 hours, they will receive a detailed safety briefing either prior to, or immediately after, the vessel gets underway. This regulatory change elevates the standard globally for approximately one third of all cruise passengers who don't embark ships in the U.S.

Further, based in part on our proposals at this June session, IMO has commenced reviewing design standards in order to make cruise ships safer, and even more damage-tolerant, through improved survivability standards.

Modern Standards for Cruise Ships

Over the past decade, the international shipping community, through the IMO and with Coast Guard leadership, has moved decisively toward a proactive approach to passenger ship safety. With cruise ships growing progressively in size and capacity, in May 2000 the IMO agreed to undertake a holistic examination of safety issues pertaining to passenger ships, with particular emphasis on large cruise ships. The outcome of this proactive initiative is an entirely new prevention- and survivability-based regulatory philosophy for cruise ship design, construction, and operation.

The U.S., through the efforts of the Coast Guard, has taken a very active leadership role throughout this initiative, putting forward many of the recommendations for action taken by the various IMO Sub-Committees. This effort identified a number of areas of concern related to cruise ships, and resulted in substantial amendments to major IMO conventions, including SOLAS, International Convention for the Prevention of Pollution From Ships (MARPOL) 73/78, International Tonnage, Standards for Training, Certification, and Watchkeeping (STCW) and Load Line conventions. These amendments address surveys, structures, stability, machinery, fire safety, lifesaving equipment, communications, navigation equipment, safety management, maritime security, pollution prevention, crew competency, watertight integrity, and safe loading.

Significant improvements under the five main pillars of the IMO initiative entered into force in July 2010 include:

- Prevention: Amendments to the STCW Code and supporting guidelines focus on navigation safety and resource management;

- Improved survivability: New SOLAS requirements for the "safe return to port" concept address essential system redundancy, management of emergencies, and casualty mitigation, including the new concept of dedicated shipboard safety centers to manage emergencies;
- Regulatory flexibility: Amendments to SOLAS provide a methodology for the approval of new and innovative safety technologies and arrangements;
- Operations in areas remote from SAR facilities: Guidelines on external support from SAR authorities, as well as guidance to assist seafarers taking part in SAR operations have been developed; and finally; and
- Health safety and medical care: Guidelines on establishing medical safety programs, and a revised Guide on Cold Water Survival.

Other recent improvements include stability and survivability of cruise ships through new probabilistic subdivision and damage stability regulations, and flooding detection systems; improved voyage planning, particularly in remote and high latitude areas; and voyage data recorders. As a separate initiative, stemming from the 2006 fire aboard the Star Princess, significant improvements have been made to the fire safety features of external areas on cruise ships. Overall, the past decade has been an enormous leap forward in cruise ship safety measures and has been largely proactive to casualties. The U.S. Coast Guard's leadership in the international community with respect to cruise ship safety measures and our support to foreign casualty investigations evidences our dedication to the world wide safety of U.S. passengers.

The Safety, Security, and Environmental Protection Net

The IMO conventions form the basis for the international safety, security, and stewardship net designed to ensure consistent standards across the world wide fleet of cruise ships. Owners and operators, vessel crews, classification societies, flag states (or their recognized organizations when delegated to act on the behalf of the flag state), and port states each have distinct roles in ensuring compliance with those standards. Each of these entities performs specific roles intended to maximize safety, security, and environmental protection.

Flag states have the primary responsibility to ensure their vessels meet international and domestic standards. They often achieve this through recognized third party organizations who certify that vessels meet design, construction, operating, and manning requirements throughout the life of the vessel.

Port states verify substantial compliance with international standards and ensure compliance with applicable domestic requirements for vessels of all flags calling in their ports. As the port state authority for the U.S., the Coast Guard has established a robust control verification program that subjects cruise ships calling in U.S. ports to a much higher level of scrutiny than other foreign flag vessels, and much higher than any other port state requires for foreign flag cruise ships in their ports.

Although we cannot provide total quality control for foreign cruise ships visiting our ports, we do take prompt action to ensure deficiencies we find during our examinations are corrected in an expeditious manner. If a deficiency is serious, we ensure it gets corrected before the vessel leaves port. When one or more deficiencies lead us to conclude a ship is substandard, we detain the vessel. A detention means the vessel cannot leave port until the serious deficiencies are corrected. We report the detention to IMO and list the vessel on international forums as a detained vessel, and we will examine the vessel more frequently for a period of three years.

Most recently, the Coast Guard detained the *Carnival Triumph* after it was found to have three serious deficiencies at its first examination after completing repairs following the February 2013 fire. As described above, the vessel was held in port until these deficiencies were corrected, we reported the detention to IMO and listed the vessel as detained on our website, and the vessel will be subject to quarterly examinations for three years. This detention demonstrates the effectiveness of our control verification program, as well as our willingness to hold substandard vessels accountable.

Coast Guard Control Verification Program for Foreign Flag Cruise Ships

All foreign flag cruise ships arriving in the United States that embark passengers or make a U.S. port call while carrying U.S. citizens as passengers must participate in the control verification process. Cruise ships that return to U.S. service after a prolonged absence are treated as if they had never been in service in the U.S. and must undergo the entire process again.

The Coast Guard control verification program includes initial, annual, and periodic examinations for foreign flag cruise ships calling in our ports. Further, it includes concept review during the very earliest stages of design and pre-construction planning by Coast Guard naval architects and fire protection engineers, mid-construction inspections at the builder's yard by Coast Guard marine inspectors, an initial operational inspection of the vessel upon completion of construction, and at least annual inspections while the vessel is in service in U.S. ports. This regime allows the Coast Guard to determine that the vessel is in substantial compliance with all applicable international and domestic standards.

The engineering review of plans for structural fire protection arrangements provides an additional level of assurance that shipboard fire safety arrangements meet international standards. After review, these same engineers visit the ship to confirm that the arrangements on the vessel are the same as those shown on the structural fire protection plans. On the basis of this initial examination, the Coast Guard issues a certificate of compliance that allows the vessel to operate in U.S. ports.

The annual examination ensures that foreign cruise ships continue to maintain the systems the Coast Guard previously examined during the initial exam in proper operating condition and that the flag administration has performed annual renewal surveys as required by SOLAS. Inspectors focus on marine environmental protection, firefighting, lifesaving, and emergency systems and witness a comprehensive fire and boat drill by the crew. In addition, inspectors examine the vessel for modifications that would affect the vessel's structural fire protection and means of escape. They also check for modifications completed without the vessel's flag administration approval. After a satisfactory annual examination, the Coast Guard re-issues a certificate of compliance.

Periodic examinations are also conducted, typically midway between the annual examinations. These examinations are more limited in scope but still compliment the more comprehensive annuals, and they are intended to ensure vessels are being operated in a safe manner. The periodic examinations focus on the performance of officers and crew, with specific attention paid to their training on and knowledge of the ship's emergency procedures, environmental protection, security, firefighting, lifesaving systems, and conduct during the drills. To ensure the overall material condition of the ship has not appreciably changed since the annual examination, inspectors randomly select sample items for examination.

Inspectors also vary the scope of the examination depending on such factors as the material condition of the vessel, recordkeeping, the maintenance of the vessel, and the professionalism and training of the crew. At every Coast Guard examination of a foreign cruise ship, the inspectors will determine whether the vessel is in substantial compliance with the international convention standards.

Investigations

Foreign vessels operating in U.S. waters are required by U.S. law to report accidents immediately. Upon accident notification, we proactively investigate casualties meeting a threshold to determine causes and issue safety recommendations to prevent recurrences.

This is a continuous improvement process which incorporates lessons learned from accident investigations to enhance cruise ship safety and ensure compliance with national and international laws.

After the *Costa Concordia* incident, and as a "Substantially Interested State" in accordance with IMO Protocols, the Coast Guard immediately offered technical expertise and support to the Government of Italy's marine casualty investigation. Similarly, following the *Carnival Triumph* fire and the *Grandeur of the Seas* fire, the Coast Guard is participating in the investigations with the vessel's flag state of the Bahamas as a Substantially Interested State.

It is long standing practice to cooperate in all manner of accident investigations involving different flag and coastal states and the Coast Guard routinely acts in this accord.

After the *Carnival Splendor* fire in November 2010, the Coast Guard reached out to Panama, the vessel's flag state, to offer assistance. In accordance with international protocols and at the request of Panama, the Coast Guard took the lead for the investigation into this casualty. While this incident did not lead to major damage to the vessel, injury or loss of life, the investigation revealed a number of major safety concerns. As a result, the Coast Guard immediately issued two safety alerts to advise the industry of potential CO_2 system problems.

The Coast Guard report of investigation which was released on July 15, 2013, also contains five safety recommendations. Three of the recommendations are addressed to Carnival and Panama (as the flag state) to ensure that the conditions which contributed to the fire, are addressed appropriately. In addition, there are two safety recommendations which are aimed at exercising and enhancing the Coast Guard's role as the Port State for this and many other foreign flag cruise ships. These recommendations will be implemented by my staff and will ensure that Coast Guard Port State Control Officers are armed with the information needed to not only evaluate the mechanical systems onboard these complex vessels, but the human element as well.

Investigations Informing the Control Verification Process and Other Actions

In its role as a Port State, the Coast Guard employs casualty investigation lessons learned where practical and appropriate to inform the Control Verification process.

For example, as a result of the *Costa Concordia* incident, we directed Coast Guard field inspectors to witness the passenger muster required by SOLAS whenever they are aboard a cruise ship conducting an initial, annual, or periodic examination. Our personnel witness these musters either immediately before or during vessel departure from port. In conjunction, the cruise industry associations announced a new emergency drill policy requiring mandatory muster for embarking passengers prior to departure from port.

As a result of the *Carnival Splendor* casualty, we are directing Coast Guard field inspectors to examine vessel CO_2 systems more closely during examinations. There was evidence that the CO_2 system had not been installed and maintained properly, and we are looking at sister vessels for similar problems. Any similar problems will require swift correction. We have also increased our expectations for the fire drills we witness during our examinations. Too often, ships perform drills for our inspectors which do not address a fire in a high-risk area such as an engine room. We will direct ships to perform an engineroom fire drill during the next examination of all vessels, and will expect such demonstrations periodically thereafter.

Following the *Carnival Triumph* fire in the Gulf of Mexico in February of 2013, we engaged aggressively in Carnival's Safety Management System (SMS) by requesting them and the vessel's flag state (the Bahamas) to hold their annual audit early, with which they complied. We participated in Carnival's company level SMS Document of Compliance audit conducted by Lloyd's Registry in April, and plan to observe one of their shipboard SMS audits. Based on the most recent audit results, we have been generally satisfied with Carnival's SMS implementation, and will continue to keep a close eye on their progress.

A more recent casualty to the *Grandeur of the Seas* yielded several observations which we are taking immediate action to correct. One involves a deluge system valve that protected the mooring deck area that had caught fire. The valve was located in an area made inaccessible due to the fire. Our inspectors will examine sister ships for similar problems. Another observation involved un-insulated aluminum deck hatches which failed and allowed the fire to affect adjacent spaces. Again, our inspectors will examine sister ships for similar problems.

Search and Rescue (SAR) and Mass Rescue Operations (MRO)

The Coast Guard has maintained a sound relationship with the cruise lines regarding search and rescue and medical evacuations. For the Coast Guard, a Mass Rescue Operation involving a cruise ship casualty offshore, with potentially thousands of passengers and crew forced to evacuate into lifeboats and the water, presents our greatest search and rescue challenge.

Working with cruise line and passenger vessel companies, the Coast Guard continues to develop and improve SAR and MRO contingency plans. In addition to internal Coast Guard SAR plans, the Coast Guard holds a copy of cruise ship SAR plans and is able to incorporate the cruise ship plans into our overall SAR planning. The Coast Guard also meets periodically with cruise line medical personnel to discuss plans for medical emergencies.

Coast Guard passenger vessel safety personnel at each of our Districts assist in the conduct and coordination of Coast Guard mass rescue exercises. Over the last five years, the Coast Guard conducted thirty-six mass rescue exercises involving passenger vessels, three of which involved a cruise ship.

Mass rescue exercises have been structured around a five-year cycle. The Coast Guard has directed that, at a minimum, each Coast Guard District conduct and/or participate in one discussion based (e.g., seminar, workshop, game, or tabletop) and one operations based (e.g., drills, functional, full scale) mass rescue exercise over a five year period.

To meet this exercise requirement the Coast Guard initiated a five-year mass rescue exercise series known as "Black Swan." The exercise series commenced in April 2013 with a full scale exercise on a passenger ship in Freeport, Bahamas, and will continue with a full scale exercise in Hawaii in 2015 and Norfolk in 2017. The scope of these exercises provides a valuable opportunity to identify and resolve the difficulties associated with rescuing hundreds or thousands of people. Black Swan will continue to focus on the exercise of Coast Guard mass rescue plans, coordination with other authorities and industry partners, notification and information processes, personnel accountability, and unique challenges of embarking thousands of survivors on rescue ships from the water, lifeboats and rafts, and rescued passenger and crew support.

Cruise Ship Security and Crime

The events of September 11, 2001, spurred the development of the Maritime Transportation Security Act (MTSA) and the IMO International Ship and Port Facility Security (ISPS) Code, both of which are rigorously enforced by the Coast Guard. The Coast Guard examines every cruise ship that visits the U.S. for compliance with MTSA and ISPS requirements during the ship's annual and periodic Control Verification exam, as well as on a random basis throughout the year during unannounced port security checks.

Despite this security compliance regime, there have been serious incidents and crimes that have affected U.S. citizens aboard foreign-flagged cruise ships. This has led to an increased focus on protecting our citizens both in port and while they are at sea. In 2010, Congress enacted the Cruise Ship Security and Safety Act of 2010 (CVSSA) which prescribes security and safety requirements for designated cruise ships.

CVSSA addresses many areas that affect personal safety and security, including: ship design; better public access to information about crime aboard cruise ships; improved precautions, response, medical care, support for victims of sexual assault; preservation of evidence necessary to prosecute criminals; and more consistent and complete reports. Some of these requirements went into effect when the President signed the legislation on July 27, 2010; however, there are areas that require implementation through the publication of regulations.

Thus far, the Coast Guard has completed the following actions with respect to implementing the CVSSA:

- The Coast Guard published policy establishing guidelines for Coast Guard Marine
- Inspectors examining cruise vessels for compliance to include physical requirements, such as: rail heights; door peep-holes (similar to hotel doors), which allow cabin occupants to see who is outside; and the passenger security guide.
- The Coast Guard established an internet-based portal (NCC@uscg.mil) to facilitate electronic submission of crime reports.
- The Coast Guard established a web link to publish cruise ship sexual assault and criminal activity data received from the Federal Bureau of Investigation (FBI) in accordance with the act: http://www.uscg.mil/hq/cg2/cgis/.
- An Inter-agency workgroup consisting of Coast Guard, FBI, and the Maritime Administration personnel completed development of a model course addressing crime scene preservation standards and curricula.
- The Coast Guard published policy promulgating training standards and curricula for the certification of passenger vessel security personnel.

Closing

In closing, let me emphasize that the Coast Guard understands and embraces our lead role in protecting our most precious cargo- people, who are carried aboard cruise ships in many of the world's most pristine marine environments. We continue to place the highest priority on enforcing compliance with safety, security and environmental regulations on those vessels that embark passengers in the United States and embark U.S. passengers world-wide.

We have a strong and effective port state control program for foreign cruise ships and will continue to ensure that vessels calling on ports in the United States are in substantial compliance with applicable international and domestic standards.

Through proactive oversight and enforcement, we participate in casualty investigations, even those taking place overseas, and we lead efforts at the IMO to improve maritime safety, security, and environmental protection standards. As those investigation results are analyzed, the Coast Guard will continue to capture the lessons learned and incorporate them into our safety regime, and continue to recommend international requirement updates where necessary. Internally, we are also changing our examination procedures to address the lessons made apparent from other recent cruise ship fire casualties and ensure our port state control examinations target areas of concern.

The Coast Guard looks forward to continued cooperation with this committee, passenger victims groups, and the passenger vessel industry to maximize cruise vessel safety, security, and environmental protection.

Thank you again for the opportunity to testify today. I will be pleased to answer any questions you may have.

In: Cruise Industry Safety and Security
Editor: Brennan T. Preston

ISBN: 978-1-63117-882-5
© 2014 Nova Science Publishers, Inc.

Chapter 3

Testimony of Ross A. Klein, Professor, Memorial University of Newfoundland, Canada. Hearing on "Cruise Industry Oversight: Recent Incidents Show Need for Stronger Focus on Consumer Protection"[*]

Oral Testimony

It is an honor to be asked to share my knowledge and insights with the U.S. Senate Committee on Commerce, Science, and Transportation. In my brief oral remarks I will identify some of the key points in my written submission.

The cruise industry has received considerable attention in the media in recent years. In 2013 alone the media reports for cruise ships: 3 running aground; 5 fires; 2 collisions; 19 mechanical problems including power loss, propulsion problems, and generator problems; 10 canceled port calls and/or changes in itinerary; 16 cruises with delayed embarkation and/or disembarkation; 2 cruises where passengers were bumped; and 8 ships that have failed U.S. health inspections.

In response to the negative publicity from these events, and Senator Schumer's call for greater consumer protection, the Cruise Lines International Association (CLIA) in late-May issued its Passenger Bill of Rights –an obvious public relations initiative. Sadly, a systematic evaluation reveals that while many of the promises on their face are reassuring to cruise passengers, a deeper look indicates the Passenger Bill of Rights is filled with empty promises. Take for example Right #5 - The right to a ship crew that is properly trained in emergency and evacuation procedures. There is a huge chasm between being properly trained and those same crewmembers demonstrating through behavior competence in executing emergency and evacuation procedures. Take for example the U.S. Coast Guard's investigation of the fire and power loss of Carnival Splendor in 2010. It indicates human error in a fire alarm being reset, leading to a 15-minute delay in activation of an automatic fire-suppression system; the crew's lack of familiarity with the engine room, which hampered their ability to locate and fight the

---

[*] This is an edited, reformatted and augmented version of testimony presented July 24, 2013 before the Senate Committee on Commerce, Science, and Transportation.

fire; and the captain ventilating the compartment where the fire began before it was fully extinguished, allowing the flames to flare again. I doubt the crewmembers were not properly trained, but what assurance does CLIA's Passenger Bill of Rights provide that training will be reflected in action. And what recourse does a passenger have when this or any Right is not realized?

Also take for example Right #1 - The right to disembark a docked ship if essential provisions cannot adequately be provided onboard. What cruise passenger would not be reassured by this, but how is this Right fulfilled when a ship is dead in the water for 3 or 4 days and being towed to port? And once the ship returns to port, who decides how quickly disembarkation will begin? Does a passenger have any right to contest a decision to keep them onboard?

Coming up with a list of "mom-and-apple-pie" rights is easy. But as they say, the devil is in the details.

Perhaps more troubling are contradictions between CLIA's Passenger Bill of Rights and the typical cruise passenger contract. There is no indication which takes precedence, especially given the restrictiveness of the passenger cruise contract with regard to rights held by a cruise passenger (particularly in comparison to the rights of the cruise line) and the extreme limitations on the cruise line's liability for almost anything that happens on a cruise ship. My written testimony systematically analyses CLIA's Bill of Rights and typical passenger cruise contracts. This analysis points to the need for better consumer protection of cruise passengers, much like the protections available to passengers on other modes of commercial transportation, including air carriers.

My written testimony also provides systematic analysis of the Cruise Vessel Security and Safety Act of 2010. I look at the implications of differences between the Act as initially introduced and the final Act passed. I also look at issues that are not adequately addressed by the current Act. One major issue is the reporting of statistics of crime on cruise ships. The original intent was that the Act would make available all reported crimes on cruise ships. In practice, there are many crimes that are either not being reported to the FBI or which the FBI chooses not to make available to the American public. Take as just one example the fact that for one 15-month period the FBI reports a single case of sexual assault on Norwegian Cruise Line; however records disclosed in discovery indicate the number was actually 23.

Access to reliable data is important for passengers who have a right to know the relative risk, including between one cruise line and another and ideally between one cruise ship and another. Through a Freedom of Information request by International Cruise Victims Association I was given 12-months of data to analyze. The analysis was illuminating. It revealed where sexual assaults occur, the identity of perpetrators and victims, and the conditions surrounding an attack (including the presence of alcohol and the high rate of victimization of children). Availability of such data is important for passengers, and access to data is essential for a proper social epidemiological analysis of the problem.

I will stop my oral testimony here. I invite all interested to read my written testimony for a deeper understanding of my insights and resulting concerns. I welcome the Committee's questions.

(Ross A. Klein, PhD, is an international authority on the cruise ship industry. He has published four books, six monographs/reports for nongovernmental organizations, and more than 30 articles and book chapters. He is a professor at Memorial University of Newfoundland in St. John's, Newfoundland, Canada and is online at www.cruisejunkie.com.

His CV can be found at www.cruisejunkie.com/vita.pdf He can be contacted at ross@cruisejunkie.com or rklein@mun.ca)

WRITTEN TESTIMONY

It is an extreme honor to be asked to share my knowledge and insights with the U.S. Senate Committee on Commerce, Science, and Transportation. My testimony focuses on the parameters I was given when I was invited to testify:

- safety and security issues relating to cruise ships (e.g., fires, collisions, and other accidents);
- safety and security of cruise ship passengers, including discussion of the Cruise Vessel Security and Safety act of 2010;
- consumer rights and issues relating to cruise ship liability, including discussion of CLIA's Passenger Bill of Rights.

I. SAFETY AND SECURITY OF CRUISE SHIPS

As the luxury liner finally made it to shore ... [passengers] expressed disgust at the way they had been treated ... Conditions inside the cabins were said to have been "beyond horrific" due to the lack of air conditioning and running water. Lavatories overflowed and they were fed on little but spam sandwiches. They were forced to sleep on deck in sweltering temperatures of up to 35C (95F) and said that the stench in the corridors and cabins was so bad it would remain with them "for a long time"... "Sheer luck has disguised the incompetence from start to finish. Some people are blissfully unaware of how lucky they are."

The alarm was first raised at around 1.30pm on Monday when an electrical fault caused a fire in the engine room and power was lost ... All passengers were told to go to their muster stations, at which point many said they feared they would have to abandon ship ... It then took three hours to conduct a roll call amid chaotic scenes and growing panic. As black smoke billowed from one of the chimneys, it became immediately clear that a fire had broken out on board.

American Gordon Bradwell, 72, from Georgia, who used to work in the travel industry, was on the cruise ship with his wife Eleanor when the engine caught fire. "It was very tense," he said. "We are just happy to have got through it. We were very hot and the sewage was very poor. Right now we're delighted to be off the ship. We are living off adrenalin right now. We have been eating dried sandwiches for three days so we are looking forward to eating a proper meal. After the fire broke out there was nothing to propel the ship along. Things deteriorated rather quickly. There was no running water so we had go back to living a primitive existence. The cabin temperature reached 110F so we had to sleep on the deck."[1]

One might think this describes the ordeal on *Carnival Triumph* in February 2013, but it is about an almost identical incident occurring a year earlier in February 2012. The *Costa Allegra* experienced an engine fire, causing a loss of all power and setting it adrift for three days in the Indian Ocean. It was finally towed to Port Victoria on the island of Mahe in the

Seychelles where passengers disembarked. The ship was decommissioned and scrapped after the incident.

A. The Nature of the Problem

The cruise industry would like us to believe incidents such as the one described above, and the eerily similar incident involving *Carnival Triumph* which had an engine fire knocking out all power and setting the ship adrift for five days[2] – finally arriving in Mobile under tow – are uncommon. The question isn't whether they are uncommon, but how common they are. Take for example the following engine fires, all involving members of the Cruise Lines International Association:[3]

- June 2009 – *Royal Princess* had an engine room fire while leaving Port Said, Egypt. The ship returned to the port the next day and after evaluation of damage the cruise was terminated.
- November 2010 – *Carnival Splendor* has engine room fire setting it adrift; the ship was finally towed to San Diego (150 miles north) even though it was 55 miles west of Punta San Jacinto, Mexico. It was a five day ordeal for passengers. Initially there was no electricity and toilets did not work, but toilets were restored by the end of the first day although there was no air conditioning and no hot food service. The ship's engine that failed had had five alarms between July 21, 2010 and November 5, 2010, most recently repaired on November 5, 2010; the fire occurred on November 8, 2010.[4]
- September 2011 – Hurtigruten's *Nordyls* suffered an engine room fire, killing two crew members and injuring 16. The ship was evacuated by lifeboat and the cruise was terminated. The *Washington Post* reported salvage teams pumped water from the cruise liner in danger of capsizing, reducing the tilt 21.7 degrees in the morning to 16 degrees in the evening.
- October 2011 – Cunard Line's Queen Mary 2 suffered an engine fire causing a loss of power while in a major storm (two other ships chose to turn back from the storm, but the *Queen Mary* decided to battle through). Staff members were given a 90 minute warning in order to prepare to deploy the lifeboats. Guests had their children dropped off and their animals picked up from the kennels. Power was restored, but people were understandably shaken up. Three weeks later the ship twice went dead in the water on a transAtalantic cruise. And again in February 2012 the ship had a total power failure and was dead in the water.
- March 2012 – *Azamara Quest* had an engine room fire, injuring five crew members (one critically), setting the ship adrift between Manila and Borneo. The ship was able to restore power and some propulsion after 24 hours and limped to Sandakan, Malaysia, arriving three days after the fire. The cruise was terminated and passengers flown home.
- April 2012 – *Adventure of the Seas* had an engine room fire causing section 6 of the ship to be temporarily evacuated. The ship was adrift for 1-2 hours and then continued on one engine.

- November 2012 – *Adventure of the Seas* had an engine room fire while crossing the Atlantic causing a brief loss of power and electricity.
- February 2013 – *Carnival Triumph* suffers an engine room fire, setting it adrift for five days without power, air conditioning, or toilets. Initial plans were to tow the ship to the closest port, Progresso, Mexico, however a decision was subsequently made to tow the ship to Mobile. NOTE: The ship was reported to have technical problems with its propulsion system affecting its cruising speed and causing a six hour delay in its return to port two weeks before;
- June 2013 – Pullmantur's *Zenith* had a disabling engine fire and had to be towed to port (Venice, Italy)

There are also ships running aground (19 since 2009) with some incidents leading to termination of the cruise. Some examples include:

- January 2009 – Hurtigruten's *Richard With* ran aground at the port of Trondheim on the west coast of Norway suffering propeller damage and taking on water through a leak in a seal. All 153 passengers were evacuated by the local emergency services from land.
- February 2009 – Quark Expeditions' *Ocean Nova* ran aground off Antarctica. Passengers were evacuated to other ships. Unofficial sources report the ship's engines were turned off for maintenance when the ship was blown aground.
- August 2010 – *Clipper Adventurer* ran aground in Canada's Northwest Passage. Passengers wer transported to Coppermine, Nunavut to be transported home.
- October 2010 – Celebrity Cruises' *Century* damaged its rudder at Villefranche-sur-Mer. Cruise terminated.
- March 2013 – Hurtigruten's Kong Harald was forced to wait for the tide to come in and lift the ship off the underground rock at the entrance to Trollfjord where it was grounded and the hull breached. Once the incoming tide freed the ship it carried on to Svolvaer, where all 258 passengers onboard disembarked and were flown home today.
- March 2013 – Coastal and Maritime Voyages' *Marco Polo* ran aground just outside Sortland in Vesterålen causing a leak in a ballast tank.
- March 2013 – Lindblad Expeditions' *National Geographic Sea Lion* hit a rock in the Las Perlas Islands, about 70 nautical miles from Panama City. The ship sustained damage to its hull and one propeller during the incident, but after clearance from the U.S. Coast Guard returned to Panama City on its own power. The cruise was terminated.

It isn't just engine fires and ships running aground. There are other problems worth note:

- March 2009 – P&O Cruises'*Aurora* experienced propulsion problems four hours after leaving Sydney. It limped to Auckland where passengers remained onboard for five days while repairs were completed. The world cruise itinerary was changed.

- April 2009 – Passengers were told upon embarkation on *Seven Seas Voyager* that most port calls between Dubai and Rome were canceled because of propulsion problems; the next two cruises canceled.
- November 2009 – *Norwegian Dawn* lost power for hours (and no air conditioning). Power was restored and the ship sailed to San Juan from where passengers were flown home. This and the next cruise were canceled.
- February 2010 – *Costa Europa* collided with pier in Sharm-el-Sheikh, ripping a hole in the side of the ship and flooding crew cabins. Three crewmembers were killed; four passengers were injured. The 18-day cruise from Dubai to Savona was terminated and passengers flown home.
- February 2010 – P&O Australia's *Pacific Dawn* was delayed in port for 18 hours because of propulsion and maintenance problems; its itinerary is changed. Two months later the ship lost power and propulsion and narrowly missed collision with a bridge in Brisbane.
- May 2010 – P&O Cruises' *Artemis* notified passengers upon boarding that engine problems require one port to be dropped from the itinerary. But once underway on the 20 day cruise, originally with ten scheduled port calls, passengers were issued a revised itinerary with four ports calls, only three of which were on the original itinerary.
- June 2010 – Celebrity Cruises' *Infinity* was delayed five or six hours because of engine problems causing a port call to be canceled. Five days later an electrical fire caused a power loss for several hours.
- February 2011 – P&O Australia's *Pacific Sun* delayed 24 hours in its arrival at Newcastle because of engine problems; several port calls canceled. Propulsion problems in November 2010 caused a 10-hour delayed arrival in Melbourne, engine problems cause a cruise to be canceled in April 2010, mechanical problems caused two ports calls to be canceled, and in November 2009 a cruise was canceled to permit repair of the propulsion system.
- March 2011 – MSC's *Opera* twice collided with pier at Buenos Aires damaging several cabins and delaying departure for 10 hours while repairs completed. September 2011 – Toilets in front and mid-ship cabins were inoperable for a day on *Carnival Imagination*. Passengers were told to use public washrooms in the aft section.
- May 2011 – MSC's *Opera* had failure of an electric panel causing power loss for 8.5 hours. The ship was towed to port and the cruise canceled.
- November 2011 – *Carnival Splendor* collided with pier in Puerto Vallarta, requiring it to stay an extra day to complete repairs; the next port call was canceled.
- January 2012 – *Costa Concordia* hits a rock off the Italian coast and capsizes killing 32 people.
- February 2012 – *Enchantment of the Seas* left Baltimore 24 hours late after unsuccessful attempts to repair an engine. The ship started the cruise on one engine, sailing at half speed, and the itinerary changed. Two weeks later the cruise had propulsion problems that left it in Port Canaveral for 27 hours for repairs, again requiring a change to the itinerary.

- March 2012 – Silversea Cruises' *Silver Shadow* collided with container ship in Viet Nam holing the cargo ship; only minor damage to the cruise ship. Passengers were frightened.
- October 2012 – Celebrity Cruises' *Summit* had a tender run aground with 93 passengers and 2 crew members. The tender suffered major damage and passengers were rescued by a fishing boat and whale-watching boat.
- November 2012 – *Saga Ruby* had engine problems that required the current cruise to be canceled.
- March 2013 – A malfunction of the backup emergency power diesel generator caused power outages and plumbing issues on *Carnival Dream* and led to a cruise being terminated in Saint Maarten and passengers flown home.
- March 2013 – Steering problems required *Carnival Elation* to have a tugboat escort to port.
- March 2013 – *Carnival Legend* was disabled and stuck in Costa Maya for a day. It finally got underway at reduced speed and dropped a port call to arrive on time at its port of disembarkation. The itinerary of the subsequent cruise was changed because of propulsion problems.
- March 2013 – *Seven Seas Voyager* suffered propulsion problems causing ports to be skipped.
- April 2013 – *Crown Princess* began a cruise with 410 cabins having toilets that would not flush. Until they were fixed, passengers needed to go to public bathrooms (even during the middle of the night).

The list can go on. Appendix 2 lists cruise ships having two or more incidents between January 2009 and June 2013. It shows 353 incidents involving mechanical problems and accidents, approximately 80 incidents per year.

The obvious question is how such events can be so common. A February 2013 in *Newsweek* gives the perspective of Jim Hall, head of the National Transportation Safety Board during the Clinton administration:

> [He] says the industry is watched over by "paper tigers" like the International Maritime Organization and suffers from "bad actors" ... "The maritime industry is the oldest transportation industry around. We're talking centuries. It's a culture that has never been broken as the aviation industry was, and you see evidence of that culture in the [Costa Concordia] accident," says Hall.
>
> Ships may seem and feel American but are mostly "flagged" in countries like the Bahamas or Panama in order to operate outside of what he says are reasonable safety standards. "It is, and has been, an outlaw industry," says Hall. "People who book cruises should be aware of that."[5]

B. Lessons to be Learned from These Events

My point is not to muckrake, listing all that goes wrong with cruise ships. My analysis instead provides insights. By knowing the problems, we can identify potential solutions. The available data raises several issues.

1. The Relative Absence of Reliable Data

"No one is systematically collecting data of collisions, fires, evacuations, groundings, sinkings," says Jim Walker, a maritime lawyer, to the *New York Times*. The article goes on to say:

> The reason for the lack of data is that cruise lines, while based in the United States, typically incorporate and register their ships overseas. Industry experts say the only place cruise lines are obligated to report anything is to the state under whose laws the ship operates."[6]

As the article points out, there remains no comprehensive public database of events at sea like fires, power failures, and evacuations except the data available at my website, Cruise Junkie dot Com.

While I take this acknowledgement as a compliment, it identifies a major gap in available information. My data is based on reports available in the public media and, on occasion, reports from passengers and/or crewmembers. There are many incidents occurring that never reach the public domain. Consequently, there is no way for passengers to know the track record of an individual cruise line or the ships comprising the line.

The data I have benefits greatly from the efforts of Senator Rockefeller who made public a list of casualty investigations by the U.S. Coast Guard for 2008 – 2012 and the Sun-Sentinel, which posted online U.S. Coast Guard data received through a Freedom of Information request. While the two datasets have considerable overlap, there are incidents on one list not appearing on the other, and incidents in my dataset that appear on neither.

Making data available is more important than simply making passengers aware. It allows a sort of social epidemiology of cruise ship incidents from which patterns can be discerned and potential solutions formulated. Rather than seeing each major incident as unique and unrelated to anything before it, a comprehensive data set permits early identification of trends or common problems. Unlike the airline industry, which is governed by the FAA, there is no similar authority when it comes to the cruise industry.

Recommendation #1: *There is need for systematic reporting of all cruise ship incidents to an independent, central authority charged with responsibility for data analysis and policy and operational recommendations.*

2. Frequency and Types of Events

There is a range of incidents occurring on cruise ships. Between January 2009 and June 2013 there were more than 350 incidents involving mechanical problems or accidents (see Appendix 1). The most frequent incidents were:

- propulsion and engine problems (average 19.59 per year) – 7 in which cruise ships were known to go adrift;
- fires (average 13.56 per year) – 6 known to require evacuation and 4 with loss of power;
- material failure and lifeboat failure (average 13.33 per year); and
- collisions (average 11.56 per year).

These four categories account for 261 incidents – all combined yielding an average 58 incidents per year. As seen in Appendix 1, less frequent incidents include loss of power (n=21), running aground (n=19), maneuverability and steering problems (n=15), experiencing a severe list (n=11), and technical (n=8) and electrical (n=8) problems. It needs to be remembered that these accounts rely on public reports, so the list is largely incomplete and underrepresents the actual frequency. For example, as relates to fires, a ship officer recently wrote to me saying:

> Every ship, almost weekly, has some type of fire incident. This could be something as simple as a cigarette butt in a trash can or a fire in the silo of the incinerator, or a grease fire, toaster fire, electrical cord fire in the galley. These are never reported because they are put out quickly, within minutes. However, there are fires happening on ships every single week. (Private correspondence)

In part related to these incidents, and in part related to weather-related factors (not including tropical storms and hurricanes), there were 104 cruises (average 23 per year) with media- reported canceled port calls, 69 cruises with media-reported itinerary changes, 25 cruises with media-reported canceled cruises, and 73 cruises with media-reported delays in embarkation/ debarkation. In sum, there are 271 incidents resulting in a cruise itinerary provided passengers when he or she booked the cruise being different than the itinerary delivered. The number is undoubtedly considerably higher given that there is no centralized collection of data on the degree to which cruise ships approximate their published itinerary, and my data does not include cruise itinerary changes caused by hurricanes or tropical storms.

Recommendation #2: *Similar to data maintained on airlines documenting "on time" performance, there should be a mechanism whereby cruise ships and cruise lines have reported their adherence to itineraries and on time performance.*

3. Discernable Insights from Data

Based on cursory analysis of the limited data available – approximately 1,500 incidents in four- and-a-half years (an average 333 per year) – there are two insights that stand out. First is that Carnival Cruise Lines is disproportionately represented. Appendix 2 shows ships with two or more mechanical incidents from January 2009 through June 2013. Not only does Carnival Cruise Lines have a higher proportion of its fleet included on the list (19 of 23 (82.6%) versus 10 of 16 (62.5%) for Princess Cruises, 10 of 21 (47.6%) for Royal Caribbean International, and 4 of 11 (36.3%) for Celebrity Cruises), but it has a higher average rate of incidents per ship listed (3.89 for Carnival Cruise Lines versus 3.40 for Princess Cruises, 3.25 for Celebrity Cruises, and 3.20 for Royal Caribbean International). An obvious question is why the rate of incidents for Carnival Cruise Lines would be 20% higher than for Royal Caribbean International; 30% higher than for Holland America Line and P&O Cruises, both of which are also owned by Carnival Corporation.

One factor may be the number and training of staff, but this is based on conjecture. An inside source in Royal Caribbean Cruises Limited wrote to me after the *Carnival Triumph* fire saying:

I've worked at RCCL for many years. Over the last 10 years they have been steadily decreasing the number of marine employees. These are the employees that navigate and maintain the engines and the main employees dealing with life saving. If there is a fire - it's the marine team suiting up and fighting the fires. If the ship is listing or sinking - it's the marine team dealing with technical systems such as water tight doors, moving tank contents from one area to another, making contact with rescue services, lowering life boats, etc.

The reason for the decrease in marine manning? It's purely driven by concern for profit. You can get rid of two marine employees who do not generate any income (they just play a major role in saving lives if something goes wrong) and replace them with a hotel employee such as a marketing and revenue manager or a maître 'd for income-generating specialty restaurants, or bar supervisors. Many times employees are cut in the marine department or doubled up in cabins so the company can revamp the crew cabins into sellable cruise guest cabins.

Approximately 5 years ago RCCL got rid of the safety officer position and combined the job with the chief officer position. There is now talk about changing the marine contracts for 3 stripe officers from 10 weeks/10 weeks off to 4 months on/2 months off so they match the hotel officer positions. The degree of technical knowledge needed, and the tremendous life saving responsibility marine officers have, is in no way equal to the demands placed on hotel officers to sell another drink. When the ship is sinking - do you want a marine officer that knows the technical systems or do you want a hotel officer selling you another beer as you are stepping into a lifeboat? (Personal correspondence)

While these comments are specific to one corporation, it raises to the forefront the degree to which this pattern is common to other cruise lines. Anecdotal accounts indicate changes of the same nature are taking place within Carnival Cruise Lines. This leads to a question requiring empirical research using reliable data. The problem is that such data is not available, largely because systematic independent oversight of the cruise industry is lacking. It is in stark contrast to the airline industry where oversight and reporting is the norm.

Recommendation #3: *There is need for greater oversight and monitoring of the cruise industry in order to monitor changing trends and to determine whether these changes are related to changes in safety and/or casualties.*

A second insight from the data is a preliminary conclusion also based in part on anecdotal information. It appears there is a pattern of incidents involving ships built on the Destiny platform (Destiny-class and Dream-class ships): my understanding is that *Carnival Destiny, Carnival Triumph, Carnival Splendor, Carnival Glory, Carnival Breeze, Carnival Dream, Carnival Liberty*, and *Carnival Magic* have all reported electrical and/or propulsion issues, power losses, and some electrical fires over the last three years or so (not all of these have been reported in the media and are thus not included in my dataset); *Costa Concordia, Costa Magica, Costa Serena* and *Costa Pacifica* have also reported similar problems during this timespan – all of these ships are Destiny platform design ships.

The relevant difference between Destiny platform and the Spirit/Vista 1/Vista 2/Signature classes is simple. Destiny platform ships have only been built at Fincantieri shipyards in Italy from a design by Fincantieri. Spirit & Vista 1 class ships originated in Kvaener Masa shipyards and were then adapted/enlarged by Fincantieri. The original blueprints had more than enough redundancy to allow for growth and design tweaks. There is limited redundancy built into the Destiny platform ships, which may be why they suffer from systemic failures.

This is illustrated in the report of the *Carnival Splendor* fire, leading to the ship losing all power and going dead in the water. The report observes that "vessel engineers were unable to restart the unaffected main generators due to extensive damage to cables in the aft engine room."[7] It goes on to state, there is "susceptibility of the Carnival Splendor and all Dream class vessels to a complete loss of power resulting from damage to a single area of electrical system components in either the forward or aft engine room." Presumably, with appropriate redundancy the main generators would have been functional.

The report also observes design flaws that cut across Dream class (and presumably Destiny platform vessels). These include air cooler drainage problems, noted as far back as October 2009 and documented problems with the CO_2 system. That these problems were identified as early as 2009, and may have been factors in the catastrophic nature of both the *Carnival Splendor* and *Carnival Triumph* fires lends convincing support for increased independent oversight of the cruise industry.

Carnival Cruise Lines appears to address the shortcoming of redundancy through its announcement April 17, 2013, of a $300 million program to enhance operating reliability, an initiative spurred by the *Carnival Triumph* fire in February 2013. As stated in the company's press release, the initiative will add an additional emergency generator on each vessel and install a second permanent back-up power system. There will also be increased fire prevention, detection and suppression systems. As well, there will be modifications to decrease the likelihood of losing propulsion or primary power.

> The modifications will include a reconfiguration of certain engine-related electrical components. On ships where these enhancements will be made, the design of specialized components will require longer lead times for completion.[8]

While the company deserves recognition of the steps being taken, an obvious question is how many of these enhancements involve adding components that were not originally included in the ship's design, but are normally included in the design of ships operated by other cruise lines and/or built and designed by other ship yards. An independent audit is the only reliable means for determining the situation.

More serious is that the company did not appear to maximize learning from the *Carnival Splendor* fire in 2010. First, a report about the incident was not issued until three years later, perhaps because responsibility rested with Panamanian authorities; this even though Carnival Cruise Lines had employed a number of experts to provide them with analysis of causes of the fire. However, a preliminary U.S. Coast Guard investigation revealed several holes in the ship's fire fighting methodology, not to mention significant errors in its firefighting operations manual.

> According to a marine advisory issue by the Coast Guard, the Splendor's firefighting instruction manual was riddled with problems, including references to "pulling" valves that actually needed to be turned to operate, incorrect descriptions of system locations, inaccurate graphics and schematics and confusing instructions such as: 'Once the fire has been extinguished, make sure that the temperature has decreased before investigate the area same time is needed to wait hours.'[9]

Recommendation #4: *Ships operating from U.S. ports should be obligatorily subject to accident investigations by the National Transportation Safety Board as a condition of using*

U.S. ports, and should be subject to the same fines and other administrative actions the NTSB is empowered to take with other modes of commercial transportation.

4. Learning from Success, Not Just Accidents

So far I have looked at what might be learned from accidents and things that go wrong on cruise ships. There is another way to look at the data; concentrate on those cruise ships and cruise lines that appear to be under-represented when it comes to incidents. For example, among the mass market cruise lines Norwegian Cruise Line and MSC Cruises appear to have much lower incidence of fires, groundings, engine failures and accidents than others in this class. It would be interesting to know what those cruise lines are doing differently than Carnival Cruise Lines and Royal Caribbean International. The problem is that cruise lines under Cruise Lines International Association (CLIA) tend to not effectively differentiate themselves with regard to such things, and the consuming public lacks reliable data on which to compare cruise lines. As an authority on the cruise industry I am often asked what cruise line or cruise ship is the safest. I can give an anecdotal response, but without adequate data it is difficult to give a fully informed response.

There are similar contrasts among cruise lines in the premium and ultra-luxury segments, however they aren't as stark as among the mass market cruise lines. It appears that Oceania Cruises has a better record than Celebrity Cruises and both have a better record than Holland America Line; all have a better record than Princess Cruises. Similarly, Seabourn Cruises appears to have fewer incidents than Silverseas Cruises and both less than Regent Seven Seas Cruises. Seadream Yacht Club has a lower incidence rate than any of the ships in the ultra-luxury category.

Again, it appears that some companies are doing a far-better job than others. Research on what they are doing, whether in staffing and training or in ship design and maintenance, is worth attention. This would naturally be something undertaken by an industry-based body, but this is unlikely to happen given the dominance in CLIA of under-achievers. As well, such research must be done by a wholly-independent researcher.

Recommendation #5: *There needs to be funded research, ideally provided by the cruise industry to a wholly independent body, to learn from those cruise lines that appear to be effective in reducing incidents and accidents.*

5. Regulation and Oversight of the Cruise Industry

Unlike the airline industry, the cruise industry is largely self-regulated. As foreign-registered vessels operated by foreign-located corporations, cruise ships are not subject to many regulations and laws in the U.S. However, cruise ships operating from U.S. ports are subject to regular safety inspections by the U.S. Coast Guard and they voluntarily participate in the Vessel Sanitation Program of the Centers for Disease Control (CDC) and report illness outbreaks affected 3% or more of passengers and/or 2% or more of crew members on ships operating from a U.S. port (ships operating from foreign ports, but sailing with a majority or U.S. passengers do not have to file illness reports with the CDC). While reports of CDC activities are available online, reports of U.S. Coast Guard inspections are not.

I received from a San Francisco-based NBC-affiliate a set of inspections (Annual Control Verification Exam) done by the U.S. Coast Guard in San Francisco from 2002 to 2012; they had been acquired through a Freedom of Information request. These reports spanning 82 pages were illuminating. It was interesting to see the types of deficiencies identified by inspectors (e.g., fuel leaks, water leaks from fire pumps, many lifeboat problems, missing or faulty equipment, faulty fire extinguishers, improper record keeping of required information, exposed live electric wires, faulty doors, mixing of segregated garbage streams (including hazardous waste), fire risks, security deficiencies, and more) and the length of time permitted for correction of some of the deficiencies. Given these are annual inspections, it is difficult to know how long deficiencies were overlooked or ignored. Of greater concern is that these inspections are not entirely unannounced, so officers and crew often prepare for them and the most obvious problems are corrected in advance.

In extreme cases, a matter identified in the Annual Control Verification Exam was referred to the vessel's Classification Society (e.g., Lloyd's Register, Bureau Veritas, Registro Italiano Navale, Det Norske Veritas), which certifies the ship's safety and seaworthiness. While these societies appear to be independent, they earn their income from cruise lines and may be conflicted when taking action that can cost the cruise line money or cause a ship to be taken out of service. For example, there is a fair number of cases where ships have been judged to have insufficient lifeboat space for the number of passengers. In some, the Classification Society has instructed the cruise line to book fewer passengers on the ship until the lifeboat(s) has/have been repaired.

In others, the Classification Society has permitted the cruise ship to accommodate passengers on inflatable rafts rather than lifeboats. It is unclear whether this is a reasonable solution if there were need for emergency evacuation, especially if like the *Costa Concordia* half of the lifeboats cannot be deployed.

There is also need for the U.S. Coast Guard to oversee and review the work of classification societies. For example, the report of the *Carnival Splendor* fire indicates:

> The firefighting manual available to officers onboard the Carnival Splendor referred to a CO2 system but not the one that was installed onboard the vessel. Related system photographs, images, schematics and diagrams were also found to be inaccurate.
> A review of CO2 system documents revealed a RINA approved test memoranda dated October 20, 2006, which established the following procedure for testing the CO2 system: 1) select the zone or line, 2) observe the shutdowns of ventilation systems, machinery and other warning alarms and then 3) move to the gas-release procedure, which included cylinder selection for the particular zone and verification of pressurization of the manifold, etc. Another document that appears to be part of a RINA approval letter dated December 28, 2008, describes the operational procedure in exact reverse order.
> In this instance, ship's crew opened the cylinder valves first. As a result, the pressure differential across the zone valve prevented opening of the ball valve.

This reminds me of publicly-reported findings in 2001 and 2004 respectively, both involving a ship approved by their Classification Society. The first involves Holland America Line's *Zaandam*. In May 2001 a crew member noticed a sprinkler head missing from a passenger cabin and upon investigation found that a branch of the sprinkler system did not connect to the main water supply. The problem was corrected.[10]

In the second, the British Marine and Coastguard Agency ordered Cunard Line's Queen Mary 2 in June 2004 to fit extra sprinklers in the ship's 1,300 passenger cabins. A BBC investigation revealed material used in the ships' bathroom units did not meet international fire safety regulations. A short-term remedy was fitting all cabins with an extra smoke detector, but the ship must also add extra sprinklers in bathrooms. The ship is estimated to contain 140,000 pounds (63,503 kilograms) of the material causing concern.[11]

Recommendation #6: *Ships should have thorough and exhaustive safety inspections by the U.S. Coast Guard without advance warning. Full reports (including all details) of cruise ship inspections by the U.S. Coast Guard should be available online.*

The importance of an unannounced, surprise inspection is demonstrated by a recent health inspection of Silversea Cruise's *Silver Shadow*. The ship had never had an inspection score of 99 in May 2012 and 95 in September 2012, however following complaints to the CDC from crewmembers a surprise inspection was done June 17, 2013, and the ship received a failing score of 84. Crewmembers had alleged that they were forced to store raw meat, salami, fish, cakes, and every kind of culinary preparations in their cabins and remote hallways to avoid inspections by the U.S. Public Health (USPH), and that some spoilable food items were kept out of the refrigerator in cabins and hallways but were served the following day to the cruise passengers. Other complaints included the alleged use of out-of-date ingredients which were served to the guests. Again, the importance of inspections being done unannounced and without advance notice can not be stressed enough.

II. SAFETY AND SECURITY OF CRUISE PASSENGERS

Previous committee hearings have dealt with safety and security of cruise passengers.[12] I won't duplicate that information here, except to summarize some important points.

A. Scope of the Problem

It is worth noting that the only comprehensive dataset for crime on cruise ships is based on data provided by the FBI in response to a Freedom of Information request by the International Cruise Victims Association. Between October 1, 2007 and September 30, 2008, the data reveals there were 115 simple assaults, 16 assaults with serious bodily injury, 89 thefts less then $10,000, 12 thefts more than $10,000, 154 sex related incidents, 7 people overboard, and 3 drug arrests. A comprehensive analysis of the data on sexual assaults on cruise ships is reported in "Sex at Sea: Sexual Crimes Aboard Cruise Ships," published in 2011 in the *Journal of Tourism in Marine Environments* (see Appendix 4).

Two areas are worth further mention here because the data is not reported elsewhere. First, is persons overboard. Since 1995, there have been 201 reports of persons gone overboard from passenger ships.[13] As shown in Appendix 3, 73.8% were male, 26.2% female. On average, males are a shade younger than females (38.85% vs 42.11%). The majority go overboard from cruise ships: 91.4% from a cruise ship, 8.6% from a ferry. While data is limited, we know that the person overboard was rescued alive in 16.7% of cases, 11% cases were a confirmed suicide, and all indications are that 3.3% of cases involve murder. Alcohol was a factor in at least 6.2% of cases, a fight with a significant other in 7.1% of cases, 2.4%

followed a significant loss in the casino, and 9.5% were witnessed and confirmed to be a fall. These numbers will be discussed further later.

The second area worth mention is drug arrests. Between January 2009 and June 2013 there were 53 media reports of drug arrests on cruise ships involving 87 people. Based on cases where data is available, we know that males are more likely to be arrested than females (83.33% vs 16.66%); the average age is the same for both genders. The largest number of individual incidents occur in Bermuda (n=27) where cruise ships are routinely searched by government officials using drug-sniffing dogs; the U.S. had 8 incidents involving the arrest of 27 individuals, in all cases the person was apprehended by Customs and Border Protection agents. Ships with the largest number arrests are *Norwegian Dawn* (9) and *Explorer of the Seas* (6) (see Appendix 4). Most frequently, drug arrests are for small amounts of marijuana, from several grams to less than an ounce.

B. The Cruise Vessel Security and Safety Act of 2010 (CVSSA)

The Cruise Vessel Security and Safety Act was introduced in 2008 following Congressional hearings in 2005, 2006, 2007, and 2008. The hearings in 2005 were convened in December by two subcommittees of the House of Representatives Committee on Government Reform: the Subcommittee on National Security, Emerging Threats and International Relations chaired by Christopher Shays and the Subcommittee on Criminal Justice, Drug Policy and Human Resources chaired by Mark Souder. The hearings had a twofold purpose. First, given the recent attack of the *Seabourn Spirit* by pirates off the coast of Somalia, they sought to determine the decision-making procedures and processes that were in place to determine the extent to which the U.S. Government responds to a ship being attacked by terrorists or pirates. The second purpose of the hearings was to determine jurisdictional conflicts that occur when U.S. citizens traveling on a foreign-flagged vessel are involved in a criminal incident. These incidents included sexual assaults, physical assaults, robbery, and missing persons. The hearings concluded with an assurance they would reconvene in March in order to hear directly from victims.

Hearings were reconvened in March 2006. The committee heard from six victims of crime on cruise ships: three victims of a sexual assault, two families with three persons overboard (one mysterious, one alcohol-related fall), and one incident involving a theft of $6,700. The committee also heard from International Cruise Victims Association (ICV), which presented 10 recommendations, many of which would be incorporated in the CVSSA; and from an expert hired by the cruise industry who claimed the rate of sexual assault on cruise ships was half the rate on land. The committee appeared to be sceptical about the reliability of crime statistics and acknowledged the absence of reliable data on persons overboard from cruise ships. Subsequent to the hearing Representative Shays introduced on June 28, 2006 HR 5707, *Cruise Line Accurate Safety Statistics Act*. The bill was straightforward. It required cruise ships that call at a port in the United States to report all crimes occurring on the ship in which a U.S. citizen is involved. It also required this information to be made available to the public on the Internet. The cruise industry didn't embrace the legislation and with the current session of Congress near-complete the legislation died in committee.

In March 2007 hearings were held by the Subcommittee on Coast Guard and Maritime Transportation of the House of Representatives Committee on Transportation and Infrastructure. Two things appear to have solidified support for the hearings. First, the *Los Angeles Times* published an article on January 20, 2007, which based on internal documents from Royal Caribbean said sex-related onboard incidents was a larger problem than the cruise industry suggested in March 2006. The documents revealed 273 reported incidents within a period of thirty-two months, including 99 cases of sexual harassment, 81 of sexual assault, 52 of inappropriate touching, 28 of sexual battery and 13 cases that fit into other categories.[14] When the company-specific numbers were subjected to the same statistical analysis as done with industry-wide data in James Fox's 2006 testimony before Congress, the rate of sexual assault was not half the average rate for rape in the U.S., but 50 percent greater than the U.S. rate.[15]

The second factor that pushed for a new round of hearings was that Representative Doris Matsui from California had a constituent, Laurie Dishman, appeal for help following non-prosecution of a rape by a security officer on a Royal Caribbean International's *Vision of the Seas*. Matsui was not only concerned about the way Laurie had been treated and her case handled, but also with discrepancies in crime statistics.

These hearings opened with the FBI and Coast Guard announcing that an agreement had just been reached with the cruise industry whereby cruise line members of the Cruise Line International Association (CLIA) agreed to report to the FBI (either a field office in the U.S. or the FBI Legal Attaché at an embassy or consulate closest to the vessel's location at the time of the incident) all crimes against Americans on their ships. To many the timing of the announcement was suspicious. As well, the agreement appeared to be a rehash of the "zero tolerance" policy announced by the International Council of Cruise Lines in 1999 and it was redundant to reporting requirements already in place. The key difference was the agreement provided a standardized form for reporting crimes that the FBI could use to establish a data set from which reports could be drawn for Congress and other government authorities. The data would not to be available to the public. The hearings also heard from ICV, Laurie Dishman, a sociologist who reported on analysis of the crime statistics presented in the *Los Angeles Times*, an attorney who represents cruise victims, and representatives of the cruise industry. At the end of the hearings the subcommittee chair, Elijah Cummings, called on CLIA and ICV to get together and to attempt to find some common ground and solutions. He said he'd prefer a solution that did not require legislation, but also said that legislation was always an option. He gave the two sides six months and said the hearings would reconvene in September.

With no solution from collaboration between ICV and CLIA, hearings were reconvened in September 2007. The day before the Congressional subcommittee reconvened September 19, 2007, Representatives Matsui and Shays with twenty-three co-sponsors introduced a House Resolution to call attention to the growing level of crime on cruise ships and the lack of federal regulations overseeing the cruise industry. The purpose of the reconvened hearings was to receive an update on the status of discussions between ICV and CLIA and to examine whether the security practices and procedures aboard cruise ships are adequate to ensure the safety of all passengers. As before, it received testimony from the FBI and Coast Guard, which discussed the implementation of the reporting framework announced at the previous hearings; from ICV and several of its members (parents of a 21-year-old who fell overboard while throwing up over a railing, two sexual assault victims, a surviving family member whose father died in a cruise ship fire); and from the cruise industry. Not surprisingly the cruise industry painted a picture that said everything was under control, that it is working diligently to improve situations raised as sources of concern by its critics, and that cruises continue to be safe.[16] The claim of safety was based in large part on the FBI receiving from cruise ships only forty-one reports of sexual assault and twenty-eight cases of sexual contact between April 1 and August 23, 2007. Together, these numbers give an annualized rate for sexual abuse on CLIA member cruise lines of 172 incidents; a rate of 56.9 per 100,000 passengers – several fold higher than the rate claimed in the 2006 hearings. The industry also used the hearings to announce formation of its survivors' working group, a group that ostensibly attempted to supplant ICV.

Less than a week after the hearings, the House Committee on Homeland Security approved by voice vote inclusion of language in the Coast Guard Authorization Act requiring cruise lines to notify the Department of Homeland Security Secretary of security-related incidents involving U.S. persons when it advises its next port of call of its arrival. Incidents required to be reported under the legislation include any act that results in death, serious bodily injury, sexual assault, a missing person, or that poses a significant threat to the cruise ship, any cruise ship passenger, any port facility, or any person in or near the port. Unlike Representative Shays' Cruise Line Accurate Safety Statistics Act, the reports would not be made public.

At the same time there was a move involving Senator John Kerry and Representatives Matsui, Shays, and Maloney to write legislation that would require cruise ships to immediately notify the FBI about crimes, suicides, and disappearances. The legislation would also provide protocols for collecting evidence. The legislation in many ways is like the agreement announced in March 2007 between CLIA and the FBI would be mandatory. A key requirement of any legislation or regulation, if it is to be useful to the public, is public disclosure. Passengers should know the history of problems and incidents on a cruise ship, much the same as they can view reports of sanitation inspections conducted on cruise ships by the Centers for Disease Control.

The Subcommittee on Surface Transportation and Merchant Marine Infrastructure, Safety, and Security of the Senate Committee on Commerce, Science and Transportation held hearings in June 2008. The hearings heard from ICV; CLIA; the Rape, Abuse, Incest and Neglect Network (RAINN); and a sociologist reporting on analysis of sexual assault data and on persons overboard. The information presented was similar to previous hearings in the House of Representatives, however RAINN discussed the need and methods for providing support to victims of sexual assault on cruise ships. The CVSSA was introduced shortly after the hearings.

1. From Hearings to Legislation

A key advocate for legislation was the International Cruise Victims Association, formed when its founders (Ken Carver whose 40 year old daughter mysteriously went missing in 2004 from *Mercury,* a Celebrity ship; Bree Smith whose 26 year old brother mysteriously went missing in on his honeymoon in 2005 from *Brilliance of the Seas,* a Royal Caribbean ship; Son Michael Pham whose parents aged 67 and 71 mysteriously went missing in 2005 from *Carnival Destiny*; the parents of 23 year old Amy Bradley who mysteriously went missing in 1998 from *Rhapsody of the Seas*, a Royal Caribbean ship; and the parents of 22 year old James Scavone who mysteriously went missing in 1999 from *Carnival Destiny*) met at the 2005 hearings. The sponsor of the CVSSA in 2008 in the U.S. House of Representatives was Doris Matsui (HR 6408); in the U.S. Senate John Kerry (S 3204). The legislation was reintroduced in 2009 as HR 3360 and S 588 and subsequently passed, becoming Public Law 111-207.

The initial version of the CVSSA reflected concerns raised in hearings and contained solutions to identified problems. However, a number of provisions of the Act when it was first introduced in 2008 and in March 2009 were changed when introduced in the Senate in June 2009, presumably partially in response to lobbying by the cruise industry or others. These changes and other elements of the legislation will guide this discussion.

2. Persons Overboard

The number of people going overboard from cruise ships is significant: between 20 and 25 a year since 2009. It is known that in 9.5% of cases the person fell overboard, however if we trust cruise industry claims – they often say a passenger has fallen or jumped even if the assertion cannot be independently corroborated – then the percentage is much higher. With that in mind, it is curious that the original version of the CVSSA stated, "The vessel shall be equipped with ship rails that are located not less than 4½ feet above the deck" (§3507 (a)(1)(A)). However the legislation passed set the height one foot lower at 42 inches. In retrospect, it would appear the original provision of 54 inches (4½ feet) may be more reasonable as an impediment to passengers falling overboard.

A second change is seen in §3507(a)(1)(D). The original proposed legislation stated, "The vessel shall integrate technology that can be used for detecting passengers who have fallen overboard, to the extent that such technology is available." Such technology is available, but there are cost implications.

The revised legislation states, "The vessel shall integrate technology that can be used for capturing images of passengers or detecting passengers who have fallen overboard, to the extent that such technology is available." While close-circuit television (CCTV) technology (used to capture images of persons going overboard) may be effective if it were monitored in real-time, it is of little use when tapes are reviewed only after it is known a person has disappeared. In addition, there are issues with whether CCTV cameras cover all relevant areas where a person may go overboard, and whether images are readily made available when requested. In a recent case in which I was retained as an expert witness we found that the CCTV images were recorded using old technology (not in a format easily viewed) and when converted the images were of limited probative value. Again, it would appear that the original legislation proposed in 2007 was more effective in identifying when a person goes overboard and in causing a response that is more likely to lead to a live rescue. Many of the 16.7% of cases where a person is rescued alive is when their disappearance is observed and reported to officers who immediately execute rescue procedures.

Data also indicates there is sufficient number of cases of persons going overboard when they are intoxicated. In two known cases the person was bending over the railing while throwing-up over the side of the ship. This is further reason for raising railing height, but also reinforces the need for stringent rules for the responsible service of alcohol; not just training, but practice.

One other concern is the way the FBI interprets the CVSSA. International Cruise Victims Association reports they have been told by the FBI that a person overboard is not necessarily a crime and thus will not be investigated and not included in the FBI's official statistics. It is difficult to understand how a determination can be made about whether a case of a person overboard is not a crime without a proper investigation. Even if CCTV videotapes show a person falling overboard, an investigation may be warranted to determine the conditions surrounding the incident, for example whether intoxication is an issue and whether the cruise ship was responsible in serving alcohol. Current wording of the CVSSA does not classify a person overboard as a crime.

Recommendation #7: Original provisions of the CVSSA regarding railing height and technology to detect passengers who have fallen overboard be reconsidered.

3. Sexual Assaults

Contrary to cruise industry claims, sexual assaults are an ongoing problem on cruise ships. Just in the past couple of months there have been media reports of a 12-year-old girl groped on *Celebrity Century* by a 30-year-old male passenger, and an 11-year-old girl molested by a crew member on *Disney Dream*. In neither case was the perpetrator arrested or prosecuted; in the latter, the crewmember was offloaded by the cruise line in the Bahamas and flown home to India at the cruise line's expense. Data from the FBI for October 2007 through September 2008 reveals that at least 18% of sexual assault victims are younger than age 18. The data was secured through a freedom of information request.

Unfortunately, reliable data is hard to come by. No comprehensive FBI data has been available since 2008. The only other data available for analysis was provided in the discovery phase of lawsuits, yielding incident reports from 1998 through 2002 for one cruise line; 1998 through 2005 for another. In a recent lawsuit involving the sexual assault of a minor a cruise line was ordered by the judge to disclose to the plaintiff's attorney all reported cases of sexual assault for the previous five years. The cruise line settled the case out of court in order to avoid complying with the court order.

There is much to be learned from incident reports of sexual assault. We know that the most frequent perpetrator among crewmembers (between 50% and 77% of sexual assaults on passengers are perpetrated by a crew member) is a room steward (34.8%) followed by dining room waiter (25%) and bar worker (13.2%). We also know that the most frequent location for the assault is a passenger cabin (36.4%) and that alcohol is a factor in 36% of incidents involving minors. Having detailed data permits identification of risk and of potential solutions or means for ameliorating the problem. However, changes to the CVSSA between the first versions to the version passed make this data much more difficult to access and thus more difficult for proper prevention and intervention. The following discussion will be organized around prevention, intervention, investigation, and prosecution.

Prevention

The best way to deal with sexual assault is to have methods of primary prevention. One of the most effective methods is for passengers to know the risk. That is why the initial version of the CVSSA not only required all sexual assaults to be reported to the FBI but that "The Secretary shall maintain, on an Internet site of the department in which the Coast Guard is operating, a numerical accounting of the missing persons and alleged crimes..." (§3507(c)(4)(A)). But the section was changed in the final version to read, "The Secretary shall maintain a statistical compilation of all incidents described in paragraph (3)(A)(i) on an Internet site that provides a numerical accounting of the missing persons and alleged crimes recorded in each report filed under paragraph (3)(A)(i) that are no longer under investigation by the Federal Bureau of Investigation" (§3507(e)(4)(A)0.

The result is that the FBI only publicly discloses those cases where they have opened a case and they have subsequently closed the case. Those incidents judged to be he said-she said, or where sufficient evidence is not available, do not have an investigation so appear to be not reported. Unlike crimes on land that are included in Uniform Crime Statistics and that reflect all complaints of a crime, crimes on cruise ships are only publicly recorded when the FBI has decided first that an investigation is warranted and second when the investigation is closed. The result is that the number of publicly reported sexual assaults on cruise ships is grossly under- reported. The one-year data for 2007-08 reported 154 sex-related incidents. In stark contrast, the FBI dataset on the U.S. Coast Guard website (which is difficult to find) reports 11 incidents in 2012 (data for 2010 and 2011 was not accessible). More illuminating is a recent case I was involved with. The FBI indicated that the cruise line (NCL) had one case of sexual assault in 15 months, but records disclosed in discovery indicated the cruise line had received (and we assume reported to the FBI in compliance with the CVSSA) 23 complaints. The change in the language of the Act effectively makes invisible the true scale of the problem of sexual assault and undermines passenger awareness of the need to protect themselves and their children.

Recommendation #8: *The CVSSA should require reported cases of sexual assault committed on a cruise ship be displayed online and broken down by cruise line and cruise ship. In addition, the raw data of cases should be made available upon request for statistical/sociological analysis in order to permit a social epidemiology of the problem.*

A provision that was not changed, but that may need to be revisited relates to crew access to passenger cabins. §3507(f)(1) states that a cruise ship shall "establish and implement procedures and restrictions concerning – (A) which crewmembers have access to passenger staterooms; and (B) the periods during which they have access; and (2) ensure that the procedures and restrictions are fully and properly implemented and periodically reviewed." While this provision is clear in its intent, it may not be specific enough in its statement. I am not sure if it effectively addresses certain incidents of sexual assault. Take for example the teenage daughter left in her parent's cabin who is walked in upon and sexually assaulted by a crew member gaining access with a room key; or the adult woman who returns to her room in the middle of the afternoon and when she walks out of the shower finds a crew member in her room and is raped; or a woman who wakes in the middle of the night and finds a crew member standing over her and is assaulted. These cases are not anomalies, but even if they were they demonstrate why there is clear need for strict restrictions on crewmember access to passenger cabins. As it stands, restrictions on access to passenger cabins by room stewards, maintenance people, minibar stockers, and others are unclear. This may be addressed in legislation that more clearly identifies parameters for when crew members have access to passenger cabins (e.g., between 9:00 AM and 11:59 AM, and between 6:00 PM and 9:00 PM). At the very least, passengers should be told what hours of the day a crewmember may have access to their cabin.

Recommendation #9: *The CVSSA should require passengers to be advised of the hours during which crewmembers may access their cabin without specific permission from the passenger.*

Another strategy for prevention, as well as useful for investigation, is CCTV cameras. There are two issues. One is that cruise ships often have real cameras and dummy cameras around the ship. Consequently, a crewmember may take a passenger to an area with no camera or a dummy camera and then assault them. This was the case when an 8-yearo-ld girl was molested on a cruise ship: a cleaner led her down a hallway with the promise he would help her find her way back to her family's cabin. He knew where there were active cameras and where there were dummy cameras.

A second related issue is where live cameras are located. In a recent case in which I served as an expert witness I raised concern about where cameras were and were not located, pointing out that cameras were not directed toward areas that I believed were high risk. The cruise line's attorney countered that the CVSSA only requires that "The owner of a vessel ... shall maintain a video surveillance system to assist in documenting crimes on the vessel and in providing evidence for the prosecution of such crimes" (§3507(b)(1). In this case the area not being covered was the entrance to public washrooms even though one data set indicates that 4.4% (n=14) of sexual assaults occur in public washrooms. While it shouldn't be necessary for an act to clearly specify where CCTV surveillance should take place, the current language of the Act is so vague that it can be effectively used to counter and/or undermine victim claims when an assault occurs. As has already been mentioned, the videotapes that were provided by the cruise line in this case were of such poor quality that they had no probative value.

Recommendation #10: *The CVSSA more clearly and specifically state requirements for CCTV surveillance and the quality and format of tape recordings.*

A final method of prevention is making passengers aware of the risk of crime on cruise ships. I have already discussed the quality of information reported on the website maintained by the U.S. Coast Guard, however the website is difficult to find and for most passengers does not alert them to the risk. Perhaps a better way to alert passengers of onboard risk is through the "Security Guide" required under §3507(c)(1)(A) of the Act. Presently the Act requires the guide to be available for each passenger, but doesn't specify how availability is achieved. The Act requires the guide to "provide a description of medical and security personnel designated on board to prevent and respond to criminal and medical situations with 24 hour contact instructions" and to describe the jurisdictional authority applicable and the law enforcement process available with respect to reporting a crime. However there is no requirement for the guide to include a clear statement of what crimes occur on cruise ships, nor for it to educate passengers in methods and/or strategies for reducing vulnerability to crime. The guide could be an effective method for forewarning passengers of known dangers.

Ironically, passengers are often advised in port lectures of things they can do to reduce the likelihood of becoming a victim to crime ashore, but there is no parallel information for how to reduce the likelihood of crime onboard the ship. It is reasonable to expect a cruise ship to alert parents to the need to supervise their children and to be aware of the risk of child sexual assault onboard, to advise adult passengers of the risk of sexual assault and the most common places and scenarios where these occur – this may include advice to keep track of one's drink to be sure it is not drugged or otherwise tampered with. The data on sexual assaults provides considerable insight into where and when sexual assaults occur; information that passengers would benefit from knowing.

Recommendation #11: *The CVSSA explicitly require the "Security Guide" be placed in plain sight in every passenger cabin and that the content of the guide include information about the types of crimes on cruise ships, where they commonly occur, and steps a passenger can take to decrease the likelihood of becoming a victim of crime.*

Intervention

Despite best efforts, it is likely some sexual assaults will occur on cruise ships. The issue then is how victims will be treated. Again, there was a critical change from early drafts of the CVSSA and the Act that subsequently passed into law. §3507(e)(3) stated,

> … make available on the vessel at all times an individual licensed to practice as a medical doctor in the United States to promptly perform such an examination upon request and to provide proper medical treatment of a victim, including antiretroviral medications and other medications that may prevent the transmission of human immunodeficiency virus and other sexually transmitted diseases.

This was replaced with §3507(d)(3) that reads:

> (3) make available on the vessel at all times medical staff who have undergone a credentialing process to verify that he or she— (A) possesses a current physician's or registered nurse's license and— (i) has at least 3 years of post-graduate or postregistration clinical practice in general and emergency medicine; or (ii) holds board certification in emergency medicine, family practice medicine, or internal medicine; … and (C) meets guidelines established by the American College of Emergency Physicians relating to the treatment and care of victims of sexual assault.

The most significant change is the required qualifications of the person providing medical care to a sexual assault victim. The original draft clearly required a physician who is licensed to practice in the United States; the change permits either a doctor or a nurse and makes no reference to where that person was trained or where they are licensed. This change is significant.

There are several reasons why this change may be of concern. First, some may believe a physician would be better able to deal with a medical issue. But more importantly is where that doctor was trained and is licensed. There has traditionally been a wide variation in medical care on cruise ships. Some cruise lines have chosen only physicians trained and licensed in the U.S., Canada, or U.K.; others have drawn physicians from a variety of countries because they are able to pay significantly less. This is not to impugn the competence of all foreign-trained physicians, but there may be issues around language (competence in English, which is important given the nuances and emotions at play in a sexual assault), issues around culture and different views about women and sexuality, and differences in knowledge of clinical guidelines common in the U.S. Perhaps more important is that when there is malpractice a physician in the U.S., Canada, or the U.K. may be easy to find, but a physician from a developing country or a non-English speaking country may be exceedingly difficult for a patient to track down.

The reference in the CVSSA to guidelines established by the American College of Emergency Physicians may be seen as a way of dealing with some of these concerns. However a review of the Policy Compendium (2013 Edition) of the American College of Emergency Physicians (ACEP) brings other issues to the forefront. The Compendium reads:

> The sexually assaulted patient, who may be an adult or child of either sex, presents special medical, psychological, and legal needs. ACEP believes that all patients who report a sexual assault are entitled to prompt access to emergency medical care and competent collection of evidence that will assist in the investigation and prosecution of the incident. ACEP has therefore developed the following guidelines:

- With the cooperative efforts of local governments, law enforcement agencies, hospitals, courts, and other relevant organizations, each county, state or other geographic area should establish a community plan to deal with the sexually assaulted patient. The plan should ensure that capable, trained personnel and appropriate equipment are available for treating sexual assault patients.
- Each community plan should address the medical, psychological, safety, and legal needs of the sexually assaulted patient. The plan should provide for counseling, and should specifically address pregnancy and testing for and treatment of sexually transmissible diseases, including HIV.
- Each hospital should provide for access to appropriate medical, technical, and psychological support for the patient. A community may elect to establish, under the supervision of a physician, an alternative medical site, which specializes in the care of the sexually assaulted patient and provides medical and psychological support capabilities when no other injuries are evident.
- A victim of sexual assault should be offered prophylaxis for pregnancy and for sexually transmitted diseases, subject to informed consent and consistent with current treatment guidelines. Physicians and allied health practitioners who find this practice morally objectionable or who practice at hospitals that prohibit prophylaxis or contraception should offer to refer victims of sexual assault to another provider who can provide these services in a timely fashion.
- Specially trained, nonphysician medical personnel should be allowed to perform evidentiary examinations in jurisdictions in which evidence collected in such a manner is admissible in criminal cases.
- Physicians and trained medical staff who collect evidence, perform in good faith, and follow protocols should be immune from civil or criminal penalties related to evidence collection, documentation of findings, and recording of the patient's subjective complaints.
- For the special diagnostic and therapeutic needs of the pediatric patient, a community plan should provide for primary referral centers with expertise and ancillary social services that support a multidisciplinary approach.
- As part of its ongoing quality management activities, the hospital should establish patient care criteria for the management of the sexually assaulted patient and monitor staff performance.
- ED staff should have ongoing training and education in the management of the sexually assaulted patient.
- ACEP supports appropriate measures to prevent sexual assault in the community.

First, and perhaps most important, is the guidelines place the emergency care physician as the primary care provider to a victim of sexual assault. Nonphyscian medical personnel may be allowed to perform evidentiary examinations, however the guidelines do not contemplate a nurse being responsible for the care received by a sexual assault victim. The CVSSA contradicts this by permitting it.

Second, the guidelines set expectations on the community, including ongoing quality management activities, however these do not appear to be part of what a cruise ship does, especially with physicians typically working a four-month (or less) contract. The infirmary on a cruise ship is not comparable to a land-based hospital and it is difficult for it to comply with the guidelines.

One guideline that is of particular note is that the ACEP expects the physician to support appropriate measures to prevent sexual assault in the community. As has already been discussed, there is much more a cruise ship can do to prevent sexual assault and to, in turn, comply with this guideline. One has to wonder whether an under-contract physician who is considered an independent contractor is in a position to effectively advocate on such a matter.

Finally, the guidelines are explicit that the psychological and safety needs of a sexual assault victim be addressed. It also has very specific expectations for how the pediatric patient will be treated, including referral centers and ancillary social services. These "best practices" are not available on a cruise ship. There are no psychological services available onboard, and cruise ships do not typically take responsibility for referring the sexual assault victim (especially a child) to appropriate therapeutic and support services. As well, a victim of sexual assault will often see their perpetrator wandering freely on the cruise ship, which seriously questions the commitment to the victim's need for feeling safe. In both cases discussed above, of the 11-year- old and 12-year-old girls recently sexually assaulted, the perpetrator was not apprehended in a timely manner (in one case the perpetrator was not apprehended at all).

While the intent of the CVSSA in referencing the ACEP guideline is laudable, it is an empty gesture when the guidelines do not fit with the setting. More appropriate would be language that addresses: 1) the qualifications of the physician charged with treating sexual assault victims; 2) the appropriate role played by nonphysician medical personnel; and 3) the provision of psychological and therapeutic services both onboard and appropriate referrals for when the victim returns home from the ship. These latter requirements may be met through a partnership with land-based organizations such as RAINN or with land-based service providers. Interestingly, based on the landscape of onboard sexual assaults I advocated in my 2002 book, *Cruise Ship Blues: The Underside of the Cruise Industry*, that cruise ships invest in having a counselor onboard a ship, both for passengers and crew. I write:

> The counselor would be someone competent in dealing with cases of sexual assault, who could serve as an ombudsperson in matters arising between passengers and staff or between shipboard employees. If a counselor is to be effective and seen as someone to turn to, it is essential that he or she be independent of the ship's hierarchical structure – a status similar to the ship's physician who on medical matters essentially answers to no one onboard, not even the captain. Counselors would need to be independent, and independently available. The simple fact is that abuses are known to occur on ships, but the information is kept within the shipboard community. The only way that information gets out is by having an outsider brought in (p. 161).

I know this was read by cruise industry executives and their lawyers, but it had no apparent effect.

Recommendation #12: *The CVSSA should require onboard physicians to be board certified in emergency medicine, family practice medicine, or internal medicine in the U.S., U.K., Canada, Australia, France, or Germany. Further, there should be clear statements about how cruise ships will treat the psychological and safety needs of sexual assault victims, especially victims who are minors.*

Investigation

Proper investigation of cruise ship crimes and preservation of evidence is critical, especially in a case of sexual assault. In addition, there needs to be proper procedures for ensuring chain of evidence requirements. Though beyond my expertise, I have to wonder whether evidence collected and secured by a shipboard safety officer will stand up in a shore side court of law. I suspect a critical issue will also be whether the safety officer is available to testify in a criminal prosecution or a civil case, especially if the case is against his/her employer.

This raises a critical issue with regard to the independence and impartiality of onboard security officers. On land when there is a sexual assault the victim can talk to their local law enforcement office, which is totally independent of the perpetrator, and they receive medical care and support services from professionals who are also independent of the perpetrator. On a cruise ship, a victim's case is investigated by an employee of the cruise line, a relationship that becomes particularly thorny when the perpetrator is also a cruise line employee – the most recent comprehensive data of sexual assaults on cruise ships indicates that the majority are perpetrated by a cruise ship employee; and then their medical care is provided by another employee of the cruise line. This situation does not engender the same level of trust a victim is likely to have when dealing with the same issue on land.

Recommendation #13: *Cruise ships should be required to have a private, independent law enforcement agent for purposes of crime investigation. These would be similar to the wholly- independent Ocean Rangers placed on cruise ships by the State of Alaska to monitor discharge of waste streams while the ship is in Alaska state waters.*

Notwithstanding the above, §3508(a) of the CVSSA states that the Secretary "shall develop training standards and curricula to allow for the certification of passenger vessel security personnel, crewmembers, and law enforcement officials on the appropriate methods for prevention, detection, evidence preservation, and reporting of criminal activities in the international maritime environment." The intent of this provision is clear, however the execution appears to be problematic. Compliance is ostensibly effected by *Model Course CVSSA 11-01: Crime Prevention, Detection, Evidence Preservation and Reporting.* This is an on-line course that takes eight hours (one day) to complete. Aside from there being no direct contact between an instructor and a student, there is a total of three hours devoted to "Crime Scene Actions," which includes techniques used by law enforcement, action required to preserve different crime scenes, and access control. There is extremely limited content on collection and preservation of evidence. The stated measure of competence for this three-hour module is that "requirements related to reporting and recording of serious crimes are correctly identified and demonstrated." It is unclear from the manual how students are tested (although it appears that the most likely method is multiple choice and other closed-choice exams) and whether the student can learn in three hours the skills and knowledge commonly possessed by crime scene investigators on shore. While the course may be useful for training support personnel to a professionally trained investigator, it appears inadequate preparation if the concern is with gathering evidence that will withstand the requirements of land-based law enforcement and a court of law.

Recommendation #14: *In the absence of a professionally qualified crime scene investigator, a cruise ship should be required to have onboard a staff person with more than adequate training in all facets of crime scene preservation, collection of evidence, and methods to ensure proper chain of evidence.*

Prosecution

The final area to consider regarding sexual assault is prosecution of the perpetrator. I have already addressed the need for evidence to facilitate prosecution. Another critical issue is to detain the offender. This may be more easily done when the perpetrator is a crewmember, however when a passenger perpetrates a sexual assault he or she should also be detained for law enforcement personnel at the next U.S. port. It is unfortunate when a crewmember is flown to his home country from a foreign port rather than having to face prosecution, especially when the crime is irrefutably caught on videotape, as was the case of the 11-year-old girl molested on *Disney Dream* in May 2013. It is equally sad that a 30-year-old man who groped a 12 year old girl can wander freely on the ship while the girl and her family are reminded of the ordeal every time they see him.

Recommendation #15: *Cruise ship personnel should take more seriously their responsibility to detain perpetrators of sexual assault until the ship arrives at its next U.S. port. Further, Congress should contemplate whether there needs to be a legislated requirement to ensure perpetrators are isolated from the general public onboard the ship and held for delivery to land- based law enforcement personnel.*

4. Other Crimes

There are two crimes for which the FBI collected data in 2007-08, but that are not required to be reported under the CVSSA. One is a theft of less than $10,000 – there were 89 in the one year period 2007-08. The other is simple assault – there were 115 in the same one year period. It doesn't seem right that these crimes are not recorded and that victim rights are apparently truncated.

As regard theft, there is the obvious fact that crew members know that a theft of less than $10,000 will not only not be prosecuted, but will not be recorded. This seems like an open door for a permissible level of crime. Why $10,000 rather than $9,800? The amount appears arbitrary. However, more importantly, by not collecting data there is no ability for analysis to discern patterns or trends that might inform interdiction or prevention. As well, there is no way to know whether the problem is increasing or decreasing, and whether the problem on cruise ships is greater or lesser than on land.

Judge Thomas A. Dickerson of the New York State 9th Judicial District makes the same point, but more eloquently:

[The Act does not] ... require the reporting of thefts which are between $1,000 and $9,999 in value. These problems may be resolved as follows. First, requiring owners to report thefts less than $10,000 would allow local law enforcement to investigate and deter future crimes. Second, mandating owners to include the recorded thefts of property valued between $1,000 and $9,999 on the USCG website would allow prospective cruise passengers to better appreciate the risks associated with cruises. An even more effective method would be to breakdown the USCG online reporting by individual cruise ships, rather than by cruise lines, as is currently required.[17]

There are similar concerns with regard to simple assault. What if the assault is a case of domestic violence (a fair proportion of which do fall within this category) – why would this not be reported and considered for prosecution, especially if the victim decides to press charges. Also, what is the fine line between a simple assault and an assault with serious bodily injury? Are cruise ship personnel expert in making this determination? I think not. But most importantly is the fact that having this data is useful both to determine changes over time as well as to compare the situation between different cruise ships and between cruise ships and incidence on land. It would seem it is in the interest of the cruise industry to have this data collected, unless they are concerned that the rate onboard their ships is higher than the rate onshore.

Recommendation #16: *The CVSSA should require reporting to the FBI of all onboard crime, including thefts less than $10,000 and simple assaults.*

III. Consumer Rights and Cruise Ship Liability

The issue of consumer rights was directly addressed by CLIA's recent announcement of its Passenger Bill of Bights. This will be discussed first. I will then shift to the broader issue of liability as it applies to cruise ships and cruise lines.

A. CLIA Passenger Bill of Rights

The CLIA Bill of Rights is as interesting for what it includes as for what it does not include. It was announced May 22, 2013 just five days before a fire on *Grandeur of the Sea;* probably motivated in large part by a series of problems before and following the media-focused fire on the *Carnival Triumph* and by Senator Schumer's stated intent to develop a passenger bill of rights. In the month before the *Carnival Triumph* fire, five ships experienced propulsion problems causing delay and/or requiring itinerary changes: *Carnival Splendor*, *Carnival Destiny*, *Carnival Legend*, *Carnival Triumph*, and P&O Cruises' *Aurora* (all ships operated by Carnival Corporation). In the several months following the *Carnival Triumph* fire there were the following:

- *Seabourn Odyssey* had a power failure and was towed to port in New Zealand;
- Cunard Line's *Queen Elizabeth* had a collision with a tug boat packed with pleasure seekers in New Zealand;

- Hurtigruten's *Kong Herald* ran aground and the cruise was canceled;
- Coastal and Maritime Voyage's *Marco Polo* was holed and canceled its cruise;
- *Carnival Dream* had generator problems and ended a cruise early, flying passengers home from Saint Maarten;
- *Carnival Legend* had propulsion problems and was stuck for a day in Costa Maya; the ship altered the itinerary on this cruise and the next because of continuing problems;
- *Carnival Elation* had steering problems and required assistance of a tug to navigate to New Orleans;
- P&O's *Ventura* had propulsion problems transatlantic and changed its itinerary;
- Regent Seven Seas' *Voyager* had propulsion problems causing significant delays;
- *Carnival Sunshine* canceled two cruises because of longer-than-anticipated time in dry dock; when the ship finally left dry dock passengers complained that work was still being done and some ship services are unavailable;
- *Celebrity Millennium* had propulsion problems that caused itinerary changes, at one point being dead in the water for three hours in the South China Sea;
- *Carnival Ecstasy* experienced a power failure;
- *Coral Princess* experienced a fire;

And then comes the Passenger Bill of Rights – no doubt a public relations initiative to counter the wave of bad publicity (notably, all but three of the problems occurred on ships operated by Carnival Corporation). In announcing the Bill of Rights CLIA stated that they detail CLIA members' "commitment to the safety, comfort and care of guests." CLIA also stated the Bill of Rights "codifies many longstanding practices of CLIA members and goes beyond these to further inform cruise guests of the industry's commitment to their comfort and care." The obvious question then is what is new about the Bill of Rights. I will address this and then consider what isn't contained in the Bill of Rights.

1. The Right to Disembark a Docked Ship if Essential Provisions Such As Food, Water, Restroom Facilities and Access to Medical Care Cannot Adequately Be Provided Onboard, Subject Only to the Master's Concern for Passenger Safety and Security and Customs and Immigration Requirements of the Port

This Right makes perfect sense if a ship is alongside a pier, however it does not consider the issue of passengers who are stranded on ships without electrical power, propulsion, toilets, air conditioning and adequate food for three to five days. What are the rights of those passengers? Getting off a ship when it is docked is an easy Right to guarantee. However there are still questions. As Senator Schumer observes in his May 21, 2013 letter to CLIA, who determines that essential provisions cannot be adequately provided? If someone on the ship or the cruise line is the decision maker, how can passengers appeal that decision? But there is also the issue of disembarking in a port that requires clearance by customs and immigration officials. A cruise ship can prevent disembarkation if local port authorities do not cooperate. What are the rights of passengers then?

The issue of landing and needing clearance from immigration officials was raised as a potential concern when *Carnival Triumph* had its fire and the company decided to tow the ship to a U.S. port rather than to a closer Mexican port. The explanation given was that many passengers didn't have passports, so disembarking in Mexico and repatriating to the U.S. could be problematic. Does the location of a ship truncate one's rights? On surface the Right sounds reasonable, but in the concrete situation with a range of conditions it isn't as straightforward.

2. The Right to a Full Refund for a Trip That Is Canceled due to Mechanical Failures, or a Partial Refund for Voyages That Are Terminated Early due to Those Failures

Again, the Right is straightforward and sounds reasonable. If a product paid for is not delivered there will be a refund. But the Right does not indicate whether the refund is in cash and how long it will take for the refund to be processed – the passenger paid for their cruise 60 – 90 days in advance of the cruise so shouldn't they be entitled to the income generated by the cruise line for the period of time it held the money on deposit? As well, how is a partial refund calculated and what mechanism is in place for a passenger to challenge the entitlement offered by the cruise line.

But there is a larger issue. What is a passenger's Right when they fly to a distant port and learn upon arrival that their ship will not depart? Will the cruise line reimburse their travel costs to the port on top of refunding the cruise fare? This is not clear from the Passenger Bill of Rights. The Passenger Bill of Rights is also not clear about a passenger's rights if a cruise line leaves port with a cruise ship that it is known will not be able to fulfill the published itinerary, as was the case on a couple of cruises listed in Appendix 2.

A related issue is how the Passenger Bill of Rights applies to a missed port and/or changed itinerary. There is a significant number of these as noted in Appendix 2 (see for example *Aurora* (March 2009), *Seven Seas Voyager* (April 2009), *Pacific Dawn* (February 2010), *Artemis* (May 2010), *Infinity* (June 2010), *Pacific Sun* (February 2011), *Enchantment of the Seas* (February 2012), *Carnival Legend* (March 2013), *Seven Seas Voyager* (March 2013), *Crown Princess* (April 2013)). Do passengers have the right to be refunded port fees, taxes, and port related services for which they have already paid when a port call skipped, and is this payment in cash rather than the typical practice of an onboard credit? Are they entitled to an additional payment for failure to deliver the published itinerary, especially when the change is due to a mechanical problem or failure? And should passengers have a right to be reimbursed for costs associated with an independently arranged shore excursion in a port call that is skipped or canceled? Finally, how are these refunds computed and by what means does a passenger have a right to dispute that computation? As the saying goes, the devil is in the details.

While the Passenger Bill of Rights appears to address canceled cruises, albeit without sufficient clarity, it does not address the much more common occurrence of port calls that are canceled. What rights do passengers have in these cases?

3. The Right to Have Available on Board Ships Operating Beyond Rivers or Coastal Waters Full-Time, Professional Emergency Medical Attention, As Needed Until Shore Side Medical Care Becomes Available

Having on board professional emergency medical attention has been a long-standing practice on cruise ships – in fact it is required by International Labor Organization Convention 164, entitled "Health Protection and Medical Care for Seafarers," requiring that ships ":engaged in international voyages of more than three days' duration shall carry a medical doctor as a member of crew responsible for providing medical care." However the qualifications of medical personnel has varied widely. In most cases a physician and/or a nurse provide medical services.

Some cruise lines have a policy of only using medical professionals trained and board certified in the U.S., Canada, or U.K. Other cruise lines, in part because the fee paid is less, draw medical professionals from a range of countries. In all cases, medical professionals are considered independent contractors – they are paid a fee by the cruise line and receive a commission based on charges for medical services and prescriptions/supplies. Though the physician wears a senior officer's uniform and is considered a member of the crew, she or he is not a cruise line employee and the cruise line claims no liability for his or her medical practice.

While the Right states a standard practice, and reiterates a requirement of the CVSSA, it does not indicate a substantial fee is charged for emergency medical attention. The Passenger Bill of Rights should have greater transparency, clearly indicating that medical services on board a ship are fee-for-service. In addition, passengers have the Right to know the limitations on medical services on board a ship. One issue is the scope of practice of the individual physician. An equally, if not more important issue, is the limited nature of a ship's infirmary. There may be limited diagnostic facility (e.g., no x-rays or complex blood tests) and there is no surgical theatre. As an experienced emergency physician on board a cruise ship told me, "my greatest fear is an ectopic pregnancy that needs emergency surgery – there is very little I can do in the middle of the ocean."

What this suggests is that the Passenger Bill of Rights should include useful information about the limits of medical care on a cruise ship so a passenger can make an informed decision and not go onboard expecting services that will not be available. In the absence of such information, the obvious question is whether a cruise ship, by the Passenger Bill of Rights, is accepting liability for cases where emergency medical attention may be inadequate or otherwise lacking in an emergency medical situation. What recourse is available to a passenger in such a case?

4. The Right to Timely Information Updates As to Any Adjustments in the Itinerary of the Ship in the Event of a Mechanical Failure or Emergency, As Well As Timely Updates of the Status of Efforts to Address Mechanical Failures

On surface this right sounds ideal – what else could a passenger expect? However the term "timely" is subjective. I have been on cruises where timely was measured in hours (sometimes many hours) whereas I as a passenger measure timely in quarter hours. It would be helpful to a passenger in understanding the Right to know what is meant by timely. Aside from that, how will these information updates be provided – via public announcements on board or by written notifications? And what recourse does a passenger have if information updates are not timely? Are they entitled to compensation or some other consideration? In many ways the Right can easily become an empty promise.

Another term requiring definition is "mechanical failure or emergency." This presumably includes a situation where a ship is dead in the water or has an extended power loss. But does it also apply to a ship that has a propulsion problem causing it to sail at reduced speeds, or a medical emergency that delays a ship and causes a change in itinerary. It would seem that what the industry should be stating is that a passenger has a Right "to timely information updates as to any adjustments in the itinerary of the ship" – full stop.

The Right leaves unstated what compensation, if any, is available to passengers when a port call is dropped or an itinerary is changed. Will they be refunded all port fees, taxes and other port use expenses associated with that port? This was addressed above. In any case, the Passenger Bill of Rights should be explicit about the parameters for what their rights are and what their rights are not.

5. The Right to a Ship Crew That Is Properly Trained in Emergency and Evacuation Procedures

This is certainly a fair expectation on the part of passengers. However, there is a huge chasm between being properly trained in emergency and evacuation procedures – there may not be basis to argue that crewmembers aren't trained – and those same crewmembers demonstrating through behavior competence in executing emergency and evacuation procedures.

Unfortunately, there is a track record of crewmembers not demonstrating this competence, not only in emergency situations but in periodic inspections by the U.S. Coast Guard and in annual U.S. Coast Guard Control Verification exams. The report of the *Carnival Splendor* fire is a good example of the point I am making. Officers were likely properly trained, however the reports says that one reason for the catastrophic nature of the fire was human error – when the fire alarm first went off on the ship's bridge, a crew member reset it, leading to a 15-minute delay in the activation of an automatic fire-suppression system. The report also faults the crew's "lack of familiarity with the engine room," which hampered their ability to locate and fight the fire, and the captain's decision to "ventilate" the compartment where the fire began before it was fully extinguished, allowing the flames to flare again.[18]

Two questions derive from these points. First, what will the cruise industry require to ensure that all crewmembers are properly trained – will current regimes of training be augmented or bolstered? How will proper training in emergency and evacuation procedures be verified? Second, what recourse does a passenger have when crewmembers do not demonstrate competence in emergency and evacuation procedures? Will the cruise line waive damage limits contained in the Passenger Contract and/or permit a passenger to file a lawsuit (including for emotional distress, mental suffering/anguish or psychological injury, presently excluded from the cruise line's liability) for demonstrated failure of competence in emergency and evacuation procedures? These should be explicitly laid out in the Passenger Bill of Rights.

6. The Right to an Emergency Power Source in the Case of a Main Generator Failure

Like other items in the Passenger Bill of Rights, the obvious question is what is included under "main generator failure" and what is excluded? We can point to *Carnival Splendor*, which had six diesel engines – a fire in one engine caused extensive damage to cables in the aft engine room that meant vessel engineers were unable to restart the unaffected main generator.[19] How can CLIA guarantee that a similar or more catastrophic event wouldn't happen on another ship? In the case of the *Carnival Splendor* it wasn't that the main generator failed, but that the cables carrying power from the generator had been destroyed. Also on the

Carnival Splendor the emergency generator apparently continued to work, but only provided power to emergency services. Does this technically comply with the right stipulated?

In the case of *Carnival Dream* in March 2013, news reports indicate the main power generator had not failed, but the backup emergency diesel generator had failed, thus causing the cruise to be terminated when the ship was in Saint Maarten. This illustrates the confusion in the language in the Right – what is it actually telling a passenger and whether what is being promised can actually be delivered? And if the Right is not fulfilled, what recourse does a passenger have?

This issue is made even more confusing when considering the number of cruise ships that have lost power and gone adrift – some for short periods of time; others for longer periods of time. How does this Right apply to a passenger in this situation? Does this Right apply to all power outages or only power outages of a certain duration and/or only power outages caused by failure of the main generator? Assuming a passenger has a Right to an emergency power source, what happens if it isn't provided; what recourse or compensation is available to them? There are many questions raised by this Right, which on surface is intended to reinforce a sense of security, but upon reflection is potentially an empty promise.

7. The Right to Transportation to the Ship's Scheduled Port of Disembarkation or the Passenger's Home City in the Event a Cruise Is Terminated Early due to Mechanical Failures

This Right is already a common practice of the cruise industry, however the Passenger Bill of Rights doesn't address two situations. First, what Right does a passenger have when a cruise ends early and passengers are returned to the port of embarkation – does the cruise line assume responsibility for the additional travel costs (and change fees on airline tickets) associated with getting from the port of disembarkation, does the cruise line assume responsibility for lodging and food expenses incurred by the passenger in getting home, and does the cruise line provide compensation for a passenger who arrives home later than scheduled thereby losing salary from missed work and having expenses for childcare etcetera? The Right to transportation doesn't appear to extend to these issues. Related to this is whether a passenger is accommodated in the same class of service on airlines and the same class of hotel that they normally choose. How long will a passenger wait for reimbursement of these costs and what mechanism is in place if there is a dispute between a cruise line and the passenger about the amount due to the passenger? Does the cruise line waive the Passenger Contract so the passenger can pursue a case in a court of law of their choosing (for example, if they live outside the U.S. or in a location remote from the court specified in the Passenger Contract's forum selection clause)?

Second, the Passenger Bill of Rights does not address the Right a passenger has when a ship arrives late in a port of disembarkation and the passenger has arranged his/her own transportation. Does a passenger in this case have the Right to have the cruise line assume responsibility for all additional travel costs (in the class of service originally booked) as well as lodging and food expenses incurred in getting home, and does the cruise line provide compensation for a passenger who arrives home later than scheduled thereby losing salary from missed work and having expenses for childcare etcetera? This is an area of rights that is not addressed at all in the Passenger Bill of Rights.

8. The Right to Lodging if Disembarkation and an Overnight Stay in an Unscheduled Port Are Required When a Cruise Is Terminated Early due to Mechanical Failures

Does this Right only apply to a cruise terminated due to a mechanical failure, or to any cruise terminated early? CLIA's choice of more restrictive language suggests there are many situations when a cruise may be terminated in an unscheduled port of call and lodging would not be provided. How does this Right interface with the Passenger Bill of Rights' #1?

This Right also says nothing about the quality of the lodging provided. Does a cot in a high school gymnasium qualify as "lodging"? Does lodging include a private bathroom? Based on past events, it is possible to imagine a range of scenarios. What Right to lodging, precisely, does a passenger have and will the cruise line assume all costs associated with that lodging? What recourse does a passenger have when the lodging provided is unacceptable.

9. The Right to Have Included on Each Cruise Line's Website a Toll-Free Phone Line That Can Be Used for Questions or Information Concerning Any Aspect of Shipboard Operations

Cruise lines already have toll-free numbers accessible from telephones in the U.S. Will access to these numbers extend to all ports of call on the cruise line's itinerary and to all countries from which passengers are drawn? More importantly, what will be done to ensure that the information provided by an operator at a toll-free number has accurate and correct information? Take for example the following correspondence I received from the parent of a passenger on *Carnival Legend* March 14, 2013:

> The ship is disabled and stuck in Costa Maya on March13, 2013. I spoke with Carnival last night about how this might effect the itinerary because my daughter is on the ship. They told me they did not know anything about an alteration in the cruise schedule and would only tell me the ship was moving. I called the ship to try to speak with my daughter today and while I did not reach her, the ship officer confirmed to me that they were in Costa Maya and not Belize yesterday. Her boyfriend called Carnival this morning as well and they denied the ship was in Costa Maya and called it a rumor. I can understand a mechanical issue that needs to be addressed although this seems to be a big problem with this company. I cannot tolerate flat out lying and misinformation that they are providing about the Legend.

What changes or initiatives are being undertaken by CLIA and its member lines in order to avoid a similar situation? What recourse does a passenger and/or his/her family have when misinformation is provided or information is withheld?

10. The Right to Have This Cruise Line Passenger Bill of Rights Published on Each Line's Website

This seems like the easiest Right to realize, however a quick survey of CLIA-member cruise line websites on July 15, 2013, found that the Passenger Bill of Rights was apparently not published on 13 of the 26 member lines' website. CLIA's May 22, 2013, Press Release (Cruise Industry Adopts Passenger Bill of Rights) states that publishing the Passenger Bill of Rights on a cruise line's website is a condition of membership in CLIA. Are these 13 members no longer members of CLIA? What right or recourse does a passenger have if they have purchased a ticket from one of these lines in the past eight weeks – does the Passenger Bill of Rights apply to them?

CLIA Passenger Bill of Rights and the Cruise Contract

There is one additional issue with the Passenger Bill of Rights. CLIA promised that the Passenger Bill of Rights would be added to Cruise Passenger Contracts. This is laudable, but this is not apparent from Passenger Contracts displayed on cruise line websites, but more importantly there is no mention of how conflicts and contradictions between the Passenger Bill of Rights and the Cruise Passenger Contract are resolved. Which has precedence? According to the standard passenger contract the cruise line has the right to alter a cruise itinerary for any reason and the passenger has no recourse. As Carnival Cruise Lines states in its hard-to-find "Cruise Cancellation and Itinerary Change Policy" states:

> In the event an itinerary change becomes necessary while the ship is at sea or when notice prior to sailing is not feasible, Carnival and/or the Master will attempt to substitute an alternative port. Carnival and/or the Master may, in their discretion and for any purpose, deviate in any direction or for any purpose from the direct or usual course, and omit or change any or all ports of calls, arrival or departure times, with or without notice, for any reason whatsoever, all such deviations being considered as forming part of and included in the proposed voyage. Carnival shall have no liability for any refund or other damages in such circumstances. [20]

In terms of itinerary changes before a ship leaves port, the policy states:

> Due to the nature of a cruise vacation, itinerary changes sometimes become necessary for safety, weather or other reasons beyond the control of Carnival. If the itinerary change is for reasons beyond Carnival's exclusive control, including but not limited to safety, security, weather, strikes, tides, hostilities, civil unrest, port closings, emergency debarkations of guests or crew, late air, sea, car or motor coach departures or arrivals, mechanical breakdowns or problems not known to Carnival, itinerary changes consistent with U.S. State Department travel warnings / advisories or other applicable US or foreign governmental advisories, guests will not be provided any compensation. Guests electing to cancel will be subject to the standard cancellation terms.

And in terms of passenger costs resulting from cruise cancellations or itinerary changes the policy states:

> Carnival shall not be liable to guests for any charges, fees or expenses paid or owed to third parties by guests (such as air travel booked by a guest directly with an airline) in connection with a cancelled cruise or an itinerary change for any reason.

Carnival Cruise Lines' Passenger Contract is even more restrictive:

> (e) If the performance of the proposed voyage is hindered or prevented (or in the opinion of Carnival or the Master is likely to be hindered or prevented) by war, hostilities, blockage, ice, labor conflicts, strikes on board or ashore, restraint of Princes, Rulers or People, seizure under legal process, **breakdown of the Vessel**, congestion, docking difficulties or any other cause whatsoever or if Carnival or the Master considers that for any reason whatsoever, proceeding to, attempting to enter, or entering or remaining at the port of Guest's destination may expose the Vessel to risk or loss or damage or be likely to delay her, **the Guest and his baggage may be landed at the port of embarkation or at any port or place at which the Vessel may call, at which time the responsibility of Carnival shall cease and this contract shall be deemed to have**

been fully performed, or if the Guest has not embarked, Carnival may cancel the proposed voyage without liability to refund passage money or fares paid in advance. (emphasis added)

These statements appear at variance with a number of items in the Passenger Bill of Rights. It appears disingenuous to promote a Passenger Bill of Rights without also clarifying how conflicts between those rights and the cruise passenger contract are to be resolved.

A common theme across all elements in the Passenger Bill of Rights is how a passenger deals with a Right that has not been fulfilled or has been directly violated. Are these rights ultimately governed by the cruise passenger contract that sets clear terms about when and how complaints and legal action must filed, and where law suits must be filed? Forum selection clauses effectively truncate a passengers rights under the Passenger Bill of Rights given the requirement that legal action can only be taken in a court located in the state where the cruise line's corporate headquarters is located (most frequently Florida). The cruise passenger contract also includes a "class action waiver," prohibiting a passenger from taking any legal action as a member of a class or as a participant in a class action. For many passengers these are impediments to taking any action and they often resign to accepting whatever the cruise line offers, if anything.

B. What the CLIA Passenger Bill of Rights Does Not Include

1. Passenger Rights

There are a number of things obviously missing from the CLIA Passenger Bill of Rights. Some of these have already been mentioned:

- There is no mention of the recourse a passenger has if one of the Rights is not fulfilled or realized.
- There is no indication of how a partial refund will be computed and whether that refund is provided in cash or, as common in the industry, as a discount on a future cruise or an onboard credit.
- There is no mention of whether the cruise line is responsible for ancillary costs when a cruise is cancelled, including change fees for airline tickets and for the costs of the tickets themselves, the cost of lodging required in travel to the passenger's home city, and support for food and incidentals associated with delays in getting from the ship to the passenger's home city.
- There is no mention of what rights a passenger has when a port of call is canceled. Some cruise lines refund "port fees and taxes," however these are given as an onboard credit rather than as a cash refund. As well, there is no transparency with regard to the amount refunded. Some cruise lines average the cost of port fees and taxes so a refund for one port is the same as the other even though actual fees can vary widely from one port to another. Also, it isn't transparent whether costs other than port taxes and fees that are not paid by the cruise line because of the canceled port call are also refunded to the passenger. There is considerable need for greater clarity and transparency around passenger rights when a port call is canceled.

- There is no mention of what rights a passenger has when a cruise itinerary is changed, such as a cruise sailing the Eastern Caribbean instead of the Western Caribbean because of propulsion problems, or a cruise going to Canada instead of the Caribbean because of weather. The Passenger Cruise Contract is clear that the cruise line has no obligation or responsibility to provide compensation in these situations. This absence of rights should be clearly articulated in the Passenger Bill of Rights.
- There is no mention of the rights a passenger has when embarkation is delayed. Does a passenger have a Right to meal vouchers or compensation for meals purchased (as is common in airline travel)? Also, after how many hours of waiting in a cruise terminal is the cruise line obligated to provide either lodging or a comfortable setting to wait? A comprehensive Passenger Bill of Rights would address these situations given the frequency of delayed embarkations.
- There is no mention of a passenger's rights when a cruise arrives late in its port of disembarkation, causing the passenger to miss transportation arrangements for their trip to their home city.

In addition there are some rights that should be directly addressed.

The Passenger Bill of Rights should clearly articulate the rights of a passenger who is "bumped" from a cruise because of overbooking or other issues. The most recent cases involve *Carnival Sunshine*, which bumped passengers on its June 7, 2013, cruise because a number of cabins were needed for contractors completing work that was not completed while the ship was in dry dock. Similarly, passengers in 78 cabins on *Grandeur of the Seas* were bumped from the July 12, 2013 (and perhaps the July 19th), sailing because cabins were needed for workers who were still making repairs following the fire earlier in the year. Some of these bumped passengers had their cruise canceled because the ship had been out of service for repairs, and here they were bumped from their replacement cruise.[21]

Similarly, the Passenger Bill of Rights should discuss a passenger's rights when they are expelled from a cruise ship, often for questionable reasons and the result is loss of cruise fare and their having responsibility for transportation from the port where they are left. Between January 2009 and June 30, 2013, there are eight cases list on my website where a passenger has been evicted or expelled (these are only ones reported in the media). These passengers have no right to appeal or recourse. The cruise line Cruise Passenger Contract gives them this unilateral, uncontestable Right to evict or expel, without liability.

The Passenger Bill of Rights does not address a passenger's rights when they miss the ship because of flight delays or because of weather conditions (such as Hurricane Sandy in the fall of 2013 when passengers lost their cruise fare because they couldn't get to the ship). The cruise lines generally take the position that this type of situation is not their problem. A passenger without trip insurance is responsible for lost cruise fares and/or additional travel costs to join the ship at a later point. Further, it there are reports that some benefits under trip insurance policies offered by the cruise line are more restrictive in the benefits they provide than insurance policies offered independent of the cruise line.

The Passenger Bill of Rights does not address a passenger's rights to have safety concerns taken seriously. Though not the first time I have received this sort of information, on June 21, 2013, I received the following from a cruise passenger:

We have just disembarked after a 7-day Alaskan cruise aboard Celebrity Solstice. We frequented the quasar dance club each night. On night two I noticed at 2300 (11pm), when the club only allows 18 and over, a crew member used a small rope to tie the handles of one of the two exits closed to prevent access. Not must looped but tied in a fashion that untying would be impossible is a smoke filled environment or panic. This room is required to have two emergency exits and this exit was clearly marked " emergency exit". This happened three nights in a row. I brought my concerns to the attention of guest services requesting to speak to the ships Safety Officer. I was told that another passenger had requested to speak with him also but he stated that he was "too busy with paperwork to speak to anyone". The guest services person apologized and drafted an email to him explaining my concerns and that I am a 28 year firefighter. That night in quasar the doors were once again tied closed. As of this writing no staff or crew has contacted me. I would encourage that all passengers be aware of their surroundings. It appears Celebrity is not concerned with safety and if this blatant example of reckless disregard for its passengers and crew in a public space is allowed to exist, then I am wondering what other safety issues exist that we did not see.

It would seem this passenger's expectations were realistic, but they were ignored. Did he have any rights? And what rights were available for this disregard of concern for fire safety?

Finally, the Passenger Bill of Rights does not address the Right to be free of sexual assault by crewmembers or cruise ship employees, or the Right to be free of other types of crime. This type of assurance seems only natural given the rate of sexual assault on cruise ships, but it is obviously one that would be difficult to fulfill (although no less difficult than some of the other rights included in the Passenger Bill of Rights). In this line of thought, the Passenger Bill of Rights should also contain a Right to contact the FBI directly from the ship when a victim of a crime. This Right is accorded by the CVSSA, so it should be provided, however most victims will be unaware of what is available to them without it explicitly being stated in something like a Passenger Bill of Rights. Alternatively, a cruise ship may be required to provide a crime victim with an information sheet outlining the rights and the options available to them, including the telephone numbers for relevant law enforcement agencies, and agencies that provide direct services or referral to services that are likely to be needed by the victim.

In sum, it appears the Passenger Bill of Rights is a public relations initiative that on its face accords more rights and protection to a passenger than is realistically the case. One problem is the many empty or nonspecific promises contained in the Passenger Bill of Rights, but a larger problem is there is no clear recourse for a passenger who believes the rights promised have not been provided. This is all based essentially based on a matter of trust, however as was observed by the Organization for Economic Co-operation and Development (OECD) in 2003, trust (or voluntary approaches) does not substantively change the status quo of the way things are done. Focusing specifically on environmental policy, the OECD notes few cases where voluntary approaches have improved the environment beyond a business as usual baseline.[22]

Recommendation #17: *Given the imprecise nature of the CLIA Passenger Bill of Rights, there is an obvious need for a legislated solution. Passenger rights can only be achieved by legislation that puts into place clear and specific measures for consumer protection, similar to those available to passengers of other modes of commercial transportation.*

This recommendation for greater consumer protection may help level the field between the rights of cruise passengers in the U.K. versus in the U.S. Unlike the U.S., there have been a number of successful lawsuits in the U.K. for "cruises from hell," with problems ranging from illness outbreaks, lapses in service, and ships having facilities that are not in proper repair or that remain under construction following time in dry dock.

2. Cruise Line Rights

While the typical Passenger Cruise Contract accords few rights to the cruise passenger, it gives many rights to the cruise line. Unfortunately, the cruise passenger contract is rarely given to the passenger when they make their booking and put down a deposit. Further, they are not usually given a copy of the passenger contract before making full payment for their cruise 60 – 90 days before the cruise. Most frequently a copy of the cruise passenger contract is provided in small print on the back of the tickets sent to a passenger to be used for boarding. By accepting the ticket the passenger acknowledges receipt of applicable brochures and agrees to abide by the terms and conditions of the cruise line's brochures and web site, including but not limited to the information contained in the "Frequently Asked Questions" and "Embarkation Information" sections.[23] At this point the passenger's rights have already been compromised – he or she cannot cancel the cruise without losing all monies paid. A cruise line would likely say that the passenger could have downloaded the passenger contract from the company's website, however a more proactive approach by the cruise line would make sense. When I buy an airline ticket I receive the passenger contract when I print or receive the ticket and I have 24 hours to cancel that ticket without loss of funds. It only seems reasonable that a cruise passenger should receive a copy of the cruise passenger contract before his or her Right to a refund passes.

As regards rights, there is an asymmetric power relationship between a passenger and a cruise ship. As already seen, the cruise line holds all of the power when it comes to itinerary changes and canceled cruises, and when it comes to crime. The cruise line similarly has full control over how to resolve customer service issues – not just evictions and expulsions, but lapses in providing the services and care a passenger is led to believe will be provided by advertising and promotional materials. The cruise contract either truncates a passenger's rights in most situations, or reinforces the cruise line's Right at the detriment of the passenger.

Some of the cruise line's rights appear unreasonable. For example, Carnival Cruise Line's contract states:

> Carnival reserves the right to increase published fares and air fare supplements without prior notice. However, fully paid or deposited guests will be protected, except for fares listed, quoted, advertised or booked in error, fuel supplements, government taxes, other surcharges and changes to deposit, payment and cancellation terms/conditions, which are subject to change without notice. In the event that a cruise fare listed, quoted or advertised through any website, Carnival sales person, travel agent or any other source is booked but is incorrect due to an electronic error, typographical error, human error or any other error causing the fare to be listed, quoted or advertised for an amount not intended by Carnival, Carnival reserves the right to correct the erroneous fare by requesting the Guest to pay the correct fare intended, or by canceling the cruise in exchange for a full refund, but in no event shall Carnival be obligated to honor any such booking resulting from the error or otherwise be liable in such circumstances.

Thus, a passenger can book a cruise only to be told later that they owe additional funds for a fuel supplement, surcharge, or government taxes. As well, if the company makes an error in booking a cruise at a fare it didn't mean to, the passenger has no right to receive the fare advertised and under which the cruise ticket was issued. This is another stark contrast with the airline industry.

The passenger contract also gives the cruise line the right to cancel the cruise contract at its discretion (and without the passengers consent) – the passenger has no reciprocal right. The cruise line also has no obligation to provide a passenger the cabin reserved when a reservation was made. As Carnival Cruise Lines' contract states, "Carnival reserves the right to move Guests to a comparable stateroom for any reason, including but not limited to, instances in which a stateroom is booked with fewer than the maximum number of Guests the stateroom can accommodate." Again, the passenger has no recourse.

Finally, the cruise line retains an exclusive right to use photographs and videotapes of a passenger onboard a ship with no limitation (including in advertising and publicity) and without the passenger's consent. Imagine taking a cruise and some time later seeing an advertisement or video with your image in a photograph or videotape (including when doing something silly or foolish). To some of us, this would be construed as a violation of privacy. Rightfully, consent should be required for use of anyone's image in a public forum.

3. Issues of Liability

In addition to issue of the cruise line's rights is the extreme limits placed on the company's liability. For claims not involving personal injury, illness, or death a passenger must give notice of claim within 30 days of disembarkation from the vessel. Claims involving personal injury, illness or death must be filed with the company within 6 months of the injury, event, illness or death and a lawsuit must be filed within a year. In all cases that legal action is taken, it must be filed in the U.S. District Court or state court where the cruise line's headquarters is located (referred to as a forum selection clause). As already mentioned, this severely limits the option available to many passengers.

Baggage and Personal Effects

Even when legal action may be initiated, there are other limits. Many passenger cruise contracts limit the liability of the cruise line for lost or damaged luggage and personal effects. For example, Carnival Cruise Lines' passenger contract states "...that the aggregate value of Guest's property does not exceed $50 USD per guest or bag with a maximum value of $100 USD per stateroom regardless of the number of occupants or bags." Consequently, a family of four whose luggage is lost by the cruise line is due only $100 – this doesn't even cover the cost of the luggage, much less the contents. A passenger can increase these limits by declaring a higher value and paying 5% of the declared value to the cruise line. In contrast, the passenger contract for an air carrier limits liability to approximately $1,500 per passenger.[24] A family of four on a cruise would have to pay $280 to the cruise line for the same level of coverage provided automatically by an air carrier.

Illness Outbreaks

Cruise lines operating out of U.S. ports and serving U.S. ports have successfully avoided liability for illness outbreaks. This has not consistently been the case in the U.K. where there are stronger consumer protection laws. Part of the cruise industry's defense is their mantra that "passengers bring the illness with them," thereby coloring itself as an unwilling victim. As Rose Abello, vice president of Public Relations of Holland America Line stated, "The ship is not sick. There are sick people getting on the ship."[25] This mantra was first used in late-2002 when there was a wave of very visible norovirus outbreaks on cruise ships, and it proved effective. Interestingly, The International Council of Cruise Lines (ICCL) laid out its strategy at the 2003 World Cruise Tourism Summit on March 3, 2003. An almost-inspirational video was shown about the situation in which the industry found itself and the way that it successfully responded on the public relations front.

At the start of the video, the industry was depicted as receiving an inordinate amount of attention for a series of norovirus outbreaks on cruise ships. Illness on cruise ships had been the topic of stories on mainstream television: Inside Edition, CNN, NBC, and many others. The industry had even become the brunt of jokes on late night television — Jay Leno and David Letterman among others. Evening news with increasing frequency showed people who had become sick on board ships.

The video described the industry's media strategy had three elements: provide talking points to cruise executives and others in a position to present the industry's position, arrange as many media interviews as possible, and flood the media with positive information about the cruise industry. It proactively distributed pictures and video footage showing ships being disinfected, and engaged in positive messaging. Carnival Cruise Lines' president, Bob Dickinson, framed the problem as part of a national epidemic and said there was no cause-and-effect with regard to norovirus on cruise ships. Colin Veitch, NCL's CEO, pointed to the incidence of norovirus in the general population to minimize the problem as unique to cruise ships. The industry also enlisted the help of third parties in its campaign, most significantly the Centers for Disease Control. It helped promote the idea that people get sick on airplanes too, but they don't experience symptoms until they get home so they don't associate it with air travel.

ICCL's video concluded with "Smooth Seas Ahead." The industry successfully fought off the negative media attention and reframed the issue. Its message was two pronged: cruises are a great vacation at a good price, and why worry about norovirus — it is as common as the common cold. You can't argue with that. The media became desensitized to the issue and most of the 79 outbreaks affecting 6,630 people in 2003 and 2004 went unnoticed. The problem continues: in 2012 the were were 34 known outbreaks affecting 5,542 passengers.

When an outbreak does happen ill passengers often are quarantined in their cabin for days; whether they receive any compensation is wholly at the cruise line's discretion. However, cruise lines are not as innocent or defenseless as they would like to appear. In 2005 and again in 2008 I argued in my books, in response to claims by the industry that the low incidence among prove that norovirus is largely a passenger problem, that there are systemic disadvantages for crewmembers to report when they are ill. This position appears to be supported by recent CDC health inspections that have identified cases where crewmembers have continued to report to work despite being ill, including in positions of food handling and food service.

The problem for passengers is that cruise lines have effectively escaped liability for illness among passengers. To my knowledge there have been no successful lawsuits in the U.S. for these outbreaks even though similar lawsuits have been successful under consumer protection laws in the U.K.

Independent Contractors

A cruise ship is populated with many independent contractors whose behavior and practice the cruise line assumes no liability. Most visibly these include medical services (physician(s) and nurse(s)), but spa and personal care services (including health and beauty staff), photographers and video diary staff, retail shop personnel, casino workers, art auctioneers, and all other concessionaires. Even though many of these people wear clothing with the cruise line's logo, and in the case of medical personnel officer uniforms, they are not considered cruise line employees. Unbeknownst to most passengers, the cruise ship has no liability for services provided and billed to the passenger's onboard account. The status of these groups as independent service providers over whom the cruise line has no authority, control, or responsibility (even though tacitly endorsed by the cruise line) needs to be more clearly visible to passengers. At the very least, there should be signage or formal notification to passengers of this fact.

Medical Care

Medical services are a bit different. In an emergency situation, the passenger has no choice but to accept the service of medical personal who the cruise line has judged to be appropriate for medical care on its ship. But the cruise ship has no liability for their practice. It is a hard concept to get one's head around given the service is offered by the cruise line and the cruise ship collects the fees. But the nature of this arrangement was supported by the Florida Supreme Court in February 2007 and by the U.S. Supreme Court in October 2007.

The case began ten years before in March 1997. Fourteen-year-old Elizabeth Carlisle was on a Caribbean cruise on *Carnival Destiny* with her family. On the second night out of Miami she developed severe abdominal pain. She consulted the ship's physician, Dr. Mauro Neri, who had finished medical school in his native Italy in 1981 and had held nine medical jobs in Italy, Africa and England in the fifteen years before joining Carnival Cruise Lines. His salary was $1,057 a month. Dr. Neri advised that Elizabeth was suffering from the flu and sent her on her way. But her pain became worse. On the third visit to the infirmary, after Elizabeth's parents specifically asked whether the problem could be appendicitis, Dr. Neri conducted his first physical exam. He responded that he was sure the problem was not the girl's appendix.

When the pain continued to grow worse Elizabeth's parents called their family physician in Michigan, who advised they return home. The family took the advice, and shortly after arriving home Elizabeth underwent emergency surgery to remove her ruptured appendix. The infection had rendered the fourteen year old sterile and caused lifelong medical problems. Elizabeth sued Carnival Cruise Lines in Florida state court, a case she lost on Carnival's motion for summary judgement. The cruise line claimed it was not responsible for the medical negligence of the doctor on board and pointed to the fine print in the passenger cruise contract to support its position.

The family appealed the Circuit Court's decision to Florida's Third District Court of Appeal, where the parents argued the cruise line was vicariously liable for the doctor's negligence. Judge Joseph Nesbitt agreed and reversed the lower court's decision. The judge held that the cruise line had control over the doctor's medical services for agency law purposes; the doctor was to provide medical services to passengers and crew in accordance with the cruise line's guidelines. And as it was foreseeable that some passengers at sea would develop medical problems (and that the only realistic alternative for such a passenger was treatment by the ship's doctor) the cruise line had an element of control over the doctor–

patient relationship. As such, the cruise line's duty to exercise reasonable care under the circumstances extended to the actions of a ship's doctor placed onboard by the cruise line. The doctor was an agent of the cruise line and his negligence was imputed to the cruise line. This invalidated the cruise ticket's purported limitation of the cruise line's liability for the negligence of its agents.

Judge Nesbitt's decision was groundbreaking. It was likely the very first case where a cruise line was held responsible for the care provided by a ship's physician. Not surprisingly, Carnival appealed the case to the Florida Supreme Court. While the court almost agreed with the lower court's assertion that times had changed and that a doctor's negligence at sea also shows negligence by the cruise line, it ultimately found in favour of Carnival. Justice Peggy Quince wrote in her opinion:

> We find merit in the plaintiff 's argument and the reasoning of the district court. However, because this is a maritime case, this Court and the Florida district courts of appeal must adhere to the federal principles of harmony and uniformity when applying federal maritime law.[26]

The case was appealed to the U.S. Supreme Court and the court refused to hear it. The Florida Supreme Court's decision was the final word. If the Carlisle family wanted to pursue the case they would have to sue the physician directly. But this would be difficult in their case, and in most involving medical malpractice on cruise ships, given that they'd first have to locate the physician in his present home. Cruise lines historically have not provided assistance with locating former staff members. In addition, malpractice cases involving treatment in international waters must be filed in the courts of the physician's country of origin, which is both difficult and expensive.[27]

Shore Excursions

Shore excursions are a major source of income for a cruise ship – the cruise ship retains 50 – 70% or more of what a passenger pays for the tour. These tours are sold onboard at a Shore Excursion Desk by staff members wearing the cruise line's uniform. But when something goes wrong on a shore excursion, the cruise line is quick to remind the passenger that they are not liable; shore excursions are provided by independent contractors. Appendix 1 indicates 14 known deaths on shore excursions (these are only incidents that have been reported in the media; there are many more than this) and five robberies ashore (some at knife or gun point) on shore excursions affecting dozens of passengers – these again are only those that have been reported in the media so they underrepresent the true number.

If there is an injury or death on a shore excursion, the cruise passenger's options are limited in U.S. courts. Their options in a court in the country where the shore excursion was offered may also offer few options. The problem is that shore excursions are largely unregulated, except by the cruise line itself, and some can be quite dangerous.

While the cruise line has no liability for shore excursions, they tend to dissuade passengers from taking tours that are independently available. They may talk about safety concerns for a tour that is not approved, and will often warn passengers that the advantage of the ship-sponsored tour is that if they are delayed the ship will wait for them. In contrast, the ship will not wait for a passenger delayed on an independent tour. While more and more passengers are choosing to make private arrangements for land- based tours, those who make advance plans may find they are out money when a ship alters its itinerary or cancels a port call.

Sexual Assaults

The issue of liability for sexual assaults reached public attention in the mid-1990s. A tort reform measure attached to the Coast Guard Reauthorization bill had passed on May 9, 1995. The amendment, for the most part written by the ICCL, was introduced by Representative Don Young. He referred to it as a "noncontroversial manager's amendment."[28] It passed the House by a vote of 406 to 12. Only afterwards did people read the final print.

One provision, directed at mounting claims from injuries and sexual assaults, limited liability to passengers and crew for "infliction of emotional distress, mental suffering or psychological injury" unless negligence or an intentional act can be proven. The American Trial Lawyers Association characterized the amendments as "dangerous legislation" that "jeopardized the safety of women on cruise ships." Opposition also came from the Women's Defense Fund, the National Organization for Women's Legal Defense Fund, the Maritime Committee of the AFL-CIO, and rape treatment centers.[29]

The amendment languished for more than a year waiting to go to a House–Senate conference where lawmakers would resolve the House and Senate versions of the Coast Guard Reauthorization Bill. Lobbying by the industry continued, including a delegation of cruise line executives led by Micky Arison in March 1996. He and Celebrity Cruise's president Richard Sasso met with Senator Larry Pressler and separately with other members of the Senate Committee on Commerce, Science, and Transportation. Pressler chaired the committee and would serve on the conference committee charged with reconciling the House and Senate versions.[30] By October 1, 1996, a compromise had been negotiated. Ernest Hollings, from the Senate's Commerce, Science, and Transportation Committee, observed before the Conference Committee that no one knew if the cruise ship people had enough votes to push the amendments through, but the cruise industry figured they were 50% there and didn't have much to lose.[31] When the Conference Committee convened, Senator Hollings threatened to kill the entire reauthorization bill if ICCL's amendments remained. In the end he capitulated after amended language was adopted for the two provisions.

In the final version, ship owners were prohibited from limiting their liability in cases involving sexual harassment, sexual misbehavior, assault, or rape in cases where the victim is physically injured. Limitations were allowed in all other situations.[32] Current passenger cruise contracts read, as does Carnival Cruise Line's, the cruise line shall not be liable to the passenger for damages for emotional distress, mental suffering/anguish or psychological injury of any kind under any circumstances, except when such damages were caused by the negligence of Carnival and resulted from the same passenger sustaining actual physical injury, or having been at risk of actual physical injury, or when such damages are held to be intentionally inflicted by the cruise line. Consequently, unless a cruise line can be found negligent, a victim of a sexual assault, whether be a crew member or a fellow passenger, has no claim for emotional distress, mental suffering/anguish or psychological injury. This position appears insensitive, especially to those (including children) victimized by a cruise ship employee.

Limit of Liability

In addition to the issues already discussed, there is one other limitation on a cruise line's liability that is worth mention; specifically that the cruise line is not liable for the intentional or negligent acts of any persons not employed by the cruise line (including independent contractors and other passengers) nor for any intentional or negligent acts of cruise ship employees committed while off duty or outside the course and scope of their employment. This last exclusion is a huge loophole given the cruise line has no responsibility when a crewmember commits a sexual assault when off duty. As well, they are not responsible when the sexual assault is not part of the scope of their employment – by its very nature, an assault would be outside the scope on one's employment. While there are a large number of lawsuits filed against cruise lines for sexual assaults, the vast majority of these are settled out of court, presumably because the cruise line wishes to avoid negative publicity. However, in how many of these cases can the cruise line effectively use the disclaimer in the passenger cruise contract?

Recommendation #18: *Given the many limits on cruise line liability, there should be a requirement that cruise lines provide passengers, in advance of when penalties accrue for cancelation, a clear statement in plain, clear English (and French or Spanish as required) of all limits on liability and laying out all rights that can be freely exercised, without limitation, by the passenger.*

Recommendation #19: *That consumer protection legislation be promulgated that extends to cruise passenger common rights and opportunities for complaint or other action similar to those available to consumers of other services, especially transportation services such as train, airlines, and other commercial carriers.*

IV. In Closing

Thank you again for the opportunity to share my observations and insights generated from my 17 years as an academic whose research has focused on the cruise industry. I welcome your questions.

V. Summary of Recommendations

Recommendation #1: *There is need for systematic reporting of all cruise ship incidents to an independent, central authority charged with responsibility for data analysis and policy and operational recommendations.*

Recommendation #2: *Similar to data maintained on airlines documenting "on time" performance, there should be a mechanism whereby cruise ships and cruise lines have reported their adherence to itineraries and on time performance.*

Recommendation #3: *There is need for greater oversight and monitoring of the cruise industry in order to monitor changing trends and to determine whether these changes are related to changes in safety and/or casualties.*

Recommendation #4: *Ships operating from U.S. ports should be obligatorily subject to accident investigations by the National Transportation Safety Board as a condition of using U.S. ports, and should be subject to fines and other administrative actions the NTSB is empowered to take with other modes of commercial transportation.*

Recommendation #5: *There needs to be funded research, ideally provided by the cruise industry to a wholly independent body, to learn from those cruise lines that appear to be effective in reducing incidents and accidents.*

Recommendation #6: *Ships should have thorough and exhaustive safety inspections by the U.S. Coast Guard without advance warning. Full reports (including all details) of cruise ship inspections by the U.S. Coast Guard should be available online.*

Recommendation #7: Original provisions of the CVSSA regarding railing height and technology to detect passengers who have fallen overboard be reconsidered.

Recommendation #8: *The CVSSA should require reported cases of sexual assault committed on a cruise ship be displayed online and broken down by cruise line and cruise ship. In addition, the raw data of cases should be made available upon request for statistical/sociological analysis in order to permit a social epidemiology of the problem.*

Recommendation #9: *The CVSSA should require passengers to be advised of the hours during which crewmembers may access their cabin without specific permission from the passenger.*

Recommendation #10: *The CVSSA more clearly and specifically state requirements for CCTV surveillance and the quality and format of tape recordings.*

Recommendation #11: *The CVSSA explicitly require the "Security Guide" be placed in plain sight in every passenger cabin and that the content of the guide include information about the types of crimes on cruise ships, where they commonly occur, and steps a passenger can take to decrease the likelihood of becoming a victim of crime.*

Recommendation #12: *The CVSSA should require onboard physicians to be board certified in emergency medicine, family practice medicine, or internal medicine in the U.S., U.K., Canada, Australia, France, or Germany. Further, there should be clear statements about how cruise ships will treat the psychological and safety needs of sexual assault victims, especially victims who are minors.*

Recommendation #13: *Cruise ships should be required to have a private, independent law enforcement agent for purposes of crime investigation. These would be similar to the wholly- independent Ocean Rangers placed on cruise ships by the State of Alaska to monitor discharge of waste streams while the ship is in Alaska state waters.*

Recommendation #14: *In the absence of a professionally qualified crime scene investigator, a cruise ship should be required to have onboard a staff person with more than adequate training in all facets of crime scene preservation, collection of evidence, and methods to ensure proper chain of evidence.*

Recommendation #15: *Cruise ship personnel should take more seriously their responsibility to detain perpetrators of sexual assault until the ship arrives at its next U.S. port. Further, Congress should contemplate whether there needs to be a legislated requirement to ensure perpetrators are isolated from the general public onboard the ship and held for delivery to land-based law enforcement personnel.*

Recommendation #16: *The CVSSA should require reporting to the FBI of all onboard crime, including thefts less than $10,000 and simple assaults.*

Recommendation #17: *Given the imprecise nature of the CLIA Passenger Bill of Rights, there is an obvious need for a legislated solution. Passenger rights can only be achieved by legislation that puts into place clear and specific measures for consumer protection.*

Recommendation #18: *Given the many limits on cruise line liability, there should be a requirement that cruise lines provide passengers, in advance of when penalties accrue for cancelation, a clear statement in plain, clear English (and French or Spanish as required) of all limits on liability and laying out all rights that can be freely exercised, without limitation, by the passenger.*

Recommendation #19: *That consumer protection legislation be promulgated that extends to cruise passenger common rights and opportunities for complaint or other action similar to those available to consumers of other services, especially transportation services such as train, airlines, and other commercial carriers.*

APPENDIX 1: SUMMARY OF CRUISE SHIP INCIDENTS, JANUARY 2009 – JUNE 2013[33]

Cancelations, Itinerary Changes, Missed Port Calls (N=271)*

Cruise with Media-Reported Canceled Port Calls	104
Cruise with Media-Reported Itinerary Changes	69
Cruise with Media-Reported Canceled Cruises	25
Cruise with Media-Reported Delayed Embarkation and/or debarkation	73

* Does not include changes caused by a hurricane or tropical storm.

Mechanical Problems (N=353)

Aground	19
Collision	37
Collision with Pier	15
Damage in Storm	5
Detained for Safety	5
Electrical Problems	8
Engine Problems	26
Fire (6 evacuation; 4 power loss)	61
Generator Problems	5
Lifeboat Failure	7
Maneuverability/Steering Problems	15
Material Failure	53
Power Loss (7 adrift, 1 towed)	21
Propulsion Problems (7 adrift)	62
Severe List	11
Technical Problems	8

Deaths on Shore (N=37)

Dive/Scuba (1 on Shore Excursion)	4
Jet Ski	1
Parasailing (3 on Shore Excursion)	3
Snorkeling (3 on Shore Excursion)	8
Swimming (7 on Shore Excursion)	13
Other	8

Miscellaneous (N=269)

Accidents Ashore (8 on Shore Excursion)	10
Bomb Threats:	14
Child Pornography Seized	8
Illness Outbreaks	189
Injuries on Shorex (n=52)	5
Passengers expelled/evicted	11
Robberies Ashore (5 on Shore Excursion)	13
Onboard Falls (3 deaths)	9
Thefts > $10K	10

APPENDIX 2: SHIPS WITH TWO OR MORE MECHANICAL INCIDENTS, JANUARY 2009 – JUNE 2013

A. Carnival Corporation (7 Companies, 45 Ships, 145 Incidents)

Carnival Cruise Lines (19 ships, 74 incidents)

Carnival Destiny (n=6)

11/18/2009	Primary motor unit 1 tripped due to malfunction
1/26/2010	Propulsion problems; itinerary changed, cruises canceled
10/22/2010	Propulsion problems; primary motor two faulty
9/10/2011	Lifeboat damaged – removed for repair
1/7/2012	Material failure
1/24/2013	Problem with stern thrusters; itinerary changed

Carnival Dream (n=3)

7/6/2011	Propulsion problems; change from Western Caribbean to Eastern Caribbean itinerary
10/7/2012	Fire
3/14/2013	Malfunction of backup emergency diesel generator, power outages and plumbing issues; cruise canceled in St. Maarten

Ecstasy (n=5)

1/19/2009	Propulsion problems; operating on half power
2/13/2009	Fire
1/28/2010	Collision with gangway
4/22/2010	Severe list to avoid buoy; damage and 60 injuries
4/18/2013	Power failure; some onboard attribute it to a fire

Elation (n=3)

10/20/2009	Propulsion problems as a result of failure with electronic control system
1/13/2011	Technical problem with propulsion system; port call skipped
3/14/2013	Steering problems; tugboat escort required

Fantasy (n=4)

1/29/2009	Equipment failure in steering system
1/5/2010	Lifeboat failure/material failure
7/27/2011	Collision with *Imagination*; minor damage
10/17/2011	Vessel maneuverability problem; arrives in port late

Fascination (n=3)

7/1/2010	Loss of power for several hours, adrift; late arrival
2/27/2011	Material failure
1/19/2013	Late return from dry dock; 7 hour delay

Carnival Freedom (n=3)

2/6/2010	Fire in crew cabin
6/27/2011	Blackout due to generator failure; fuel oil filters cleaned, fuel oil purifiers started and chemical treatment added to the both service tanks.
8/21/2011	Material failure

Carnival Glory (n=3)

5/15/2011	Vessel maneuverability
11/14/2012	Material failure
12/2/2012	Propulsion problems

Holiday (transferred to Iberocruises in 2010) (n=4)

1/20/2009	Material failure
2/6/2009	Technical problem causing reduced speeds; dropped port call on this and next cruise
3/9/2009	Material failure
4/11/2009	Material failure

Imagination (n=3)

7/13/2010	Fire in the elevator machinery room leaving two passenger elevators and one crew elevator inoperable
7/27/2011	Collision with Fantasy
9/28/2011	Toilets in front and midship inoperable for day

Carnival Legend (n=10)

3/21/2009	Smoke and fire system on Deck B-A-1 in fault and not operating properly
6/21/2009	Unpalatable water in cabins
9/30/2009	Collision with *Enchantment of the Seas*; minor damage
2/7/2010	Maneuverability problems given malfunctioning azipod
2/14/2010	Mechanical problems cause seven-hour delay leaving Tampa, itinerary changed; vessel pitched when leaving Roatan, maybe caused by touching channel wall
7/11/2010	Loss of propulsion on port azipod while entering port; faulty circuit breaker tripped
1/17/2012	Material failure
1/29/2012	Technical problem with starboard azipod causes late arrival (5 hours) and delayed embarkation (2 hours)
3/14/2013	Disabled and stuck in Costa Maya; a day later underway with reduced speed and changed itinerary
3/16/2013	Propulsion problems; changed itinerary

Carnival Liberty (n=4)

4/26/2010	Problems with palatable water in cabin
11/5/2010	Two diesel generators shutdown because of malfunction

| 1/15/2012 | Technical problem, severe list |
| 11/25/2012 | Loss of electrical power |

Carnival Miracle (n=3)

1/10/2010	Lifeboat material failure
1/28/2010	Collision with pier at Port Zante (St. Kitts); stay overnight for repairs and arrive late for disembarkation
1/18/2011	Lifeboat material failure

Carnival Paradise (n=2)

| 8/31/2012 | Material failure |
| 10/1/2012 | Partial loss of propulsion; power loss |

Carnival Pride (n=2)

| 5/16/2009 | Fire in battery room |
| 3/31/2011 | Blown from mooring at Port Canaveral; delayed departure |

Sensation (n=2)

| 2/9/2012 | Burst pipe floods 10 – 20 cabins; departure delayed 4 – 5 hours |
| 5/22/2012 | Fire |

Carnival Splendor (n=7)

11/8/2009	Delay in Long Beach (7 hours) to repair fire door
11/25/2009	Collision with *Radiance of the Seas* in Puerto Vallarta
12.17/2009	Collision with pier in Puerto Vallarta, stayed until 3:30PM next day for repairs; next port call canceled
2/18/2010	Sharp turn (radar missed some small yachts in path) causes flooding onboard
11/8/2010	Fire lasting several hours knocks out all power, ship towed back to San Diego; this and next 8 – 10 cruise canceled
1/6/2013	Itinerary changed to permit two days in Puerto Valllarta for repair of damage to propulsion system
1/13/2013	Cruise delayed one day given repair of propulsion system; itinerary changed

Carnival Triumph (n=4)

3/14/2010	Vessel maneuverability
11/18/2010	Oil leak from shaft seal of forward bow thruster; disabled until repairs made
1/27/2013	Technical problem with propulsion system affecting cruising speed; 6 hour delay in return to port
2/10/2013	Disabling fire, adrift for days with no power/electricity, towed to port; cruise canceled

Carnival Victory (n=2)

| 1/17/2010 | Failure of UPS battery charger |

1/20/2013   Propulsion problem; leaves port almost 24 hours late, itinerary change

Costa Cruises (1 ship, 2 incidents)
Costa Europa (n=2)
3/5/2009   Propulsion problems lead to passenger revolt; ports missed
2/26/2010   Collision with pier in Sharm-el-Sheikh killing three crew and injuring four passengers; cruise canceled

Cunard Line (1 ship, 6 incidents)
Queen Mary 2 (n=6)
7/22/2009   Broke from mooring lines; damage to stern, four hour delayed departure
9/23/2010   Loss of electric and all power for an hour after explosion in electric panel
10/5/2011   Fire causes power loss in major storm, damage onboard; arrive in NYC 2 hours late
10/17/2011   Went "dead in the water" twice during transatlantic cruise
2/4/2012   Total power failure, "dead in the water"
10/23/2012   Material failure

Holland America Line (7 ships, 21 incidents)
Maasdam (n=4)
3/17/2009   Fire in crew galley
5/22/2009   Severe list caused by pilot error
8/8/2012   Sewage and refuse from ship washes up on shore at Nahant, MA
6/13/2013   Port forward propulsion system malfunctioning; 2.5 hour delayed departure and sailing at reduced speed

Prinsendam (n=2)
9/11/2010   Major damage from storm – 50 windows blown out (with flooding) and dent in prow of ship
12/17/2010   Lifeboat failure

Ryndam (n=2)
11/18/2012   Material failure
6/8/2013   Fire – 40 minute wait for all clear after initial alarm

Statendam (n=2)
12/21/2009   Engine problems, changed itinerary
9/22/2012   Fuel pump explosion causes two hour power outage

Westerdam (n=2)
5/11/2011   Collision with ice; damage 15 feet below water line
10/28/2011   Fire

Zaandam (n=6)

1/13/2009	Alternator of #5 generator exploded causing switchboard to ground out; emergency generator started 43 second later
7/13/2010	Fire
7/28/2010	Loss of electrical power
8/11/2010	Material failure
6/7/2011	Material failure
10/19/2012	Mechanical problems and/or flooding onboard

Zuiderdam (n=3)

7/8/2010	Material failure
2/9/2012	Fire in engine room
9/25/2012	Material failure

P&O Cruises (4 ships, 12 incidents)

Artemis (n=2)

| 4/7/2010 | Engine problems, skipped St. Barts |
| 5/8/2010 | Engine problems, itinerary changed from 10 ports to 4 ports (Pax advised when boarding that there were engine problems and 1 port would be skipped) |

Aurora (n=4)

3/3/2009	Propulsion problems – Broke down 4 hours after leaving Sydney. Stuck in Auckland (with passengers aboard) for five days for repairs. Itinerary changed
9/18/2009	Mechanical problems and loss of bow thruster; changed itinerary
9/30/2011	Electrical problems delay for three hours departure from Portland, ME
2/8/2013	Fault with port propeller shaft. Delayed in Auckland, dropped two port calls

Oriana (n=4)

8/5/2010	Delayed four hours in Dubrovnik; computers crash causing loss of steering system
8/7/2010	Fire on tender
11/30/2010	Engine breakdowns; missed port call
6/2/2011	Collision with pier

Ventura (n=2)

| 10/18/2012 | 60 mm crack on full width of deck 14; passengers advised to not use balconies |
| 3/17/2013 | Propulsion problems cause missed ports and itinerary changes |

P&O Australia (3 ships, 10 incidents)

Pacific Dawn (n=3)

| 1/8/2009 | Engine problems; arrival in Sydney 10 hours late |
| 2/15/2010 | Propulsion and maintenance problems cause 18 hour delayed departure; itinerary changed |

| 4/10/2010 | Loss of power and propulsion; near miss collision with bridge |

Pacific Pearl (n=2)

| 2/2/2011 | Three-meter-across chandelier falls three storeys into café area in atrium |
| 2/3/2011 | Lack of running water and working toilets |

Pacific Sun (Left fleet in 2012) (n=5)

11/10/2009	Cruise canceled to permit repair of propulsion system
3/13/2010	Mechanical problems cause canceled port calls at Suva and Denarau
4/21/2010	Engine problems; cruise canceled
11/2/2010	Propulsion problem; 10 hour delayed arrival at Melbourne
2/28/2011	Engine problems, 24 hour delayed arrival at Newcastle; several ports canceled

Princess Cruises (10 ships, 34 incidents)

Caribbean Princess (n=9)

10/16/2009	Severe list, storm damage
4/5/2010	Severe list, steering malfunction
5/9/2010	Collision with gangway; departure delayed several hours
8/8/2010	Material failure
2/4/2012	Engine problems - delays
2/25/2012	Material failure
3/12/2012	Engine problems – next two cruises canceled
6/8/21012	Technical fault; remain in port overnight, itinerary changed
12/15/2012	Loss of electrical power

Coral Princess (n=3)

3/19/2009	Propulsion problems; missed port
8/19/2011	Turbine oil system failure; switch to diesel electric power
5/2/2013	Fire

Crown Princess (n=3)

6/20/2009	Fire in passenger cabin
7/17/2012	Electrical fire in passenger cabin
4/13/2013	Toilets in 410 cabins not operational

Dawn Princess (n=3)

6/15/2010	Propulsion breakdown, adrift for 2.25 hours; restored and sailing at reduced speed
7/16/2010	Engine problems; missed port call
10/27/2011	Mechanical problem; missed port call

Emerald Princess (n=2)

| 7/26/2010 | Electrical failure leads to propulsion problems; no A/C; repaired in 6 hours |

5/17/2011   Collision with fuel barge damages several lifeboats

Golden Princess (n=3)
1/22/2009   Near-collision with fishing vessel
3/22/2009   Fire in engine room
3/28/2012   Vessel maneuverability

Royal Princess (n=2)
6/18/2009   Fire in engine room as leaving Port Said, passengers called to muster
                   stations; cruise and next cruise canceled
4/9/2010   Break in fire hose fitting causes extensive damage to restaurants;
                   water leaked all the way down to crew decks

Sapphire Princess (n=4)
7/12/2010   Severe list to avoid collision with whale
2/4/2011   Loss of electrical power
2/26/2011   Material failure
9/7/2011   2 pleasure boats swamped and float dock damaged by ship's wake
                   when maneuvering in Ketchikan Harbour

Star Princess (n=3)
3/21/2011   Material failure
7/1/2012   Material failure
8/2/2012   Material failure

Sun Princess (n=2)
7/25/2012   Material failure
8/27/2012   Transformer blown leading to loss of power adrift for 3.5 hours

B. Royal Caribbean Cruises Limited

Celebrity Cruises (4 ships, 13 incidents)
Century (n=4)
10/15/2010   Rudder damaged, stranded in Villefranche-sur-Mer; cruise canceled
10/22/2011   Vessel maneuverability problems
3/25/2012   Engine problems, late departure and late arrival
10/28/2012   Fire

Infinity (n=3)
6/22/2010   Material failure
6/26/2010   5-6 hour delayed departure because of engine problems, canceled port
                   call; five days later an electrical fire causes power loss for several
                   hours
8/23/2012   Material failure

Millennium (n=2)

3/9/2009	Cruise canceled to allow repair of problem with bearing on propeller shaft
4/9/2013	Electrical problem adversely affects propulsion, dead in water for 3 hours; port call at Hanoi canceled

Summit (n=4)

1/10/2009	Electrical problem causes cruise to be shortened by one day and itinerary changed
2/27/2010	Material failure
4/9/2011	Loss of electrical power
10/5/2012	Tender runs aground with 93 passengers and 2 crew, sustains major damage

Pullmantur (1 ship, 2 incidents)

Zenith (n=2)

8/18/2009	Fire while docked in Stockholm, evacuated; departed one day late, itinerary changes
6/25/2013	Fire in engine room disables ship; towed to port

Royal Caribbean International (10 ships, 32 incidents)

Allure of the Seas (n=2)

1/29/2012:	Fire in incinerator area
4/12/2012:	Fire in engine room, section 6 of ship evacuated; drift 1-2 hours and then operated on 1 engine

Brilliance of the Seas (n=2)

10/13/2009	Windows broken out in storm and 35 passenger cabins flooded, delayed departure from Barcelona
12/12/2010	Severe list while entering Alexandria, Egypt; 30 passengers injured

Enchantment of the Seas (n=5)

7/21/2009	Material failure
3/23/2010	Load sharing problem shuts down engine 4
7/27/2011	Steering gear pump failure on pump #4
2/20/2012	Propulsion problems – one propeller broken; delayed departure by 24 hours, changed itinerary, sailing at half speed
3/10/2012	Propulsion problems; spent 27 hours in Port Canaveral to accommodate repairs, itinerary changed

Explorer of the Seas (n=7)

2/5/2009	Propeller damaged causes change in itinerary on this cruise and next
4/14/2009	Changes in itinerary for several upcoming cruises; too late to cancel, no explanation
9/30/2009	Collision with *Carnival Legend*; minor damage
1/13/2010	Delayed departure because delayed arrival from drydock

3/14/2010   Severe list due to human error; injuries and considerable damage
9/14/2012   Collision with *Norwegian Star* when mooring line breaks; minimal
                   damage
10/29/2012   Sailed into Hurricane Sandy

Grandeur of the Seas (n=3)
2/26/2009   Loss of two engines; material failure
7/30/2009   Loss of power due to malfunctioning power inverter; loss of electrical
                   power
5/27/2013   Fire; cruise canceled

Jewel of the Seas (n=3)
8/3/2010   One hydraulic motor not working forcing reduced speeds; itinerary
                   changes
12/7/2010   Collision with 500 meter long 2 foot wide flexible plastic pipe,
                   becoming wrapped around front of ship
9/6/2012   4.5 hour delay leaving Cape Liberty; no reason given

Legend of the Seas (n=2)
2/9/2009   Pulled into Key West for unscheduled stop because of faulty azipod
                   and leaking oil (needed boom around ship); repaired by day's end
1/30/2012   Fire in bar (Café Promenade)

Majesty of the Sea (n=4)
8/13/2010   Lifeboat malfunction when lowered; damaged and release of oil
9/30/2011   Vessel maneuverability
11/2/2011   Material failure
11/7/2011   Material failure

Oasis of the Seas (n=2)
5/7/2010   Emergency generator damaged; given three months to repair
11/16/2012   Vessel maneuverability

Radiance of the Seas (n=2)
11/25/2009   Collision with *Carnival Splendor* in Puerto Vallarta; minor damage
1/27/2011   Ship is operating under USCG COTP due to one of two main
                   propulsion azipods not working; repairs anticipated in fall 2011

C. Prestige Cruise Holdings (3 Companies, 5 Ships, 14 Incidents)

Norwegian Cruise Line (2 ships, 4 incidents)
Norwegian Dawn (n=2)
11/27/2009   Loss of power for hours (no A/C), ship disembarks in San Juan
                   instead of Miami; this and next cruise canceled

| 8/27/2010 | Leaves Bermuda 11 hours early because engine problems cause slower speeds; want to arrive in NYC on time |

Norwegian Star (n=2)

| 4/28/2012 | Collision while docking |
| 9/14/2012 | Collision with *Explorer of the Seas* when mooring line breaks; minimal damage |

Oceania Cruise (1 ship, 3 incidents)

Regatta (n=3)

6/20/2011	Material failure
7/24/2011	Material failure
10/19/2012	Electrical outage; delayed return to port (NYC) by several hours

Regent Seven Seas Cruises (2 ships, 7 incidents)

Seven Seas Navigator (n=2)

| 10/25/2011 | Material failure; one day delayed departure from Charleston, itinerary change |
| 11/9/2011 | Material failure |

Seven Seas Voyager (n=5)

3/22/2009	Propulsion problems (fishing net caught in azipod), reduced speed; many ports canceled
4/1/2009	Passengers told upon embarkation that most port calls canceled from Dubai to Rome because of propulsion problems; following two cruises canceled
12/14/2009	One azipod fails so sailing at reduced speed; port call canceled
10/4/2010	Podded propulsion system fails; passengers flown home from Athens, 2 cruises canceled
3/17/2013	Propulsion problem; skipped ports and itinerary changes

D. Independent Cruise Lines

Avalon Waterways (1 ship, 3 incidents)

Avalon Tranquility (n=3)

7/23/2009	Collision with the tall ship Schoenbrunn, a 1912-built paddlesteamer
9/5/2011	Collision with cargo ship – holed, cruise ended
12/13/2011	Fire in generator room

Celebration Cruises (1 ship, 2 incidents)

Bahamas Celebration (n=2)

| 2/1/2012 | Maneuverability problems |
| 3/30/2012 | Maneuverability problems |

Fred Olsen Cruises (1 ship, 2 incidents)
Black Watch (n=2)

10/21/2009	Severe list – navigational error while entering La Coruna Harbour (Spain)
8/12/2010	Collision with iceberg – damage superficial

Mediterranean Shipping Company (MSC) (2 ships, 5 incidents)
Opera (n=3)

3/30/2011	Collision with pier (twice), damage to several cabins; delayed 10 hours for repairs
5/15/2011	Failure of an electric panel causes power loss for 8.5 hours; towed to port and cruise canceled
5/27/2011	Detained by UK authorities for noncompliance with safety regulations

Poesia (n=2)

1/7/2012	Ran aground in Bahamas; waited for high tide to refloat
1/10/2012	Collision with pier while leaving Jamaican port

Saga Cruises (1 ship, 3 incidents)
Saga Ruby (n=3)

10/12/2009	Collision with pier, emergency repairs to bow; itinerary changes
11/11/2012	Engine problems; remainder of cruise canceled
1/7/2013	Mechanical problems with crankshaft; current world cruise delayed ten days

Silversea Cruises (1 ship, 2 incidents)
Silver Shadow (n=2)

3/19/12	Collision with container ship off Vietnam; major damage to container ship, minor damage to cruise ship
9/9/2012	Material failure

Thomson Cruises (1 ship, 3 incidents)
Thomson Dream (n=3)

7/25/2010	Plumbing/sewage problems
1/17/2011	Starboard engine fire
5/20/2012	Severe list following two maneuvers caused by "slip of the hand"; major damage

Travel Dynamics International (1 ship, 3 incidents)
Clelia II (n=3)

12/26/2009	Propeller damaged, loss of power; escorted to port, next cruise canceled
9/1/2010	Loss of electrical power (human error)
12/9/2010	Wave in storm breaks bridge window; damage to electronics, affecting engine performance

Voyages of Discovery/Coastal and Maritime Voyages (1 ship, 4 incidents)
Discovery (n=4)

10/15/2009	Engine problems; port missed
12/05/2009	Delayed return from drydock; itinerary changed
3/4/2013	Ship detained in UK for safety issues; cruise canceled
5/7/2013	Deep cleaning after illness outbreak delays departure; itinerary change

APPENDIX 3: SUMMARY OF PERSONS OVERBOARD, JANUARY 1995 – JUNE 2013 (N=210)*

A. Gender

Male	73.8%
Female	26.2%

B. Age by Gender

Total		Male		Female	
Mean	Range	Mean	Range	Mean	Range
39.82	14 – 90	38.85	14 - 90	42.11	15 - 79

C. Vessel

Cruise	91.4%
Ferry	8.6%

D. Passenger vs Crew

Passenger	75%
Crew	25%
E. Rescued	16.7%
F. Alcohol	6.2%
G. Suicide	11.0%
H Murder	3.3%
I. Fall	9.5%
J. Casino loss	2.4%
K. Fight	7.1%

* The data contained in this table is based on available information. Details were not consistently available for each incident. See www.cruisejunkie.com/Overboard.html for details.

APPENDIX 4: DRUG BUSTS, JANUARY 2009 – JUNE 2013[34]

A. Gender

Male	83.33%
Female	16.66%

B. Age by Gender

Total		Male		Female	
Mean	Range	Mean	Range	Mean	Range
38.5	19 – 74	38.6	19 – 74	38.25	20 – 54

C. Drug Busts by Country (N=53)

Bermuda	27
US	8
	(27 persons)
Belize:	6
UK	6
St. Kitts-Nevis	2
Jamaica	1
Cayman Islands	1
Australia	1
Spain	1
	(9 persons)

D. Drug Busts by US State/City

Florida	3
	(17 persons)
Baltimore	2
Alaska	1
US Virgin Islands	1
Puerto Rico	1

E. Ships with 2 or More Drug Busts

Norwegian Dawn	9
Explorer of the Seas	6
Black Watch	3
Enchantment of the Seas	3
Summit	3
Allure of the Seas	2
Bahamas Celebration	2
Grandeur of the Seas	2
Grand Princess	2
Norwegian Gem	2
Poesia	2

End Notes

[1] Ward, V. 2012. "Costa Allegra: Passengers Tell of 'Hell' On-board. *The Telegraph* (March 1).

[2] See Brown, R., K. Severson, and B. Meier. 2013. "Cruise Line's Woes are Far From Over as Ship Makes Port," *New York Times*, (February 15).

[3] All of these events are reported at Events at Sea (www.cruisejunkie.com/events.html)

[4] See United States Coast Guard. 2013. *Report of Investigation into the Fire Onboard the Carnival Splendor which Occurred in the Pacific Ocean Off the Coast of Mexico on November 8, 2010, which Resulted in Complete Loss of Power*, MISLE Incident Investigation Activity Number: 3897765 (July 15).

[5] Conant, E. 2013. "Carnival from Hell: The Warning Signs Before the Triumph Disaster," *Newsweek* (February 22).

[6] Rosenbloom, S. 2013. "How normal are cruise mishaps," *New York Times* (May 8, 2013).

[7] United States Coast Guard. 2013. *Report of Investigation into the Fire Onboard the Carnival Splendor which Occurred in the Pacific Ocean Off the Coast of Mexico on November 8, 2010, which Resulted in Complete Loss of Power*, MISLE Incident Investigation Activity Number: 3897765 (July 15).

[8] See "Carnival Cruise Lines announces fleetwide $300 million program to enhance operating reliability and guest comfort." April 17, 2013. Online at: http://carnival-news.com/2013/04/17/carnival-cruise-lines-announces-fleetwide-300-million-program-to-enhance-operating-reliability-and-guest-comfort/

[9] Wolfe, K.A. 2013. "Horrific Carnival cruise gets D.C.'s attention," *Politico* (February 27).

[10] Seatrade Insider. 2001. "Another Ship Sprinkler Problem," Seatrade Insider (June 5).

[11] BBC News. 2004. "Urgent Safety Work Starts on QM2," BBC News (June 26).

[12] Testimony before the Senate Committee on Commerce, Science and Transportation, Hearings on "Oversight of the Cruise Industry," March 1, 2012; Testimony before the Subcommittee on Surface Transportation and Merchant Marine Infrastructure, Safety, and Security, Senate Committee on Commerce, Science and Transportation, June 19, 2008; Testimony before Subcommittee on Coast Guard and Maritime Transportation, Committee on Transportation and Infrastructure, Hearings on "Crimes Against Americans on Cruise Ships, March 27, 2007.

[13] See www.cruisejunkie.com/Overboard.html

[14] Yoshino, K. 2007. "Cruise Industry's Dark Waters: What Happens at Sea Stays There as Crimes on Lineres Go Unresolved," *Los Angeles Times* (January 20).

[15] Klein, R. A. 2007. "Crime Against Americans on Cruise Ships," Testimony Before the Committee on Transportation and Infrastructure, United States House of Representatives, Subcommittee on Coast Guard and Maritime Transportation, March 27.

[16] Dale, T. 2007. "Cruise Ship Security Practices and Procedures," Testimony Before the Committee on Transportation and Infrastructure, United States House of Representatives, Subcommittee on Coast Guard and Maritime Transportation, September 19.

[17] Dickerson, T.A. and S. L. Sgroi. 2012. "Recent Developments in Maritime Law," Presented at the Joint Judicial Seminar Program for the Appellate Divisions for the First and Second Judicial Departments," April 25. Available at: <www.nycourts.gov/courts/9jd/TacCert_pdfs/Dickerson_Docs/recent_dev_maritimelaw.pdf>

[18] Dolan, J. 2013. Crew Error Cited in Carnival Ship Fire that Led to Nightmare Tow," *Los Angeles Times* (July 16).

[19] U.S. Coast Guard. 2013. Report of Investigation into the Fire Onboard the *Carnival Splendor which Occurred in the Pacific Ocean off the Coast of Mexico on November 8, 2010, which Resulted in Complete Loss of Power.* MISLE Incident Investigation Activity Number 3897765.

[20] See http://www.carnival.com/about-carnival/legal-notice/port-cancellation-policy.aspx

[21] It is worth mention that Royal Caribbean Cruises Limited, in anticipation of these hearings and concern that the facts might paint an unkind picture, sent an email to all employees asking them to write their Senator with the following text: Dear Senator, As one of your constituents and an employee of_____, one of the major cruise lines serving North America, I am contacting you today out of concern regarding the July 24 Senate Commerce Committee hearing regarding the cruise industry. As an individual who is intimately familiar with cruising, it is apparent to me that there has been a great deal of misinformation and distortion regarding the industry in recent months. As one of your constituents, I am concerned that the industry will be unfairly portrayed at this hearing. As someone that works in the cruise line industry, I know firsthand that cruising is extremely safe and well regulated at the national level, by the U.S. Coast Guard, and by international authorities. Additionally, the cruise industry directly benefits businesses in all 50 states, generating over 355,000 jobs and over $42 billion in economic impact. It provides $17.4 billion in wages to American workers each year. I would greatly appreciate your support to ensure that the cruise industry receives a fair and balanced hearing. Thank you for your time and attention to this matter and your service to our nation. Sincerely, Your Name

[22] Organization for Economic Co-operation and Development. 2003. *Voluntary Approaches to Environmental Policy: Effectiveness, Efficiency, and Usage in Policy Mixes*, Paris:OECD.

[23] See section 2(d) of Carnival Cruise Lines' passenger contract.

[24] Coverage under the Warsaw Convention is approximately US$1,663; under the Montreal Convention US$20 per kg for loss of or damage or delay to checked baggage, and US$400 for unchecked package.

[25] LaMendola B. and T. Steighorst. 2002. "Cruise Lines Blame Passengers for 3rd Viral Outbreak on Ship," *Sun – Sentinel* (November 12).

[26] Supreme Court of Florida. 2007. *Carnival Corporation vs. Darce Carlisle, Case No. SC 04-393*, February 15.

[27] Chen, S. 2007. "Trouble at Sea: Free-Agent Doctors," *Wall Street Journal* (October 24).

[28] Glass, J. 1996. "Compromise on US Cruise Tort," *Lloyd's List* (October 1), p. 1.

[29] Fox, L. and B. R. Fox. 1995. "Anchored in the Docks, *Washington Post* (October 8), p. E4.

[30] Rowe, S. 1996. "There Oughta Be a Law," *Miami New Times* (March 21).

[31] Ibid.

[32] Glass, J. 1996. "Compromise on US Cruise Tort," *Lloyd's List* (October 1), p. 1.

[33] Data based on media and other reports as recorded at Cruise Junkie dot Com

[34] Data based on media and other reports as recorded at Cruise Junkie dot Com

In: Cruise Industry Safety and Security   ISBN: 978-1-63117-882-5
Editor: Brennan T. Preston   © 2014 Nova Science Publishers, Inc.

Chapter 4

TESTIMONY OF MARK ROSENKER, PANEL OF EXPERTS MEMBER, CRUISE LINE INTERNATIONAL ASSOCIATION. HEARING ON "CRUISE INDUSTRY OVERSIGHT: RECENT INCIDENTS SHOW NEED FOR STRONGER FOCUS ON CONSUMER PROTECTION"[*]

Chairman Rockefeller, Ranking Member Thune and distinguished members of the committee, thank you for inviting me to testify today. My name is Mark Rosenker and I am a Former Chairman of the United States National Transportation Safety Board and a retired United States Air Force Reserve Major General. I also served as Deputy Assistant to President George W. Bush and Director of the White House Military Office. I welcome the opportunity to testify before this committee, which served as my authorizing committee during my tenure as chairman of the National Transportation Safety Board.

I am testifying today in my capacity as a member of the independent Panel of Experts established by the Cruise Lines International Association, or CLIA. The independent Panel of Experts was put in place as part of the Global Cruise Industry Operational Safety Review, which was launched in January 2012 by the industry in the wake of the Concordia incident. The Review was introduced as part of the cruise line industry's efforts to execute on their stated commitment to continuous improvement and innovation in shipboard operations and safety. It focused on the critical human factors and operational aspects of maritime safety.

The Review was introduced to identify best practices and develop new policies that could be implemented rapidly on an industry-wide basis to further enhance the safety of passengers and crew. It took the lead in identifying additional best practices for industry-wide implementation and ultimately, formal submission to the International Maritime Organization, as appropriate, that could strengthen the cruise industry's safety record. [See appendix] The International Maritime Organization is an international maritime regulatory body with 170 Member States including the United States, which mandates global standards for the safety and operation of cruise ships. The Review was guided by a task force consisting of senior industry executives from CLIA member lines with responsibility for maritime

---

[*] This is an edited, reformatted and augmented version of testimony presented July 24, 2013 before the Senate Committee on Commerce, Science, and Transportation.

safety. To commence the Review, CLIA's member lines took a detailed look at existing safety procedures and practices. Senior cruise line executives undertook internal reviews of their own operational safety practices and procedures concerning issues of navigation, evacuation, emergency training, and related practices and procedures.

The independent Panel of Experts was formally appointed in April 2012 to provide an impartial assessment of the recommendations developed by the Review. Collectively, those of us on the Panel of Experts bring well over a century of experience in transportation and safety to the table. Our backgrounds include senior positions with a diverse mix of organizations. Each Panel member has deep experience in the maritime, regulatory and accident investigation fields and the Panel is balanced geographically with equal representation from the United States and Europe. The three other members of the panel are Rear Admiral (Ret.) Stephen Meyer, Dr. Jack Spencer, and Willem de Ruiter.

Stephen Meyer is a retired Rear Admiral in the Royal Navy. He is a former commander of a number of Royal Navy Ships and was the former head of the United Kingdom Marine Accident Investigation Branch.

Dr. Jack Spencer is the former Director of the Office of Marine Safety at the National Transportation Safety Board. Dr. Spencer has more than 40 years of experience with the U.S. Coast Guard, American Bureau of Shipping, and National Transportation Safety Board. For 30 years, he has been on United States delegations to the International Maritime Organization.

Willem de Ruiter is former head of the European Maritime Safety Agency (EMSA). In 2003, Mr. de Ruiter was appointed as the first executive director of EMSA and charged with building up the organization. He joined EMSA after a distinguished career in the Dutch government and at the European Commission.

The independent Panel of Experts was formally appointed in April 2012 to provide an impartial assessment of the Review's recommendations. I took this panel extremely seriously and approached it with the same unwavering commitment that I had as NTSB Chair to raise the bar of safety even higher for this safe sector.

The Panel takes a very active view of the issues being discussed and policies being developed by CLIA that relate to all aspects of maritime safety. We are a deliberative body that is independent of CLIA's technical and regulatory advisory committees. Our advice, counsel and recommendations have covered a wide range of topics and are delivered to CLIA's Board of Directors, Executive Committee, and other advisory committees as appropriate. We are all experienced professionals and we find our views to be well-received and that candor is a hallmark of our confidential deliberations. We are a group of highly critical and deeply committed experts and we are never bashful about sharing what we are thinking either as individuals or as a Panel. At times our deliberations between the Panel members have been very spirited. This has further assisted CLIA in highlighting for their members the various thoughtful perspectives of complex safety issues and the related policy implications.

As someone with four decades of experience in the transportation and technology industries, I've always known that the cruise industry is governed by an extremely extensive framework of safety regulations. Every aspect of the cruise industry is heavily regulated and monitored under United States, European Union, and international maritime law to protect the safety of passengers and crewmembers. Regulations start with the design and construction of the ship and extend to the operation of the vessel, the emergency equipment on board, and scenarios for emergency situations, including the evacuation of a ship. Cruise ships are also subject to multiple layers of enforcement at the international, flag State and port State level.

The Panel played an active role and provided many new and innovative ideas and recommendations that were incorporated into the final policies and other initiatives, in addition to providing independent, expert analysis of proposed policies. As the Panel gained more experience working together, our commitment to the process grew and the value of our role became even clearer over time, as our engagement in the issues and policy development began to produce tangible results. It is without question that we are working with a talented and deeply committed group of cruise industry professionals that share the Panel's values toward maritime safety. If I did not believe this to be the case, I would most certainly not be associated with these efforts, nor would any of my colleagues that serve on the Panel.

During the course of the Review, my fellow panelists and I examined safety-related shipboard systems and observed safety drills aboard one of the world's largest cruise ships. We visited the state-of-the-art full bridge simulator at the Resolve Maritime Academy to see how technology can strengthen safety and supplement training on cruise ships. We held a session with officials at Airbus to draw from their efforts related to Crew Resource Management, Simulation Training, and Safety Culture. We met with leaders of the Review multiple times to review, analyze, and discuss recommended changes to cruise industry safety practices and offered our own ideas based on our individual and collective experiences.

As a member of the Panel of Experts during last year's Review, my role was to provide an impartial assessment of the recommendations developed by the established Task Force of cruise line experts, before they were ultimately implemented and then submitted for formal consideration to the IMO. Additionally, as Panel members we shared numerous, wide-ranging recommendations and suggestions that were incorporated into the industry's policies, as well as into other important ongoing efforts that have not specifically resulted in published industry-wide policies.

All ten policies that resulted from the Review were incorporated into IMO standards. Those ten policies, in the order in which they were introduced, are as follows:

The *Passenger Muster Policy* requires musters for embarking passengers prior to departure from port and was launched with immediate effect on February 9, 2012. On occasions when guests arrive after the muster has been completed, the policy dictates that they are promptly provided with individual or group safety briefings. This practice exceeds existing legal requirements – which require that musters occur within 24 hours of passenger embarkation.

Under the *Passage Planning Policy,* each passage plan is to be thoroughly briefed to all bridge team members who will be involved in execution of the plan well in advance of its implementation. The passage plan will be drafted by the designated officer and approved by the master. This policy was effective upon its announcement on April 24, 2012.

To minimize unnecessary disruptions and distractions on the bridge, the *Bridge Access Policy* requires bridge access be limited to those with operationally related functions during any period of restricted maneuvering or when increased vigilance is required such as arrival/departure from port, heavy traffic, or poor visibility. Further, member lines are to take steps to prevent distractions to watchkeeping during these periods. This policy was effective upon its announcement on April 24, 2012.

The *Excess Lifejackets Policy* ensures that the number of lifejackets carried is far in excess of the number of persons actually onboard a ship. In addition to the statutory requirements of carriage of lifejackets for each person onboard and certain specified extras, the cruise industry adopted a policy of carrying additional adult lifejackets onboard each cruise ship in excess of current legal requirements. As a result, the number of additional adult lifejackets provided must not be less than the total number of persons berthed within the ship's most populated main vertical fire zone.

All of the additional lifejackets addressed in this policy are to be stored in public spaces, at the muster stations, on deck or in lifeboats, and in such a manner as to be readily accessible to crewmembers for distribution as may be necessary in the event of an emergency. This policy was effective upon its announcement on April 24, 2012.

The *Nationality of Passengers Policy* was developed in response to the request of governments at the May 2012 meeting of the IMO Maritime Safety Committee meeting. This policy prescribes that the nationality of each passenger onboard is to be recorded, kept ashore and made readily available to search and rescue personnel as appropriate. This policy was effective upon its announcement on June 26, 2012.

Under the *Common Elements of Musters and Emergency Instructions Policy,* member cruise lines have specified 12 common elements that are to be communicated to passengers in musters and emergency instructions. In addition to current legal requirements, this policy specifically requires that musters and emergency instructions are to include the following common elements:

1) When and how to don a lifejacket
2) Description of emergency signals and appropriate responses in the event of an emergency
3) Location of lifejackets
4) Where to muster when the emergency signal is sounded
5) Method of accounting for passenger attendance at musters both for training and in the event of an actual emergency
6) How information will be provided in an emergency
7) What to expect if the Master orders an evacuation of the ship
8) What additional safety information is available
9) Instructions on whether passengers should return to cabins prior to mustering, including specifics regarding medications, clothing, and lifejackets
10) Description of key safety systems and features
11) Emergency routing systems and recognizing emergency exits
12) Who to seek out for additional information

This policy was effective upon its announcement on June 26, 2012.

To facilitate training for lifeboat operations, the *Lifeboat Loading for Training Purposes Policy* requires that at least one lifeboat on each ship is to be filled with crewmembers equal in number to its certified number of occupants at least every six months. Under this policy, for safety considerations, the loading of lifeboats for training purposes is to be performed only while the boat is waterborne and the boat should be lowered and raised with only the lifeboat crew onboard essential for safe operation. All lifeboat crew and embarkation/boarding station crew are to be required to attend the lifeboat loading drill. If not participating inside the lifeboat, crew members are to observe the loading of the lifeboat to its certified number of people and its operation. Taking into account safety consideration, the policy also includes specific provisions for ships with crew sizes less than three hundred. This policy was effective upon its announcement on September 20, 2012.

Operational safety can be enhanced by achieving substantive consistency in bridge operating procedures among commonly owned ships, for example by providing that bridge personnel who may rotate among such ships can be familiarized with a common set of procedures. The *Harmonization of Bridge Procedures Policy* requires that bridge operating procedures are to be harmonized as much as possible, both within individual companies and among brands within a commonly owned and operated fleet. Under this policy, each member operating multiple ships and each cruise line brand that is commonly owned and operated with another brand is to harmonize their respective procedures for bridge operations. This policy was announced on November 15, 2012 and its implementation has been completed.

The *Location of Lifejacket Stowage Policy* complements the Excess Lifejackets policy under which oceangoing cruise ships carry additional adult lifejackets onboard far exceeding the number of persons actually onboard the ship. Under this new policy lifejackets equal to or greater than the number required by international regulations and the ship's flag State are to be stowed in close proximity to either muster stations or lifeboat embarkations points on newly-constructed ships. Consequently, lifejackets will be readily accessible by crewmembers for distribution to passengers in the event of an emergency. This policy further enhances shipboard safety as passengers will have even greater access to lifejackets in the event of an emergency. This policy was announced on November 15, 2012 and goes into effect with newly-constructed cruise ships for which the building contract is placed on or after July 1, 2013.

The Securing Heavy Objects policy requires that oceangoing members include procedures in their Safety Management Systems to secure heavy objects either permanently, when not in use, or during severe weather. This policy was announced on November 15, 2012 and its implementation is now complete.

When I was Chairman of the National Transportation Safety Board, I closely monitored trends in safety across every sector of transportation. I've been able to apply my experiences and knowledge of transportation safety to the panel as we evaluated the suggested policy and best practice improvements. Each of the individual Panel members brings unique and in-depth strengths to the Panel as a whole; one of my greatest strengths is a broad view of transportation safety that includes but reaches far beyond the maritime sector.

I can say unequivocally that the cruise industry has been very receptive to our input. I've also been impressed with the level of collaboration of this industry with its regulators and other key stakeholders to enhance safety practices and procedures. The cruise industry works continually with the IMO, other global maritime authorities, classification societies, and shipbuilders to implement and enhance what are already stringent safety standards. My involvement on this panel has given me confidence that the industry is engaged in proactive and responsible relationships with regulators across the globe.

Along with the other members of the Panel of Experts, I've been extremely impressed with the speed with which the industry adopted the ten policies developed by the Review, all of which exceed current regulatory requirements. Further, I believe that CLIA's initiative to combine these ten policies related to the Review with an additional ten new and existing industry-wide policies is a very positive and aggressive step for a trade association to take. We specifically advised CLIA as they considered this initiative, including with relation to developing a comprehensive Compendium of Policies; their methods of CEO-level verification of policy implementation; and their use of Safety Management Systems to ensure the sixteen policies related to safety and environmental protection were subject to a regulatory internal and external auditing scheme. These are exactly the types of proactive and innovative actions that I, and my fellow Panel members, have encouraged this industry to take. As an avid cruiser, I also feel it is important that consumers understand that cruise vacations are extremely safe. This industry is highly regulated that is continuously subjected to tremendous oversight, wherever they operate.

As members of the Panel of Experts, our work isn't done because the Operational Safety Review is completed. We continue to advise and assist the cruise industry in providing ideas, guidance and impartial analysis as it continues to review and seek improvements to shipboard operations and safety. We remain actively engaged by providing our advice through CLIA's Board of Directors, Executive Committee and other Advisory Committees. This has ensured that while the formal structure of the Operational Safety Review wound down, the cruise industry could still benefit from our active input and expertise.

So thank you again for the opportunity to testify today and I look forward to your questions.

APPENDIX

MARITIME SAFETY COMMITTEE
90TH Session
Agenda Item 27

MSC/90/27/1
February 29, 2012
Original: English

PASSENGER SHIP SAFETY
Cruise Industry Operational Safety Review
Submitted by Cruise Lines International Association (CLIA)

SUMMARY

Executive summary: This document describes the work undertaken immediately following the Concordia incident, under the leadership of the Cruise Lines International Association, to address operational safety. This work will continue and recommendations will be provided to the industry, IMO, and governments on an ongoing basis.

Strategic direction: 5.1

High-level action: 5.1.1

Planned output: None

Action to be taken: Paragraph 16

Related document: MSC 90/1/Rev.1; MSC 90/27

Background

1. In response to the Concordia incident, and as part of the industry's continuous efforts to review and improve safety measures, the Cruise Lines International Association (CLIA), speaking on behalf of the global cruise lines industry, announced the launch of a Cruise Industry Operational Safety Review on 27 January 2012, although it had begun prior to that date.

2. As best practices are identified via this Review, they will be shared on an ongoing basis among CLIA members and any appropriate recommendations will be shared with the IMO.

Support for the Secretary-General's Efforts

3. In expressing his condolences to the families of those lost in the Concordia incident, the Secretary-General stated his determination to work with others to ensure that such an accident could be prevented in the future and has pledged that the Organization will consider seriously the lessons to be learned and will take action, as appropriate, in the light of those findings.

4. CLIA specifically supports the views expressed by the Secretary-General in his 30 January 2012 press statement on this subject.

5. The Secretary-General indicated in that statement that he had opened a channel of communication with passenger ship operators – through the Cruise Lines International Association (CLIA) – and that he welcomed the response to his request to hold meetings with him to discuss the safety of cruise passenger ships in general and, in particular, any findings and recommendations from their own internal review of current - practices and safety procedures in the operation of passenger ships.

6. This Review is intended to complement the efforts and goals of the Organization and to also be completely consistent with the Secretary-General's description of the on-going communications and operational safety initiatives of the global cruise industry.

Description of the Cruise Industry Operational Safety Review

7. The Review will include a comprehensive assessment of the critical human factors and operational aspects of maritime safety.

8. Key components of the Review include:

    I.   An internal review by CLIA members of their own operational safety practices and procedures concerning issues of navigation, evacuation, emergency training, and related practices and procedures.

    II. Consultation with independent external experts.

    III. Identification and sharing of industry best practices and policies, as well as possible recommendations to the IMO for substantive regulatory changes to further improve the industry's operational safety.

    IV. Collaboration with the IMO, governments and regulatory bodies to implement any necessary regulatory changes.

9. More specifically, an example of how one major cruise line intends to proceed with their internal review in three distinct phases might be useful for the Committee:

- First Phase: Bridge operating procedures; Emergency response procedures; and Abandon ship
- Second Phase: Lessons learned; Communications shoreside and with local authorities; Remote monitoring of voyages and status of ship; and Newbuild implications
- Third Phase: Emergency responses to fire, flooding, collision, and grounding; Damage control equipment; Training; Safety Management System; Audit procedures; and Corporate emergency response

10. Each cruise line will conduct their internal review in accordance with their own Safety Management System.

Outputs of the Cruise Industry Operational Safety Review

11. The first output of the Review was the cruise industry's Passenger Muster Policy, announced on 9 February 2012 and made immediately effective, serves as an example of the type of best practices and procedures that may be expected as outputs from the Review.

12. That Passenger Muster Policy is offered to this Committee for them to consider and reads as follows:

"Current legal requirements for conducting a muster of passengers are found in the International Convention for the Safety of Life at Sea (SOLAS) and mandate that a muster for embarking passengers occur within 24 hours of their embarkation. Notwithstanding the legal requirement, CLIA's member cruise lines have identified a best practice effective immediately that calls for conducting the mandatory muster for embarking passengers prior to departure from port. On occasions when guests arrive after the muster has been completed, CLIA's policy is that they be promptly provided with individual or group safety briefings that meet the requirements for musters applicable under SOLAS. This practice exceeds existing legal requirements and has been adopted by CLIA's membership as a formal policy to help ensure that any mandatory musters or briefings are conducted for the benefit of all newly embarked passengers at the earliest practical opportunity."

13. Additional outputs from the Review will be provided as appropriate to the Organization via its relevant Committees and Sub-committees.

Conclusion

14. CLIA is fully committed to understanding the factors that contributed to the Concordia incident and is proactively responding to all maritime safety issues.

15. The Cruise Industry Operational Safety Review will enable the industry to do so in a meaningful and expedited manner.

Action requested of the Committee

16. The Committee is invited to consider the information provided in this submission and take action as appropriate.

MARITIME SAFETY COMMITTEE
90th session
Agenda item 27

MSC 90/27/2
13 March 2012
Original: ENGLISH

PASSENGER SHIP SAFETY
Cruise Industry Operational Safety Review
Submitted by the Cruise Lines International Association (CLIA)

SUMMARY

Executive summary: This document describes certain specific initial outputs from the Cruise Industry Operational Safety Review, which was undertaken immediately following the Concordia incident, under the leadership of the Cruise Lines International Association, to address operational safety. This work will continue and recommendations will be provided to the industry, IMO, and governments on an ongoing basis.

Strategic direction: 5.1

High-level action: 5.1.1

Planned output: None

Action to be taken: Paragraph 9

Related document: MSC 90/1/Rev.1; MSC 90/27; MSC 90/27/1; MSC-MEPC.3/Circ.3; and Res. MSC255(84)

Background

1. In response to the Concordia incident, and as part of the industry's continuous efforts to review and improve safety measures, the Cruise Lines International Association (CLIA), speaking on behalf of the global cruise lines industry, announced the launch of a Cruise Industry Operational Safety Review on 27 January 2012, although it had begun prior to that date.

2. As best practices are identified via this Review, they will be shared on an ongoing basis among CLIA members and any appropriate recommendations will be shared with the IMO.

3. In CLIA's previous submission, MSC 90/27/1 we described the basic framework for the Review and reported on the first output, which was our Passenger Muster Policy.

Outputs of the Cruise Industry Operational Safety Review

4. The first output of the Review was the cruise industry's Passenger Muster Policy, announced on 9 February 2012 and made immediately effective, serves as an example of the type of best practices and procedures that may be expected as outputs from the Review.

5. In the interim, the cruise industry has developed three additional outputs which CLIA wishes to share with this Committee:

I.   The cruise industry is of the view that we, along with the rest of the maritime community, would benefit from increased reliability and transparency with regard to marine casualty information. Specifically, we believed the relevant information contained in the IMO database would benefit from some additional verification. Accordingly, CLIA recently undertook an effort with the IMO Secretariat to harmonize the information in Annex I of the GISIS Marine Casualties and Incidents module to ensure that no recent and known "very serious casualties," alternatively referred to as "very serious marine casualties," involving one or more fatalities on a cruise passenger ship were inadvertently omitted. This action resulted in adding and verifying basic information on a total of fifteen marine casualties in the database, but did not result in the removal of any existing marine casualties or associated data.

II.   Consistent with the above actions regarding Annex I of the GISIS Marine Casualties and Incidents module, CLIA is of the view that a mandatory obligation to provide information on the occurrence of very serious casualties is beneficial to Member States, the maritime industry, and the public at large. As we worked through reconciling existing IMO casualty data with the best data presently available to our industry, we found substantial inconsistency in reporting. Thus, to assist Member States in their ongoing efforts to consider improvements to maritime safety through examination of casualties, we respectfully wish to draw attention to the existing provisions in the mandatory IMO Casualty Investigation Code (Res. MSC.255(84)) and those in MSC-MEPC.3/Circ.3.

III.   Thus, recognizing that it is not procedurally appropriate for CLIA to propose an amendment to a mandatory instrument, we request that Member States consider revising SOLAS Chapter XI-1, Regulation 6 to expressly and more clearly emphasize the mandatory reporting requirements regarding "very serious casualties." We believe that Member States would find this to improve the breadth and depth of reporting, providing them a better foundation for prevention of future casualties.

6. Additional outputs from the Review will be provided as appropriate to the Organization via its relevant Committees and Sub-committees.

Conclusion

7. CLIA is fully committed to understanding the factors that contributed to the Concordia incident and is proactively responding to all maritime safety issues.

8. The Cruise Industry Operational Safety Review will enable the industry to do so in a meaningful and expedited manner.

Action requested of the Committee

9. The Committee is invited to consider the information provided in this submission and take action as appropriate.

MARITIME SAFETY COMMITTEE
90th session
Agenda item 27

MSC 90/27/11
10 April 2012
Original: ENGLISH

PASSENGER SHIP SAFETY
Cruise Industry Operational Safety Review
Submitted by the Cruise Lines International Association (CLIA)

SUMMARY
Executive summary: This document describes a specific additional output from the Cruise Industry Operational Safety Review, which was undertaken immediately following the Concordia incident, under the leadership of the Cruise Lines International Association, to address operational safety. This particular output relates to the subject of Carriage of Additional Lifejackets onboard. This work will continue and recommendations will be provided to the industry, IMO, and governments on an ongoing basis.   *Strategic direction:* 5.1   *High-level action:* 5.1.1   *Planned output:* None   *Action to be taken:* Paragraph 10   *Related document:* MSC 90/1/Rev.1; MSC 90/27; MSC 90/27/1; MSC 90/27/2; and MSC 90/27/12

Background

1. In response to the Concordia incident, and as part of the industry's continuous efforts to review and improve safety measures, the Cruise Lines International Association (CLIA), speaking on behalf of the global cruise lines industry, announced the launch of a Cruise Industry Operational Safety Review on 27 January 2012, although it had begun prior to that date.

2. As best practices are identified via this Review, they will be shared on an on-going basis among CLIA members and any appropriate recommendations will be shared with the IMO.

3. In the first of CLIA's previous submissions, MSC 90/27/1, we described the basic framework for the Review and reported on the first output, which was our Passenger Muster Policy.

4. In MSC 90/27/2 and 90/27/XX, CLIA reported upon a series of additional outputs of the Review.

Outputs of the Cruise Industry Operational Safety Review

5. The first outputs of the Review, as mentioned above, were reported in MSC 90/27/1, 90/27/2, and 90/27/12.

6. The cruise industry has developed an additional output of the Review, applicable to all of the oceangoing ships we represent, which CLIA wishes to share with this Committee:

Carriage of Additional Lifejackets Onboard:

I.   The International Convention for the Safety of Life at Sea (SOLAS), as well as flag State regulations, require that passenger ships on international voyages carry an approved lifejacket (Personal Flotation Device–PFD) for every person onboard the ship.

II.   SOLAS requires that lifejackets suitable for children must also be carried in a number equal to 10% of the number of passengers onboard, provided that the number of children's lifejackets carried must not be less than the number of children onboard.

III.   Lifejackets must also be carried for the persons on watch and must be stored on the bridge, in the engine control room and at any other manned watch station.

IV.   An additional number of lifejackets equal to 5% of the persons onboard must also be carried and stored in conspicuous places on deck or at muster stations.

V.   Under certain circumstances, additional lifejackets must also be carried, and stored at muster stations or in public spaces, when it is likely that persons may not be able to return to their staterooms to retrieve the lifejacket stored there.

VI.   Some flag States have similar requirements for domestic or non-international voyages.

VII.   CLIA's members have adopted a policy of carrying additional adult lifejackets onboard each cruise ship in excess of these legal requirements.

VIII.   Under this policy the number of additional adult lifejackets to be provided must not be less than the total number of persons berthed within the ship's most populated main vertical fire zone.

IX.   Implementation of this policy ensures should result in spare lifejackets being carried are far in excess of the number required by SOLAS.

X.   Some smaller cruise ships may be constructed with only one main vertical fire zone that is utilized for accommodation spaces.

XI.   For these vessels, CLIA's policy is that the maximum number of excess lifejackets provided need not exceed fifty percent of the total number of persons carried by the vessel.

XII. Extra lifejackets for children in excess of legal requirements, in a number equal to 10% of the number of passengers berthed within the most populated main vertical zone, must also be carried on international voyages under this policy.

XIII. All of the additional lifejackets addressed in this policy are to be stored in public spaces, at the muster stations, on deck or in lifeboats, and in such a manner as to be readily accessible to crewmembers for distribution as may be necessary in the event of an emergency.

XIV. Lifejackets carried for persons on watch, and at remotely located survival craft stations, are to be carried in accordance with SOLAS and other applicable flag State regulations.

7. Additional outputs from the Review will be provided as appropriate to the Organization via its relevant Committees and Sub-committees.

Conclusion

8. CLIA is fully committed to understanding the factors that contributed to the Concordia incident and is proactively responding to all maritime safety issues.

9. The Cruise Industry Operational Safety Review will enable the industry to do so in a meaningful and expedited manner.

Action requested of the Committee

10. The Committee is invited to consider the information provided in this submission and take action as appropriate.

MARITIME SAFETY COMMITTEE
90th session
Agenda item 27

MSC 90/27/12
10 April 2012
Original: ENGLISH

PASSENGER SHIP SAFETY
Cruise Industry Operational Safety Review
Submitted by the Cruise Lines International Association (CLIA)

SUMMARY
Executive summary: This document describes certain specific additional outputs from the Cruise Industry Operational Safety Review, which was undertaken immediately following the Concordia incident, under the leadership of the Cruise Lines International Association, to address operational safety. These particular outputs relate to the subjects of Passage Planning and Personnel Access to the Bridge.

> This work will continue and recommendations will be provided to the industry, IMO, and governments on an ongoing basis.
>
> *Strategic direction:* 5.1
> *High-level action:* 5.1.1
> *Planned output:* None
> *Action to be taken:* Paragraph 10
> *Related document:* MSC 90/1/Rev.1; MSC 90/27; MSC 90/27/1; and MSC 90/27/2

Background

1. In response to the Concordia incident, and as part of the industry's continuous efforts to review and improve safety measures, the Cruise Lines International Association (CLIA), speaking on behalf of the global cruise lines industry, announced the launch of a Cruise Industry Operational Safety Review on 27 January 2012, although it had begun prior to that date.

2. As best practices are identified via this Review, they will be shared on an ongoing basis among CLIA members and any appropriate recommendations will be shared with the IMO.

3. In the first of CLIA's previous submissions, MSC 90/27/1, we described the basic framework for the Review and reported on the first output, which was our Passenger Muster Policy.

4. In MSC 90/27/2, CLIA reported upon a series of additional outputs of the Review, which were all related to reporting of marine casualties.

Outputs of the Cruise Industry Operational Safety Review

5. The first outputs of the Review, as mentioned above, were reported in MSC 90/27/1 and 90/27/2.

6. The cruise industry has developed two additional outputs of the Review, applicable to all of the oceangoing ships we represent, which CLIA wishes to share with this Committee:

Passage Planning:

I.   Since 1999, CLIA's member lines have been subject to international guidance concerning passage planning in accordance with IMO Resolution A.893(21), Guidelines for Voyage Planning, adopted on 25 November 1999.

II. CLIA has adopted a policy that the guidance elements set forth in this resolution are deemed to be the mandatory minimum requirements in the development of passage plans by all member lines.

III. In addition, CLIA's policy recognizes the Bridge Procedures Guide published by the International Chamber of Shipping as a compilation of best practices valuable resource that should are to be utilized by all ship operators, either as a component of their Safety Management Systems or Bridge Resource Management procedures.

IV. Under this policy each passage plan is to be thoroughly briefed to all bridge team members who will be involved in execution of the plan well in advance of its implementation.

V. The passage plan will be drafted by the designated officer and approved by the master.

VI. CLIA's policy is that all members are to take steps to help ensure bridge team members are asked and encouraged to raise any operational concerns without fear of retribution or retaliation.

Personnel Access to the Bridge:

VII. To minimize unnecessary disruptions and distractions to bridge team members in accomplishing their direct and indirect duties during any period of restricted maneuvering, or while maneuvering in conditions that the master or company bridge procedures/policy deems to require increased vigilance (e.g. arrival/departure from port, heavy traffic, poor visibility), CLIA's members have adopted a policy that bridge access is to be strictly limited to those with operational functions only during these periods.

VIII. Further, member lines are to take steps to prevent distractions to watchkeeping during these periods.

IX. Any deviation from this policy requires prior approval of senior management ashore.

7. Additional outputs from the Review will be provided as appropriate to the Organization via its relevant Committees and Sub-committees.

Conclusion

8. CLIA is fully committed to understanding the factors that contributed to the Concordia incident and is proactively responding to all maritime safety issues.

9. The Cruise Industry Operational Safety Review will enable the industry to do so in a meaningful and expedited manner.

Action requested of the Committee

10. The Committee is invited to consider the information provided in this submission and take action as appropriate.

MARITIME SAFETY COMMITTEE
91st session
Agenda item 7

MSC 91/7/1
24 September 2012
Original: ENGLISH

PASSENGER SHIP SAFETY
Cruise Industry Operational Safety Review
Submitted by Cruise Lines International Association (CLIA)

SUMMARY
Executive summary: This document provides additional outputs from the Cruise Industry Operational Safety Review and proposes a revision to include these additional outputs in the annex to MSC.1/Circ.1446.   *Strategic direction:* 5.1   *High-level action:* 5.1.1   *Planned output:* None.   *Action to be taken:* Paragraph 14   *Related documents:* MSC 90/27

Background

1   1. In response to the Concordia incident, and as part of the industry's ongoing efforts to review and improve safety measures, the Cruise Lines International Association (CLIA), speaking on behalf of the global cruise lines industry, announced the launch of a Cruise Industry Operational Safety Review (hereinafter "Review") on 27 January 2012, although it had begun prior to that date. As best practices are identified via this Review, they will be shared on an on-going basis among CLIA members and as appropriate to the Organization.

2   2. In the first paper on this subject (MSC 90/27/1), CLIA provided the Committee with an overview of the basic framework of the Review and also reported on the first output, a CLIA policy on passenger muster prior to departure from port. Since then, we have provided the Committee with additional outputs, including:

I.   The need for consistent reporting and additional verifying of marine casualties and incidents, in particular very serious casualties, with a concomitant recommendation that Member States consider revising SOLAS regulation XI-1/6 to emphasize the mandatory reporting requirements of very serious casualties (MSC 90/27/2);

II.   CLIA policies on passage planning and personnel access to the bridge (MSC 90/27/12); and

III.   CLIA policy on carriage of additional lifejackets on board (MSC 90/27/11).

3. The Committee, having considered the information provided in the Cruise Industry Operational Safety Review, invited Member Governments to recommend that passenger ship companies conduct a review of operational safety measures with the aim to enhance the safety of passenger ships, taking into consideration the recommended interim measures of an operational character listed in the *Recommended interim measures for passenger ship companies to enhance the safety of passenger ships* (MSC.1/Circ.1446), on ships flying their flag, on a voluntary basis and with all possible urgency and efficiency (Resolution MSC.336(90)).

Outputs of the Cruise Industry Operational Safety Review

4. As part of the ongoing Review, the cruise industry has developed three additional outputs as laid out below in paragraphs 5-9.

Common Elements of Musters and Emergency Instructions

5. Regulations 8 and 19 of SOLAS Chapter III require musters and emergency instructions to be provided for passengers. In addition to the legal requirements, CLIA oceangoing members have adopted a policy that musters and emergency instructions are to include the following common elements:

I.   When and how to don a lifejacket.
II.   Description of emergency signals and appropriate responses in the event of an emergency.
III.   Location of lifejackets.
IV.   Where to muster[†] when the emergency signal is sounded.
V.   Method of accounting for passenger attendance at musters both for training and in the event of an actual emergency.
VI.   How information will be provided in an emergency.
VII.   What to expect if the Master orders an evacuation of the ship.
VIII. What additional safety information is available.
IX.   Instructions on whether passengers should return to cabins prior to mustering, including specifics regarding medications, clothing, and lifejackets.
X.   Description of key safety systems and features.
XI.   Emergency routing systems and recognizing emergency exits.
XII.   Who to seek out for additional information.

Recording the Nationality of Passengers

6. Regulation 27 of SOLAS Chapter III requires that all persons on board be counted prior to departure; details of those who have declared a need for special care or assistance in an emergency be recorded and communicated to the Master prior to departure; names and gender of all persons on board, distinguishing between adults, children and infants be recorded for search and rescue purposes; and that all of this information be kept ashore and made readily available to search and rescue services when needed.

7. To further facilitate the effective and immediate availability of key information in the event of an emergency situation, CLIA oceangoing members have adopted a policy that, in addition to the information required by SOLAS, the nationality of each passenger onboard is also to be recorded, kept ashore and made readily available to search and rescue services when needed.

[†] The terms "muster" and "assembly" are used interchangeably and therefore are synonymous for this purpose.

Life Boat Loading for Training Purposes

8. To facilitate training for lifeboat operations, CLIA oceangoing members have adopted a policy that at least one lifeboat on each ship is to be filled with crewmembers equal in number to its certified number of occupants at least every six months. Under this policy:

I. for safety considerations, the loading of lifeboats for training purposes is to be performed only while the boat is waterborne and the boat should be lowered and raised with only the lifeboat crew onboard;

II. lifejackets should be worn;

III. all lifeboat crew and embarkation/boarding station crew are to be required to attend the lifeboat loading drill; and

IV. if not placed inside the lifeboat, those crew members are to observe the filling of the lifeboat to its certified number of people.

9. This policy applies to ships with crew sizes of three hundred or greater, with lifeboats installed. Ships with crew sizes of less than three hundred are to conduct similar and equivalent training evolutions, at appropriate intervals, that are consistent with operational and safety considerations.

Proposed revision to MSC.1/Circ.1446

10. CLIA recommends the Committee consider revising MSC.1/Circ.1446 such that these three additional outputs (paragraphs 5-9) would be included among the other recommended interim measures contained in the annex to that circular.

Conclusion

11. CLIA is fully committed to understanding the factors that contributed to the Concordia incident and is proactively responding to all maritime safety issues. The Cruise Industry Operational Safety Review has enabled the industry to do so in a meaningful and expedited manner.

12. Since the Review began, CLIA has provided the Committee with several outputs, including 7 new policies regarding passenger muster prior to departure from port; passage planning; personnel access to the bridge; carriage of additional lifejackets on board; common elements of musters and emergency instructions; recording the nationality of passengers; and life boat loading for training purposes. In addition, CLIA has provided the Committee with an output of the Review regarding marine casualty reporting.

13. Additional outputs from the Review will be provided as appropriate to the Organization via relevant Committees and Sub-Committees.

Action requested of the Committee

14. The Committee is invited to:

I. consider the information provided in this document;

II. consider revising the annex to MSC.1/Circ.1446 (paragraph 10); and

III. take action as appropriate.

MARITIME SAFETY COMMITTEE
92nd session
Agenda item 6

MSC 92/6/1
13 February 2013
Original: ENGLISH

PASSENGER SHIP SAFETY
Cruise Industry Operational Safety Review
Submitted by Cruise Lines International Association (CLIA)

SUMMARY
Executive summary: This document provides additional outputs from the Cruise Industry Operational Safety Review and proposes a further revision to include these additional outputs in the annex to MSC.1/Circ.1446/Rev.1.   *Strategic direction:* 5.1   *High-level action:* 5.1.1   *Planned output:* None.   *Action to be taken:* Paragraph 17   *Related documents:* None.

Background

15. In response to the Concordia incident, the global cruise industry launched a comprehensive Cruise Industry Operational Safety Review (hereinafter "Review") and identified a number of best practices, which have been shared among CLIA members and with the Organization.

16. In the first paper on this subject (MSC 90/27/1), CLIA provided the Committee with an overview of the basic framework of the Review and also reported on the first output, a CLIA policy on passenger muster prior to departure from port. Since then, we have provided the Committee with additional outputs, including:

I.   The need for consistent reporting and additional verifying of marine casualties and incidents, in particular very serious casualties, with a concomitant recommendation that Member States consider revising SOLAS regulation XI-1/6 to emphasize the mandatory reporting requirements of very serious casualties (MSC 90/27/2);

II. CLIA policies on passage planning and personnel access to the bridge (MSC 90/27/12);

III. CLIA policy on carriage of additional lifejackets on board (MSC 90/27/11);

IV. CLIA policies on musters and emergency instructions (MSC 91/7/1);

V.   CLIA policy on recording the nationality of passengers (MSC 91/7/1); and

VI. CLIA policy on life boat loading for training purposes (MSC 91/7/1).

17. The Committee, having considered the information provided, invited Member Governments to recommend that passenger ship companies conduct a review of operational safety measures with the aim to enhance the safety of passenger ships, taking into consideration the recommended interim measures of an operational character listed in the *Recommended interim measures for passenger ship companies to enhance the safety of passenger ships* (MSC.1/Circ.1446/Rev.1), on ships flying their flag, on a voluntary basis and with all possible urgency and efficiency (Resolution MSC.[...](91)).

Outputs of the Cruise Industry Operational Safety Review

18. As part of the Review, the cruise industry has developed three additional outputs as laid out below in paragraphs 5-13.

Securing Heavy Objects

19. CLIA's oceangoing members have adopted a policy to incorporate procedures into their Safety Management Systems (SMS) to help ensure the securing of heavy objects either permanently, when not in use, or during heavy/severe weather, as appropriate. Under this policy, a person or persons are to oversee a deck by deck inspection to identify unsecured and potentially hazardous heavy objects. Integral to the procedures is a list of identified objects which have a significant potential to cause injury.

20. Shipboard personnel should apply good seamanship in identifying additional items to be secured. Attention should be given to muster[‡] stations, evacuation routes, and lifeboat embarkation stations as a ship emergency could give rise to conditions that differ from ship motions caused by heavy/severe weather.

21. Consideration should also be given to development of a guidance document to assist in the identification of heavy objects and the most adequate methods for securing them. An example of this guidance document is attached in the annex. This annex is only intended to provide an example for one method of implementing this policy.

22. Practices and procedures for securing heavy objects should be monitored by each Head of Department and/or as otherwise specified by the ship's command structure, and during routine shipboard inspections and audits.

23. Heavy/severe weather should be clearly defined under the company policy taking into account the size of the ship, operational profiles, and other information. In defining heavy/severe weather, appropriate deference should be given to the judgment of the Captain.

Harmonization of Bridge Procedures

24. Operational safety can be enhanced by achieving substantive consistency in bridge operating procedures among commonly owned ships, for example by providing that bridge personnel who may rotate among such ships can be familiarized with a common set of procedures.

[‡] The terms "muster" and "assembly" are used interchangeably and therefore are synonymous for this purpose.

25. CLIA's oceangoing members have adopted a policy that bridge operating procedures are to be harmonized as much as possible, both within individual companies and among brands within a commonly owned and operated fleet. Under this policy and best practice, each CLIA member operating multiple ships and each cruise line brand that is commonly owned and operated with another brand is to harmonize their respective procedures for bridge operations, taking into account any unique operating characteristics of specialty ships (e.g., expedition ships; sail powered ships; etc.)[§]

Location of Lifejacket Stowage

26. In addition to CLIA's policy on excess lifejackets (MSC 90/27/11), CLIA's oceangoing members have adopted an additional policy to reflect best practices for the stowage of lifejackets onboard newly-constructed cruise ships (e.g., cruise ships for which the building contract is placed on or after 1 July 2013). Under this policy, a number of lifejackets equal to or greater than the number required onboard under the relevant international and flag State regulations, are to be stowed in close proximity to either muster[#] stations or lifeboat embarkation points, and be readily available for use in case of emergency.

27. Implementation of this policy will continue to result in spare lifejackets being carried in excess of the number required by the International Convention for the Safety of Life at Sea (SOLAS).

Proposed revision to MSC.1/Circ.1446/Rev.1

28. CLIA recommends the Committee consider revising MSC.1/Circ.1446/Rev.1 such that these three additional outputs (paragraphs 5-13, annex) would be included among the other recommended interim measures contained in the annex to that circular.

Conclusion

29. Since the Review began, CLIA has provided the Committee with several outputs, including 10 new policies regarding various operational safety matters. In addition, CLIA has provided the Committee with an output of the Review regarding marine casualty reporting.

30. CLIA is fully committed to understanding the factors that contributed to the Concordia incident. Ongoing innovation in safety has been a hallmark of our industry for decades and we are fully committed to continuous improvement of shipboard operations and safety. The global cruise industry continuously reviews operational safety and works closely with the Organization as well as flag States, Recognized Organizations and others to enhance maritime safety.

[§] And giving due regard to any relevant flag State requirements.

[#] The terms "muster" and "assembly" are used interchangeably and therefore are synonymous for this purpose.

Action requested of the Committee

31. The Committee is invited to:
    I.   consider the information provided in this document;
    II. consider revising the annex to MSC.1/Circ.1446/Rev.1 (paragraph 14); and
    III. take action as appropriate.

* * *

ANNEX

SAMPLE STRUCTURE OF A GUIDANCE DOCUMENT TO ASSIST IN THE IDENTIFICATION OF HEAVY OBJECTS AND THE MOST ADEQUATE METHOD FOR SECURING THEM

Guidance document(s) should consider the following three elements, in addition to any other relevant information.

1.   *Heavy Objects.* The following list is an example of some heavy objects that may be identified and secured in accordance with company policy. In this sample listing, the objects are grouped by those that should be permanently secured, always secured when not in use, and those to be secured in heavy weather. Heavy objects that have been identified include, but are not limited to, the following:

1.1. Heavy objects that should be permanently secured.
1.1.1. Heavy plant pots, sculptures, TVs, cash machines, laundromat equipment, slot machines, and game machines such as in teen recreation areas.
1.1.2. Display stands and racks.
1.1.3. Treatment tables, heavy standalone product displays, treadmills, exercise weight racks, and weight lifting machines.
1.1.4. Pianos, lounge speakers, and back-stage scenery equipment.
1.2. Heavy objects that should be secured at all times when not in use.
1.2.1. Trolleys and forklift trucks.
1.2.2. Paint rafts, gangways, and deck trash containers.
1.2.3. X-ray scanners.
1.2.4. Cylinder heads, pistons, charge air coolers, heavy chemical containers, and heavy fan impellers.
1.2.5. Gas bottles (refrigerant, oxygen, acetylene, CO_2, etc.)
1.3. Heavy objects not otherwise secured that should be secured for heavy weather.
1.3.1. Loose objects on display.
1.3.2. Temporary decorations.
1.3.3. Items brought aboard temporarily as part of shows.
1.3.4. Materials/equipment onboard as part of repairs/refurbishment.

2. *Securing Methods.*

2.1. Consideration should be given to the strength and appropriateness of each point of attachment to which the heavy objects are secured.

2.2. Consideration should be given to the following list of securing methods. Additional securing methods appropriate to the objects to be secured should be identified and used as necessary. Examples are as follows; however, additional methods should be identified and included as appropriate.

A—Latch type gate hook and eye bracket mounted on bulkhead or vertical surface.

B—Ratchet strap and eye brackets mounted on bulkhead or vertical surface. C—Rope secured to object and adjacent suitable securing surface.

D—Contained in metal rack-type shelving system.

E—Suction cup and bracket, ratchet strap, chain, etc.

F—Permanent securing such as bolting to bulkhead or deck.

3. *Various.* A list of specific heavy objects that have been identified by the company during surveys and inspections and that require particular attention.

MARITIME SAFETY COMMITTEE
92nd session
Agenda item 6

MSC 92/6/9
24 May 2013
Original: ENGLISH

PASSENGER SHIP SAFETY
Comments relating to the Costa Concordia incident:
The importance of shoreside management to maintaining shipboard safety
Submitted by Cruise Lines International Association (CLIA)

SUMMARY

Executive summary: This document provides comments relating to the Costa Concordia incident.

Strategic direction: 5.1, 5.2, 5.4

High-level action: 5.1.1, 5.1.2, 5.1.3, 5.2.1, 5.2.2, 5.4.1

Planned output: None

Action to be taken: Paragraph 25

Related documents: MSC 92/6/1; MSC 92/6/3; MSC 91/7/1; MSC 90/27/1; MSC 90/27/2; MSC 90/27/11; MSC 90/27/12

Background

This document is submitted in accordance with paragraph 6.14 of the *Guidelines on the organization and method of work of the Maritime Safety Committee and the Marine Environment Protection Committee and their subsidiary bodies* (MSC-MEPC.1/Circ.4/Rev.2), and provides comments relating to the Concordia incident and in particular the importance of shoreside management to maintaining shipboard safety.

2. Comments related to Italy's report on the safety technical investigation regarding the Concordia marine casualty investigation are in document MSC 92/6/10.

Discussion

3. The role of shoreside management is critical to the proper development and function of an effective Safety Management System. An integrated approach is used by the cruise industry to maintain shipboard safety; one that recognizes an essential connection with senior shoreside officials.

4. Notwithstanding substantive progress made to date, the cruise industry continues to establish and implement operational and management measures that are robust enough to minimize the potential for a recurrence of the type of navigational incident recounted in document MSC 92/6/3. For example, the cruise industry takes very seriously its responsibility to address issues surrounding the authority of the Master with regard to maneuvering a large cruise ship and the naturally related responsibility in management of the company to ensure safety. These efforts are ongoing and take the form of both industry-wide cooperation and company-specific actions.

5. Some specific elements that have already been addressed and will continue to be evaluated on an ongoing basis via the cruise industry's efforts include:

I.   senior management level of engagement in safety-related matters;
II. senior management commitment to a company-wide culture of safety;
III. integration of shoreside management responsibilities into the company's Safety Management System; and
IV. CEO-level direct engagement in CLIA's Member Policy Verification Program.

6. Recall the prior CLIA submissions to the Committee on various outputs from the Cruise Industry Operational Safety Review.[‖] As part of the cruise industry's ongoing efforts to continually improve operational safety, a wide range of additional items were also considered but have not to this point resulted in industry-wide policies. Instead, with regard to these items, information and best practices have been shared among our members and incorporated into their own relevant policies and procedures as appropriate.

7. Efforts to evaluate and improve in these areas remain ongoing within our standing committee structure and other appropriate mechanisms within our industry. Examples of areas, closely related to the role of shoreside management, that continue to be under consideration include:

[‖] See MSC 92/6/1; MSC 91/7/1; MSC 90/27/1; MSC 90/27/2; MSC 90/27/11; and MSC 90/27/12 (CLIA)

I.   discretion of the Master with regard to non-safety related voyage modifications;

II. bridge procedures during maneuvering and shipboard emergencies;

III. voyage plan change and general bridge procedure review practices and policies;

IV. hiring, evaluation, and training practices for Masters; and

V.   expectations and policies on when a Master may personally abandon their ship.

8. It is the cruise industry's approach that these types of issues are very much the responsibility of shoreside management to develop and successfully implement via effective shipboard practices and procedures. For a Safety Management System to be genuinely effective and within the true spirit of the ISM Code, it must carefully integrate the roles carried out by both professional shipboard staff and the shoreside management that both lead and support them. The cruise industry continues to fully embrace such an approach and commits to continuous improvement in this regard.

Conclusion

9. The cruise industry looks forward to working with all engaged stakeholders to identify and prioritize areas where additional improvements can be made and to develop any necessary standards that will further the shared goal of continuous improvement of maritime safety.

Action requested of the Committee

10. The Committee is invited to consider the comments provided in this document and take action as appropriate.

* * *

MARITIME SAFETY COMMITTEE
92nd session
Agenda item 6

MSC 92/6/10
24 May 2013
Original: ENGLISH

PASSENGER SHIP SAFETY
Comments relating to the Costa Concordia incident:
Specific comments on Italy's recommendations
Submitted by Cruise Lines International Association (CLIA)

SUMMARY
Executive summary: This document provides comments relating to the Costa Concordia incident.

> *Strategic direction:* 5.1, 5.2, 5.4
> *High-level action:* 5.1.1, 5.1.2, 5.1.3, 5.2.1, 5.2.2, 5.4.1
> *Planned output:* None
> *Action to be taken:* Paragraph 25
> *Related documents:* MSC 92/6/1; MSC 92/6/3; MSC 91/7/1; MSC 90/27/1; MSC 90/27/2; MSC 90/27/11; MSC 90/27/12

Background

1. This document is submitted in accordance with paragraph 6.14 of the *Guidelines on the organization and method of work of the Maritime Safety Committee and the Marine Environment Protection Committee and their subsidiary bodies* (MSC-MEPC.1/Circ.4/Rev.2), and provides comments relating to the Concordia incident and in particular Italy's Report on the safety technical investigation regarding the Concordia marine casualty investigation, as presented in the Marine Casualty and Incident Module of GISIS under Incident Reference No. C0008482 (hereafter "the Report").

2. Comments related to the importance of shoreside management to maintaining shipboard safety are in document MSC 92/6/9 (CLIA).

Discussion

3. The Report contains 20 recommendations grouped into 6 functional areas covering stability; vital equipment & electrical distribution; emergency power generation; operational matters; evacuation analysis; and search and rescue. Seven are for new ships only, while 11 are for both new and existing ships. The two SAR recommendations, which are external to the ship, will not be discussed in this document. CLIA welcomes the opportunity to discuss the Report, consider the recommendations made by Italy, and develop a comprehensive way forward to further improve safety.

4. Below is a summary of CLIA's preliminary comments regarding Italy's recommendations as contained in the Report.

Stability (Section 6.2.1.)

5. *Double skin.* Future discussions regarding the need for double skin to protect compartments containing equipment vital for the propulsion and electrical propulsion should also take into consideration requirements and guidance relating to SOLAS Safe Return to Port and Probabilistic Damage Stability, as appropriate.

6. *Limiting down flooding points.* If this recommendation is aimed at mitigating progressive flooding, CLIA is of the view that it may need to be clarified. CLIA notes that the Report indicates the water reached the bulkhead deck in the aft area after about 40 minutes following the incident.

7. *Computerized stability.*

I.   In the discussion of computerized stability support for the master in case of flooding, it is important to distinguish between systems having static inputs (manual, by crew) from those having dynamic inputs (automated, in near real time).

II.   Many cruise ships currently have computerized stability support systems on board that are based primarily on static inputs. Such systems require manual intervention and input by ship's crew in order to display damage stability information.

III. Dynamic simulation would likely entail *inter alia* fitting and interfacing of flooding sensors on existing ships. CLIA believes that such a proposal needs an in-depth discussion among subject matter experts. To our knowledge, such systems are currently not available to handle dynamic inputs, in near real time, displaying predictive dynamic damage simulation.

8. *Interface between flooding detection and stability computer.* See paragraph 7.

Vital equipment and electrical distribution (Section 6.2.2.)

9. *Discontinuity between compartments.* This recommendation relates to new ships. In addition, CLIA members have initiated a preparedness risk assessment to *inter alia* identify ways to preserve functional integrity of essential systems for existing ships.

10. *Bilge pumps.* The recommendation regarding bilge pumps is far too vague e.g., "huge quantities of water" cannot be defined. Also, there may be additional aspects to consider when discussing this proposal such as power source and requirements to feed additional pumps.

11. *Relocation of main switchboard.* CLIA notes that there are existing regulatory constraints regarding location of main switchboards in relation to other spaces/equipment. Such requirements may affect aspects of this recommendation regarding relocation of main switchboards. Any future development of new/revised requirements would need to be discussed by experts and carefully considered.

12. *Relocation of UHF radio switchboard.* CLIA agrees in principle that the preservation adequate communications in an emergency is required. CLIA is of the view that the basis of the Italy proposal to relocate the UHF switchboard above the bulkhead deck is not clear. Therefore, CLIA believes that other more effective and efficient options may exist to accomplish the intended goal. A number of different solutions should be discussed and evaluated by experts.

Emergency power generation (Section 6.2.3.)

13. *Increasing EDG capacity.* It should be clarified whether increasing EDG capacity would apply to existing certified emergency diesel generators or to the "second emergency diesel generators" mentioned in paragraph 14.

14. *Second EDG.* CLIA agrees in principle with providing increased emergency power supply to support additional selected services. However, the recommendation regarding a second EDG is not clear whether the intent is to apply existing regulations (statutory EDG) to the second EDG or to allow for flexibility in the requirements applicable to the second EDG. When establishing new requirements for the "second emergency diesel generator," this proposal should be carefully considered in relation to the multiple technical and operational

aspects involved. Therefore, CLIA recommends that any further consideration of this item be made by the relevant technical sub-committee(s).

15. *EDG functional tests.* Italy proposes that both emergency diesel generators be tested weekly for at least two hours under a load of at least 50%. While generally in favor of enhancing functional testing aimed at improving reliability of EDGs during emergencies, the basis for Italy's proposal is not clear and therefore further consideration is needed in the relevant technical sub-committee(s), including input from engine manufacturer(s).

16. *Emergency light in cabins.* Italy's proposal regarding emergency light in cabins suggests that these lights should be fed by both UPS and emergency power. Although cruise ships are provided with such emergency lights in cabins, CLIA would like to inform the Committee that not all of the lights are fed by the emergency source of power. In some installations, a light is powered by stand-alone battery. CLIA is of the view that as long as the goal is achieved (e.g., lighting the exit) and that a process is in place to ensure that lights work in an emergency, that a requirement for feeding from emergency power is not necessary.

Operational matters (Section 6.3.4.)

17. *Bridge management.* CLIA supports consideration of development of training requirements that reflect established principles such as function-based bridge management and collective decision making. CLIA is looking forward to considering this matter, perhaps in the STW sub-committee.

18. *Bridge team management certification.* Italy's recommendation regarding bridge team management certification is unclear.

19. *Principles of minimum safety manning.* CLIA notes there is a lack of details in Italy's recommendation. Nevertheless, CLIA agrees that the current principles of Minimum Safe Manning do not adequately reflect reality on passenger ships and therefore supports in principle the need for further consideration on this matter.

20. *Muster list.* CLIA does not support the Italy proposal to show certification requirements in muster lists. CLIA notes that under the ISM Code, the Company is already required to ensure crewmembers are duly certified according to the duties and responsibilities assigned onboard. Cruise ships already have procedures/processes in place that ensure compliance with such requirements. In addition, robust systems are in place to ensure that those responsible for assigning emergency duties to the crew can easily verify the certifications required to cover such duties. CLIA believes that this proposal could result in the addition of unnecessary and redundant information to an already "overpopulated" document.

21. *Inclusion of inclinometer data in VDR.* CLIA agrees in principle with the Italy proposal to include inclinometer data in the VDR.

Evacuation analysis (Section 6.3.4.)

22. *Evacuation analysis at early stage of project.* CLIA notes that evacuation analysis is currently not on any sub-committee agenda, and that MSC 92 may consider whether to send a new work item to FP. CLIA looks forward to participating in the discussion at the relevant sub-committee, should the Committee decide to place this on the work programme.

23. *Embarkation ladders.* CLIA supports in principle consideration for additional embarkation ladders. However, CLIA believes that in this regard careful consideration should be given to a number of important aspects, such as:

I.   the positioning of additional ladders that could impact other LSA;
II. the difficulties for un-trained persons to utilize the ladders in conditions other than Concordia high-side, etc.; and
III. "blanket" requirements may be difficult to meet.

CLIA suggests that other individual means of evacuation should also be included in the discussion on how to achieve the goal, with the focus of identifying improvement in their design and functions, if needed.

Conclusion

24. The cruise industry looks forward to working with all engaged stakeholders to identify and prioritize areas where additional improvements can be made and to develop any necessary standards that will further the shared goal of continuous improvement of maritime safety.

Action requested of the Committee

25. The Committee is invited to consider the comments provided in this document and take action as appropriate.

* * *

In: Cruise Industry Safety and Security
Editor: Brennan T. Preston

ISBN: 978-1-63117-882-5
© 2014 Nova Science Publishers, Inc.

Chapter 5

TESTIMONY OF GERALD CAHILL, PRESIDENT AND CEO, CARNIVAL CRUISE LINES. HEARING ON "CRUISE INDUSTRY OVERSIGHT: RECENT INCIDENTS SHOW NEED FOR STRONGER FOCUS ON CONSUMER PROTECTION"[*]

Good afternoon Chairman Rockefeller, Ranking Member Thune, and Members of the Committee. I appreciate the opportunity to appear before the Committee to discuss Carnival Cruise Lines' ("Carnival") commitment to the safety and security of our guests. It is Carnival's number one priority.

Carnival operates 1500 cruises per year, carrying nearly 4.5 million guests. Our parent company Carnival Corp & plc serves nearly 10 million guests annually. Our business is built on being able to offer a safe, enjoyable, and affordable cruising experience to millions of middle-class American families each year. Safety, security, and guest satisfaction not only is important to us, but our success relies upon it.

Over our forty-one year history, Carnival has an excellent safety record. We work hard to provide our guests with safe and memorable vacation experiences. Our goal is to exceed the regulatory requirements of our industry to ensure that our guests are confident that they will enjoy a fun cruise vacation. To that end, I will focus my testimony on some of the steps that we take with respect to safety and security.

REGULATION OF THE CRUISE INDUSTRY

Because of the international nature of the cruise industry, there are several layers of oversight and regulation designed to insure the safe and reliable operation of cruise ships around the world. At the global level, the International Maritime Organization (IMO), which is part of the UN, is responsible for creating standards for all ships operating around the world.

---

[*] This is an edited, reformatted and augmented version of testimony presented July 24, 2013 before the Senate Committee on Commerce, Science, and Transportation.

IMO has adopted several conventions that address and regulate various areas of vessel operations, which in turn, are ratified and enforced by Flag and Port States. These conventions address, among other things: all aspects of safety; ship design and equipment; fire protection, training and watch keeping; communications; search and rescue; navigation; and, environmental protection.

The Flag State of each vessel is primarily responsible for enforcing international requirements, as well as additional regulations imposed by the Flag State. All Port States the vessel calls upon also ensure the vessel is in compliance, which further strengthens what the IMO and Flag State provide. Cruise ships, like other vessels, are subject to regular inspections and audits from both the Flag and Port States.

In the U.S, the Coast Guard is both the primary regulator and the principal enforcement agency of the laws, regulations, and international treaties applicable to cruise ships. The U.S. is a party to IMO and has adopted the conventions described above. The Coast Guard conducts announced and unannounced inspections of cruise ships that operate out of US ports in order to ensure compliance by ships operating in U.S. waters. Therefore, cruise ships operating in the U.S. are subject to numerous local, state, and federal laws and regulations, including those related to safety.

SAFETY AND SECURITY

Carnival takes our compliance with all laws and regulations very seriously. Carnival has safety management systems in place that meet or exceed all regulatory requirements. Further, our parent company in 2006 established at the Board-level, a Health, Environmental, Safety & Security ("HESS") Committee to assist the Board in fulfilling their responsibility to supervise and monitor HESS policies, programs, initiatives at sea and onshore, and compliance with HESS legal and regulatory requirements. In addition, the HESS Committee oversees audits of each of our ships annually to ensure compliance. Our HESS policy includes our commitments to:

- Protecting the health, safety and security of our passengers, guests, employees and all others working on behalf of Carnival;
- Protecting the environment, including the marine environment in which our vessels sail and the communities in which we operate;
- Fully complying with or exceeding all legal and statutory requirements related to health, environment, safety and security throughout our business activities; and
- Assigning health, environment, safety and security matters the same priority as other critical business matters.

Carnival engages in regular training to ensure compliance as well. As an example, all officers and crewmembers on Carnival's ships undergo regular safety and emergency training, which meets or exceeds all regulatory requirements. Carnival Corporation and Carnival plc also operate their own Center for Simulator Maritime Training (CSMART), in Almere, Netherlands, which features a broad portfolio of maritime training courses, including courses dedicated to bridge resource management, in which Carnival participates. The facility is one of the most advanced of its kind in the maritime industry and has been praised by the U.S. Coast Guard.

Carnival has a professional Shoreside Security Department that provides training and support to shipboard security staff on each vessel. The Security Department consists of former law enforcement professionals. Training includes week-long annual shoreside training sessions for all shipboard Senior Security Officers, with curriculum based on the CVSSA model course 11-01 designed by the FBI and U.S. Coast Guard. Support includes pre-employment evaluation and incident response assistance and guidance. In addition, the Security Department serves as liaison to the FBI, U.S. Coast Guard, and local law enforcement agencies for reporting and investigation of incidents.

GLOBAL OPERATIONAL SAFETY REVIEW IMPLEMENTATION

The cruise industry, through the Cruise Lines International Association ("CLIA"), initiated a comprehensive Global Operations Safety Review with the purpose of identifying additional practices that could strengthen the cruise industry's already exceptional safety record. CLIA received input and guidance from an independent panel of experts with extensive experience in the maritime, regulatory and accident investigation fields. As a result, ten new industry-wide policies that exceed current international regulatory requirements were developed. Carnival has approved and has implemented these policies, which have also been submitted to IMO for consideration.

The new policy recommendations that exceed current international regulatory standards are:

- Passenger Muster policy;
- Passage Planning policy;
- Personnel Access to the Bridge policy;
- Excess Lifejackets policy
- Recording the Nationality of Passengers policy;
- Lifeboat Loading for Training Purposes policy;
- Harmonization of Bridge Procedures policy;
- Location of Lifejacket Stowage policy; and
- Securing Heavy Objects policy.

OPERATING RELIABILITY AND GUEST COMFORT ENHANCEMENTS

Immediately after the Carnival Triumph incident, Carnival announced a comprehensive review of its entire fleet, which was overseen by our parent company. While no one was injured as a result of the incident, our guests clearly went through an uncomfortable experience. As part of that review, Carnival is implementing a $300 million program to significantly enhance emergency power capabilities, take advantage of new fire safety technology, and improve the level of operating redundancies across its entire fleet. Carnival's ships have been and are safe. The changes made as a result of the review are primarily to improve comfort and guest convenience.

All of Carnival's ships have strong systems in place to respond to emergency situations. We meet or exceed all regulatory requirements. However, as we do on an on-going basis, we are applying lessons learned through our operational review after the Triumph fire, and by taking advantage of new technologies, we identified multiple areas for enhancement across our operations. These enhancements reinforce our commitment to safe and reliable operations and to provide an enjoyable cruise experience for the nearly 4.5 million guests who sail with us each year.

The actions by Carnival will expand the availability of hotel services for the comfort of our guests in the rare instance of a shipboard event that involves the loss of main power. In addition, the plan will reinforce key shipboard operating systems to further prevent a potential loss of primary power.

INCREASED EMERGENCY GENERATOR POWER

The initial increase in emergency generator power across Carnival's fleet of 24 ships is projected to be completed by November. An additional emergency generator will be installed on each vessel to provide for 100 percent of stateroom and public toilets, fresh water and elevators in the unlikely event of a loss of main power. Upon completion of the initial phase, the line will install a second permanent back-up power system on each ship to provide an even greater level of hotel and guest services if main power is lost. These additional services will include expanded cooking facilities and cold food storage, as well as internet and telephone communications.

INCREASED FIRE PREVENTION, DETECTION AND SUPPRESSION SYSTEMS

The company will also make additional investments in the newest and most technically advanced fire prevention, detection and suppression systems. This includes upgrading the existing water mist fire suppression systems already in place on Carnival vessels to the newest generation. When triggered, this high-pressure water mist system instantly creates a larger and thicker blanket of water droplets than the present system. As the water droplets evaporate, the system also rapidly cools any hot areas to prevent the possibility of a fire restarting.

ENHANCED OPERATING REDUNDANCIES

All of Carnival's ships have two separate, redundant engine rooms. The company's operational review has identified modifications to further decrease the likelihood of losing propulsion or primary power, as happened on Carnival Triumph in February. The modifications will include a reconfiguration of certain engine-related electrical components to improve and enhance operational redundancies.

NEW SAFETY & RELIABILITY REVIEW BOARD

Carnival also announced the formation of a Safety & Reliability Review Board comprised of outside experts with significant expertise in marine and occupational safety, reliability and maintenance, marine regulatory compliance and quality control/assurance. The company already receives oversight and input from outside regulatory authorities and industry experts, as well as the HESS Committee. The new Review Board will provide an additional, independent third-party perspective, drawing from deep experience across a number of relevant fields and organizations.

Carnival's review board will include five external members with specific expertise in the areas of marine and occupational safety, reliability and maintenance, marine regulatory compliance and quality control/assurance. Four highly esteemed maritime and transportation industry experts, including two former U.S. Navy Flag Officers, already have been appointed. These experts will help us drive continuous improvement and further ensure the safe and reliable operation of our fleet.

PASSENGER BILL OF RIGHTS

Carnival, along with 25 other CLIA North American member cruise lines, has formally adopted the Cruise Industry Passenger Bill of Rights, which details our industry's commitment to the safety, comfort and care of our guests. The voluntary implementation of the Bill of Rights formalizes many longstanding industry practices and is currently in effect for all U.S. passengers who purchase their cruise in North America, regardless of itinerary.

We expect the impact of the Bill to be a positive one for Carnival because we have already taken great strides to deliver across all areas described in the Bill throughout our fleet. The Bill serves to underscore our already-existing commitment to our guests.

The Bill covers the following set of passenger rights:

- The right to disembark a docked ship if essential provisions such as food, water, restroom facilities and access to medical care cannot adequately be provided onboard, subject only to the Master's concern for passenger safety and security and customs and immigration requirements of the port.
- The right to a full refund for a trip that is canceled due to mechanical failures, or a partial refund for voyages that are terminated early due to those failures.
- The right to have available on board ships operating beyond rivers or coastal waters full-time, professional emergency medical attention, as needed until shore side medical care becomes available.
- The right to timely information updates as to any adjustments in the itinerary of the ship in the event of a mechanical failure or emergency, as well as timely updates of the status of efforts to address mechanical failures.

- The right to a ship crew that is properly trained in emergency and evacuation procedures.
- The right to an emergency power source in the case of a main generator failure.
- The right to transportation to the ship's scheduled port of disembarkation or the passenger's home city in the event a cruise is terminated early due to mechanical failures.
- The right to lodging if disembarkation and an overnight stay in an unscheduled port are required when a cruise is terminated early due to mechanical failures.
- The right to have included on each cruise line's website a toll-free phone line that can be used for questions or information concerning any aspect of shipboard operations.
- The right to have this *Cruise Line Passenger Bill of Rights* published on each line's website.

CONCLUSION

Nothing is more important than the safety and comfort of our guests, and we will devote the full resources of our company to meet that commitment. As I have said, our continued success depends on our ability to offer a safe, comfortable, and affordable cruising experience to millions of middle-class American families each year. We strive every day to improve our performance in all areas so that our guests have confidence in their choice of Carnival, and we will continue to do so.

In: Cruise Industry Safety and Security
Editor: Brennan T. Preston

ISBN: 978-1-63117-882-5
© 2014 Nova Science Publishers, Inc.

Chapter 6

STATEMENT OF ADAM M. GOLDSTEIN, PRESIDENT AND CEO, ROYAL CARIBBEAN INTERNATIONAL. HEARING ON "CRUISE INDUSTRY OVERSIGHT: RECENT INCIDENTS SHOW NEED FOR STRONGER FOCUS ON CONSUMER PROTECTION"[*]

Good Afternoon, Mr. Chairman, Senator Thune and Members of the Committee. My name is Adam Goldstein and I am President and Chief Executive Officer of Royal Caribbean International which operates 21 cruise ships around the world with four new ships on order.

Royal Caribbean International is one of six brands owned by Royal Caribbean Cruises Ltd., ("Royal Caribbean") the world's second largest cruise company. Our company operates a total of 41 ships globally. Last year, our brands carried nearly 5 million guests, visiting approximately 425 different destinations throughout the world. Approximately 50 percent of our worldwide revenue is currently generated by cruises in and out of the United States — down from 76 percent in 2006. We believe that this trend will continue as rapidly growing foreign markets offer significant growth and profitability.

Last week, members of this Committee's staff visited one of our ships, *Grandeur of the Seas,* while she was docked in Baltimore, Maryland. The staff toured the engine rooms, the bridge, the medical facility, and observed firsthand some of the important safety features such as back-up power generation and fire suppression systems. At the Committee's request, the US Coast Guard also participated in the ship tour and explained its role in inspecting cruise ships to further ensure the safety of all guests and crew.

The Committee staff were also briefed on our extensive environmental programs and observed our Advanced Wastewater Purification, or AWP, system. Royal Caribbean has invested over $150 million in our AWP systems. As a result, the wastewater that we discharge into the ocean is purified to a standard that exceeds leading municipal, federal and international standards.

With regard to air emissions, Royal Caribbean began working with manufacturers several years ago to develop Advanced Emissions Purification, or AEP, systems to clean or "scrub"

---

[*] This is an edited, reformatted and augmented version of a statement presented July 24, 2013 before the Senate Committee on Commerce, Science, and Transportation.

the sulfur from fuel emissions before they are emitted from the ship. While we have had some success with the two scrubbers in which we have invested, we are now pleased to be expanding this research project to additional vendors and to additional ships within our fleet, including *Grandeur of the Seas.*

With the extraordinary support and cooperation of the United States Environmental Protection Agency and the United States Coast Guard, as well as the Canadian Government, Royal Caribbean has been able to develop an approach designed to benefit the broader maritime industry. We anticipate that successful development of this AEP technology will allow marine engines to achieve sulfur reductions below that required by regulatory standards.

Mr. Chairman, the cruise industry has been at the forefront of not only maritime wastewater treatment and emissions reduction technology, but other environmentally responsible initiatives. Royal Caribbean, and the cruise industry as a whole, has adopted practices and procedures that are substantially more protective of the environment than are required by regulation. On our website, we post our annual Stewardship Report which provides the public with updates on our performance in nine key areas of stewardship, including safety and security, energy and air emissions, water and wastewater, and medical operations.

Also on our website -- and on those of my colleagues from Carnival and Norwegian -- the public will find a compilation of allegations of crime that occur onboard our ships around the world, on all itineraries, by all guests and crew. In 2010, Congress passed the Cruise Vessel Security and Safety Act, or CVSSA, which required the US Coast Guard to maintain a public website disclosing the allegations of crime onboard US-based cruises, provided those allegations were the subject of a closed FBI investigation.

As you know, Mr. Chairman, there are those who have taken issue with this limitation so, in the spirit of transparency, the three largest cruise lines — making up over 85 percent of the cruise industry — voluntarily agreed to expand that reporting by posting all allegations in each of the CVSSA categories on our websites, regardless of whether an investigation was opened or closed. We will have this reporting posted on our websites by August 1st and it will date back to the last quarter of 2010 when the CVSSA was passed.

We are proud of this initiative and believe that it addresses many of the concerns raised with the limited public reporting required by the CVSSA. By providing these statistics, as well as the land-based rates of crime, consumers will be able to see for themselves that cruise ships are among the safest venues when compared to any landside communities or destinations.

At Royal Caribbean, we recognize that there is no such thing as perfect safety but there is perfect commitment to safety and that is our goal every minute of every day. While we are proud of our safety record and of our high rate of guest satisfaction, we understand that incidents do happen, such as the recent fire onboard Royal Caribbean International's *Grandeur of the Seas.*

Grandeur of the Seas set sail from Baltimore, Maryland on Friday, May 24th of this year for a 7-night Bahamas cruise. On Sunday morning, May 26th, the ship made its scheduled port call in Port Canaveral, Florida then set sail again that evening, bound for the Bahamas. Unfortunately, just before 3 o'clock in the morning on Monday, May 27th, the ship experienced a fire, requiring us to cancel the remainder of the cruise as well as six subsequent sailings. The cause of the fire remains under investigation.

This incident was the first to occur subsequent to the cruise industry's adoption of a "Passenger Bill of Rights." As the Committee may know, your colleague Senator Charles Schumer recommended that the industry adopt a 6-point Bill of Rights to protect those guests whose vacations are disrupted by mechanical issues on a cruise ship. Our industry trade association, the Cruise Lines International Association, or CLIA, welcomed this recommendation, expanded the Bill of Rights to 10-points, and its member cruise lines adopted it within weeks. In the wake of the fire onboard *Grandeur of the Seas,* Royal Caribbean exceeded our obligations under the Bill of Rights in terms of compensating and accommodating our guests.

While compensating our guests for the stress and inconvenience caused by such an incident is important, clearly, our immediate onboard response is of far greater importance. First and foremost, we must address and successfully resolve any immediate threat such as a fire. As required by international regulations, our crew members conduct extensive training and drills to address emergency situations and are well-prepared to act quickly and decisively in the event of a real emergency. Once the threat is eliminated, crew members can and should ensure the comfort of the guests. In the case of *Grandeur,* none of the guests or crew members were seriously injured and the ship never lost power. While I am certain the fire caused stress and fear among guests, I am pleased that many guests took the time to write to Royal Caribbean to commend the crew's response to both the fire and the comfort and care of the guests.

In addition to the emergency response drills and the pre-departure muster drill, each ship in our fleet is equipped with emergency backup systems that activate in the event there is an interruption in the main power systems. Each ship in our fleet is equipped with multiple high capacity pumps that are capable of removing large amounts of water that may enter the ship. Each ship in our fleet has two or more propellers, each operated by a separate propulsion motor. Each ship in our fleet has three or more generators and each generator has its own separate power cable.

I believe it is important to note that, in addition to what our individual companies are doing, many of these "best practices" have been set forth by the industry's trade association, CLIA, for adoption by its diverse and global membership. As the second largest cruise company, Royal Caribbean plays a significant role in CLIA and I would like to briefly advise the Committee of recent developments at CLIA.

CLIA represents the interests of 26 cruise lines, as well as 16,000 travel agencies, and hundreds of port authorities, destinations, and various industry business partners. Over the course of the past year, CLIA has successfully globalized its membership so that the policies developed for its members operating in North America will extend to CLIA members operating worldwide. CLIA now provides the single platform for a unified approach to industry policy and advocacy with representation in North America, South America, Europe, Asia, and Australia. Prior to December 2012, nine separate trade associations represented the global cruise industry.

As a result of CLIA's aggressive efforts, our industry around the world is more focused on higher standards of safety and security than ever before. Last year, CLIA directed an industry-wide Operational Safety Review, a comprehensive assessment of the critical human factors and operational aspects of maritime safety. As a result of that review, the global cruise industry introduced ten new safety policies — each of which exceeded current international regulatory requirements upon their announcement and each of which have now been included in formal standards for Passenger Ship Safety promulgated by the International Maritime Organization, or IMO.

For example, passenger ships were required to conduct muster drills within 24 hours of guests embarking on a ship; CLIA identified as a 'best practice' conducting the muster drills prior to departure from port. CL1A's membership adopted this as a formal policy and IMO has now adopted it as an international regulation.

Royal Caribbean is proud to play a leadership role in CLIA and has been supportive of its relentless efforts towards continuous improvement for the global industry. CLIA's commitment to Safety, Security, Environmental Stewardship, Medical Care, and Public Heath makes for a stronger, more consistent and more unified cruise industry in these critical areas of our operations. I am sure my colleagues from Carnival and from other member cruise lines will join me in saying that we are proud of all that CLIA has accomplished and we will continue to support its efforts to develop global policies, to address international issues, and to provide strategic communications for its worldwide audience.

I appreciate the opportunity to testify before the Committee this afternoon and look forward to working with you and your staff in the future.

I am happy to respond to any questions you may have.

INDEX

D

S

T

U

V

W

X